Everyday White People Confront Racial & Social Injustice

WARREN J. BLUMENFELD

ABBY L. FERBER

JANE K. FERNANDES

AFTERWORD/MICHELLE FINE

DIANE J. GOODMAN

FOREWORD/PAUL C. GORSKI

HEATHER W. HACKMAN

GARY R. HOWARD

KEVIN JENNINGS

FRANCES E. KENDALL

PAUL KIVEL

JAMES W. LOEWEN

PEGGY McINTOSH

JULIE O'MARA

ALAN RABINOWITZ

ANDREA RABINOWITZ

CHRISTINE E. SLEETER

Everyday White People Confront Racial & Social Injustice

15 Stories

Edited by Eddie Moore Jr., Marguerite W. Penick-Parks, and Ali Michael

STERLING, VIRGINIA

Published by Stylus Publishing, LLC
22883 Quicksilver Drive
Sterling, Virginia 20166-2102

Library of Congress Cataloging-in-Publication Data
Everyday white people confront racial and social injustice: 15
stories/edited by Eddie Moore, Jr., Marguerite W. Parks, and Ali
Micheal. -- First Edition.
    pages cm
Includes bibliographical references and index.
ISBN: 978-1-62036-207-5 (cloth: alkaline paper)
ISBN: 978-1-62036-208-2 (paperback: alkaline paper)
ISBN: 978-1- 62036-209-9 (library networkable e-edition)
ISBN: 978- 1-62036- 210-5 (consumer e-edition)
1. United States--Race relations. 2. Whites--United States--
Biography. 3. Political activists--United States--Biography. 4. Civil
rights workers--United States--Biography. 5. Minorities--Civil
rights--United States. 6. Anti-racism--United States. 7. Social
justice--United States. I. Moore, Eddie, Jr. II. Parks, Marguerite W.
III. Michael, Ali.
E184.A1A493 2015
305.800973--dc23
2014042529

ISBN: 978-1-62036-207-5 (cloth: alkaline paper)
ISBN: 978-1-62036-208-2 (paperback: alkaline paper)
ISBN: 978-1- 62036-209-9 (library networkable e-edition)
ISBN: 978- 1-62036- 210-5 (consumer e-edition)

Printed in the United States of America

All first editions printed on acid-free paper
that meets the American National Standards Institute
Z39-48 Standard.

Bulk Purchases

Quantity discounts are available for use in workshops and for
staff development.
Call 1-800-232-0223

First Edition, 2015

To my family E3, Jax, and Laura. —Eddie Moore Jr.

To my daughters. —Marguerite Penick-Parks

To Tina and Sami. —Ali Michael

And to all the everyday White people seeking ways to make change. May this book be a resource and an inspiration on your journey.

CONTENTS

Foreword

It is one thing to be a racial justice activist bent on reshaping an unjust world. It is something else altogether to be a racial justice activist who fights racism even as its aggressions and oppressions are bearing down upon her or him. In other words, when it comes to the experience of racial injustice and its impact on individuals or communities, my expertise is purely theoretical, which is a kind way of saying I'm relatively clueless. On the other hand, on subjects like White entitlement and bigotry, I am well groomed. When it comes to deflecting responsibility and exerting White supremacy implicitly or to participating actively and unapologetically in a hyperracist corporate-consumer capitalism even as I pretend to despise it, my family, teachers, coaches, and others equipped me with an impressive spectrum of expertise and skills.

In a recent essay, I briefly described the troublingly incremental process that led me to reach the still incomplete understanding I now have of structural racism and my role in it:

> Learning about racism, for me, has been a continual process of the same basic routine. Just when I think I have somewhat of a grasp of what racism is, some new bit of consciousness comes along and whacks me right in the hind end, reminding me that I don't know squat. Like many White people, my introduction to conversations about racism started with the assumption that it was purely interpersonal. *If we can just figure out how different racial groups can get along with one another, everything will be cheery and sweet.* Then—*whack!*—oh, it's *institutional*, it's bigger than individual relationships. I started to wrap my mind around that, and then—*whack!*—oh, it's *global*, it's connected to a history of imperialism. . . . [Then] recently, a couple of experiences conspired to give me the latest whack, and it flattened me. . . . Every day I participate in pervasive systems of oppression, not just through microaggressing or reaping the "benefits" of White privilege as they normally are understood, but by consuming mindlessly in ways that exploit already disenfranchised communities. (Gorski, 2013, p. 2)

I believe that many White people see me as an expert on racial justice and White hegemony, despite all my tripping and foot dragging, because of the creative ways I'm able to share the understandings I picked up—almost all of

---

them from people of color—along that journey. What I find more notable and instructive than the distance I have traveled is the amount of time I spent at each stop before I allowed myself to be nudged forward a little farther, almost always, again, by a person of color. What stands out even more to me is how I have dodged a sense of urgency; how it took me 40 years, for example, to recognize—not to *understand* to any appreciable degree, but just to *recognize*—that mindlessly participating in a global consumerist-capitalist system that exploits low-income people of color all over the world, which is something I do every day in a million ways, makes me just as complicit with structural racism as I have been at every other step along my path.

Perhaps there is something to be learned by White readers from the transitions in my story, from how I moved from one level of consciousness to another, from the bits of understanding that somehow survived all the waves of denial and cognitive dissonance. In fact, the chapters in this book are full of inspirational and lesson-rich stories about the expanding awareness of White social justice advocates and activists who grappled with their socializations and fought cognitively and spiritually against the pervasive temptations and immediate rewards of complying with structural racism. Indeed, as I read my fellow contributors' chapters, I was emboldened by their collective reminder of how fleeting the immediate rewards of this compliance can be. I came to learn that the pervasive temptations of racial ignorance and inaction, understood a different way, actually are temptations to desert my truest instincts toward community and humanity in exchange for the mostly material, counterspiritual benefits of White privilege. That is a beautiful, critical lesson—one among many to be gleaned from the stories in this book.

Equally critical, although perhaps less beautiful, are the lessons to be learned from the gaps and dodges and leisurely paces I and many of the most recognized White racial justice advocates and activists took as we pieced together our present understandings of and responses to racism. I am reminded of a compelling but rarely acknowledged lesson I learned from my good friend Peggy McIntosh (1989)—one of the people I respect most in this world for her humility and conviction—through her famous knapsack article: that she came to think about what she called "White privilege" only through her work examining sexism and male privilege. She spent many, many years working on the latter before her come-to-consciousness moment about her own whiteness and role in racism. It came to her, it seems, when she was ready for it to come to her. There is nothing particularly unique about this dynamic. There is something unique about Peggy, though, and her willingness to share that lesson with us, in a sense implicating herself as a step toward racial justice. We all, to some extent, tend to home in on the oppressions that target us most voraciously and drag our proverbial feet a little when it comes to the oppressions that benefit us, even if they benefit us in the most spiritually deleterious ways. But the lesson there for me, in addition to *what* she came to understand, was always *how* she came to understand it. The lesson for me, despite my commitments to racial justice, is what am I choosing not to see? And why?

In my view, the best potential of this book lies in the opportunity it provides White readers who imagine themselves as racial justice activists to focus their critical lens—not merely to celebrate the good that many of the contributors to this volume have done but to reflect upon the leisure and privilege that some of the most well-known White racial justice activists and scholars have used to develop a racial justice consciousness. The greatest gift the contributors give us is a willingness to lay themselves bare so that we can grow as much from learning about the hesitancies and stumbles as from celebrating the breakthroughs and triumphs.

For example, mirroring my own experience, many of the chapters in this book hint, at least implicitly, at interest convergence—the critical race theory principle that White people will invest in racial justice only to the extent that the investment benefits them, always stopping short of compromising their own privilege and status. They demonstrate how even those White racial justice activists or educators or scholars or consultants, whom some people see as experts or role models, including me, have had the luxury of choosing how or when or under what circumstances to act on our consciousness. In fact, the implicit nature of the interest convergence theme in several chapters is itself a demonstration of the contributors' individual and collective privilege. I urge you, as a reader, to not see us as people to be celebrated or emulated. Nothing is that simple. Instead, learn from our challenges and reluctances so that you might catch yourself following those leads and decide instead to quicken your pace.

Learn from our "detours" (Olsson, 1997), from the unjust reliance so many of us had on people of color to nudge us along. Remember, there are no heroes in this book. We are tripping and stumbling along, full of contradictions. In my opinion, it's in the tripping and stumbling and the leisurely pacing where the most important lessons in this book hide. It's in the recognition, once again, that White supremacy and structural racism inform *everything*, including the ways White people known for their contributions to racial justice choose to tell their coming-to-awareness stories and engage in racial justice work.

Consuming This Book With a Critical Lens

Having read all the chapters that you are about to read, I am excited for you. In these pages are powerful lessons full of inspiration, beautifully complex coming-to-consciousness narratives, and fantastic nuggets of wisdom from some of my favorite people. Still, as honored as I am to have been invited to write this foreword, and as moved as I am by the humility of the contributors, I've wondered whether the world needs this book. Not a single contributor whose words fill these pages is lacking for attention or space or voice in racial justice circles. Several of the contributors acknowledge this reality with endearing levels of understanding in their chapters. For many of us, me included, the fact that we're recognized as authorities on race and racism at all can be attributed to a large extent to our whiteness and, for some of us, to the fact that we had ample leisure time and adequate financial resources to complete advanced degrees, write books and articles, and make presentations at pricey conferences and other events. Privilege begets privilege, and a book full of the voices of relatively well-known white people talking about their racial justice activism should be understood as *evidence of* this at least as much as it is understood to be a *response to* it.

Like every contributor to this book, in addition to being involved in a variety of activist movements, I have made part of my living doing racial justice work. In that way I have profited from the very oppression I abhor. Many of us, including me, have accepted keynote fees to speak at conferences that the average community activist never could afford to attend. Sure, a good many of us also have spent considerable time—perhaps even the majority of our time—doing racial justice work as unpaid community activists and organizers. Still, the very fact that any of us makes a living fighting conditions to which we as White people contribute and from which we as White people benefit highlights a troubling incongruence. Similarly, the fact that we are well known enough, thanks in many cases to work—books, keynotes, workshops, consulting—for which we are compensated financially, to be invited to contribute to this book is itself a symptom of the racialization of racial justice. And that is precisely the kind of fascinating, troubling complexity taken on by the contributors to this book.

Still, I worry. I worry that some White readers with myriad reading options will seek safety and comfort in a book full of White people's voices when they ought to be reading Audre Lorde or Arundhati Roy or Gloria Anzaldúa or Michelle Alexander. I worry that White university professors will be delighted to see so many of their favorite writers or scholars or facilitators in one book, think how fantastic it would be for their White students to have White racial justice role models, and assign this book in their classes, forcing students of color to spend money buying a book they don't need to own or read. I worry that for some White readers, my contribution to this book will foster the mistaken notion that I am exceptional among White people or that there's something unique about the White confessional—about presumably enlightened White people pouring the contents of our White privilege knapsacks onto the floor for everybody to rifle through. I worry that racial justice and White privilege work, in many contexts, are industries just as much as they are movements, and that clever turns of phrase and easily digestible frameworks about race have become profitable commodities in the "diversity awareness" marketplace.

And I worry—actually, I *know*—that White people like me who have the leisure time to write essays and books (and book chapters) about race or who have the opportunity to make a living as diversity consultants or university professors are the primary beneficiaries, financially and otherwise, in that marketplace.

So, with all my worrying, why did I agree to write this foreword?

First, I agreed because I trust the editors—Eddie, Marguerite, and Ali—implicitly. I know, based on conversations I have had with them throughout the process of assembling this book, that they have challenged the contributors to share not just the triumphs of their work and consciousness but the tripping and the stalling and the tight, tight grips on White privilege that don't disappear when a White person commits his or her life to racial justice. Second, among the contributors, people like Heather Hackman and Paul Kivel have influenced me and my activism in deep and beautiful and lens-changing ways. But most important, I agreed to write this foreword because this book has the potential to help disrupt the unjust pattern of White people relying on the patience and lived knowledge of people of color to learn not just about racism but about subtle forms of White complicity with racism, even among—*especially* among—White people who think of themselves as antiracists.

The chapters in this book, if consumed with a critical lens, may demonstrate that sort of disruption.

The Sociopolitical Context of the White Antiracism Narrative

Here, then, is my brief, disruptive contribution. As much as anything, this book highlights the privilege—what I call the *institutional likeability*—associated with being a racial justice activist who is White. For example:

- I am often offered money, praise, and other rewards for going into communities and organizations and saying things that people of color in those communities have been saying, sometimes for generations, and often at their own personal and professional peril.
- I was able to build a career out of doing social justice work without being seen as self-absorbed and self-serving. Rather, I'm often seen as brave for doing the work for which many people of color are criticized.
- I can retreat when the work gets too heavy. Again, it's one thing to do racial justice work, and it's something else altogether to be doing racial justice work while experiencing the weight of racism.

- I am often credited for ideas, concepts, and frameworks related to social justice that did not originate from me even when I say they did not originate from me.
- I can be seen as a change agent simply by writing essays or books about racism, by teaching courses about racism at a university, by speaking at plush diversity conferences, or by doing cultural competence or diversity consulting, regardless of whether I do any racial justice work for which I am not financially compensated and regardless of how I spend the rest of my time.
- I have the option of softening my racial justice message for particular types of audiences if doing so will help me sell more books or have a higher likelihood of being hired as a facilitator or consultant without making people of my own racial group more vulnerable to racism.
- And so on.

From an intersectional perspective, each of these luxuries is elevated or humbled for each contributor depending on her or his other identities. For me, they're elevated by my cismaleness and my mostly heterosexuality, for example.

Here then is that critical lens. For each contributor to this book, the luxuries are there, more or less, and the richest lessons are inseparable from that reality. This acknowledgment, I think, is a decent point of departure for readers who do not seek infallible heroes or role models but little bits of triumph in stories that remain saturated with privilege, even by their very presence in this book.

Paul C. Gorski
Associate Professor
Integrative Studies
New Century College
George Mason University

References

Gorski, P. (2013). Consumerism as racial and economic injustice: The macroaggressions that make me, and maybe you, a hypocrite. *Understanding & Dismantling Privilege,* 4(1), 1–21.

McIntosh, P. (1989, July/August). White privilege: Unpacking the invisible knapsack. *Peace and Freedom,* 10–12.

Olsson, J. (1997). *Detour-spotting for white-racists.* Retrieved from Racial Equity Tools website: http://www.racialequitytools.org/resourcefiles/olson.pdf

Introduction

Eddie Moore Jr., Marguerite W. Penick-Parks, and Ali Michael

The original title for this book was *Polished Gems* because we felt it aptly framed the people and the content in the book. The people are activists and academics who contributed to the very foundation of antiracism and social justice action that we all stand on today. The knowledge and ideas generated by these contributors over years of challenging and complicated work are replete with gems that will inspire and guide readers. But the contributors featured here do not think of themselves as jewels and do not want others to do so either.

On the contrary, they are everyday White people; they are just folks. They started out in different places, including New York City during the Great Depression; Waco, Texas, in the 1950s; Las Vegas, Nevada, in the 1960s. They started out in homes like many White people's. Some were exposed to the subtle racist jokes of neighbors and their parents' friends; others were encouraged to stay in their places, not to make waves; some witnessed the overt and violent racism targeting loved ones and caregivers; and others knew little of racism as young children, so concerned were they with their own survival. Few of the people in this book started out knowing a thing or two about racism. Like many White people in the United States, it was something they had to learn by recognizing and admitting their ignorance and

1

then putting themselves in positions of apprentice, protégé, and student. It was a personal and long-term journey that continues to this day.

In this book the contributors lend their unique gifts to our mutual struggle to fight White supremacy, White privilege, and other forms of racial oppression. We wanted to capture their voices in a way that made their personal life experiences and knowledge accessible to everyone. Too often the world of academia takes control of our stories, putting them physically and intellectually out of reach. Sometimes we need to stop and take a moment to look beyond the theory, lecture halls, and textbooks to listen to the stories of our fellow human beings, no matter their titles or accolades. As one contributor said to an editor when presented with the idea for the book, "Stories are sacred." Each story shares who the contributors are and how they came to be a part of the social justice world. Through their stories we see different paths, different challenges, and different roles. But throughout their stories we also see one common cause—the struggle to create a world in which all people have the opportunity to be whomever they choose to be.

The idea for this book arose from years of listening to the very people featured in it, in workshops, caucuses, and coffeehouses at the White Privilege Conference (WPC), a space where even keynote speakers show up as learners, eager to learn from others and to consider their own blind spots. The conference is grounded in Dr. Eddie Moore Jr.'s collaborative relationship model that demands that everyone is a learner, and everyone has something to teach. When the WPC started in 1999 at Cornell College in Mount Vernon, Iowa, with 150–200 participants, no one anticipated it would explode into the national and international conference it has become, a place of collaboration and idea generation, a central location for building a movement in pursuit of equity and justice. It is our hope that the vision of the conference Moore has—a vision of how to address issues of power, privilege, white supremacy, race, and systemic inequalities—will also be realized through the collaboration manifested in this book. In 2014 more than 2,400 people who recognize that collaborative action comes from the ground up attended WPC 16. And in the 16 years of these conferences each of these contributors has been side by side with other everyday participants advocating for peace, equity, and justice.

The folks in this book have become well known because they have found a way to speak and write about racism and oppression in a way that resonates and leads to real change and action. But while we know their academic work and we read their theoretical works, very rarely do they have the opportunity to share what personally drives them in this work. As one contributor put it,

> My role in this work is made possible because of my privilege, and it took me a long time to acknowledge that. But once I acknowledged that, I was able to realize the flipside of that: that without whites in this fight, it continues to be a fight about the other, never a fight about us.

Or as Christine Sleeter writes in her chapter, confronting racism as a White person requires becoming "an *antiracist racist*." Becoming antiracist doesn't make anyone less White or less a holder of racial privilege. But these contributors demonstrate how to use one's whiteness and one's privilege strategically to work against oppression.

Multicultural educators and historians have routinely called for the inclusion of White antiracists in the teaching of multicultural history. White students often do not see a role for themselves in the work because they do not have access to the stories of White people who came before them. While there are numerous recognized role models of color who have confronted racism in politics and throughout history, White antiracists are not well known. Geneva Gay, Beverly Daniel Tatum, and Gloria Ladson-Billings have all written about the need for White students to have White antiracist role models they can relate to, and yet there are very few resources teachers can use to meet that need. We created this book to help fill that void.

For this book we asked the contributors to explore the following questions: (a) How did you get into this work? (b) What have you learned? and (c) What do you recommend for future generations? We ask how they started in this work because it is critical for Whites to see a variety of paths into the social justice field. There is no right way to come to this path; as you will see in these stories, no one was born into it. Yet one by one, in their own unique ways, these contributors found their way. We ask them what they learned, knowing that this learning has been hard won. Many of them have received hate mail, been publicly criticized, and their work has been demeaned. Whites who enter this field need to recognize the link between privilege and supremacy and be willing to speak for what is right, enduring the criticism and vitriol reserved for those who challenge the status quo.

All the contributors to this book have been in the field of social justice for 25 years or more. One of the book's goals is to let readers know that people really don't know what they are doing when they enter this field, and no one is mistake free. The contributors share their stories so others can be inspired, not by academic words but by personal experiences. They do not see themselves as special, but they represent generations of everyday White people who choose to make confronting racial and social injustice a part of who they are. The following paragraphs introduce the contributors and their stories. Just as each contributor found his or her own path into this work, each story is unique. We hope that in the many and varied stories you read here, you find people and moments that inspire you and connect you to a movement that belongs to us all.

Foreword. In his richly critical foreword, Paul C. Gorski steps back from this volume and questions what it means to publish a book of stories from White people, each of whom already has space in the public sphere to tell his or her story. With clairvoyance and zest, he reminds us of all the ways that privilege makes a book like this possible and of the many voices of people of color that merit, but do not have access to, such a platform. Using himself as an example, Paul charts a new accounting of White privileges, the privileges of the White antiracist activist who benefits from what he calls *institutional likeability.* With humility and a keen awareness of power dynamics, Paul models the critical self-reflection that antiracist action requires of White people. Finally, in an endorsement made all the more powerful by his critique, he reminds us that White people need to do their own work, and in that respect, there's a lot to be learned from those who came before.

Gorski is the founder of EdChange and is an associate professor at George Mason University, where he led the development of the new social justice and human rights program. He is a longtime activist, educator, and writer, focusing on social justice issues ranging from poverty and racism to animal rights and environmental justice. He lives in Falls Church, Virginia, with his cats, Unity and Buster.

Chapter 1: "Real-izing Personal and Systemic Privilege: Reflection Becoming Action." One's earliest education in racism often happens in childhood. It is a lesson so rooted in and supported by social norms that it can crystallize in a moment and take a lifetime to unlearn. Because so much of this early training happens in childhood, adults attempting to live an antiracist life have to be willing to grapple with subconscious messages they absorbed early. Peggy McIntosh shares the earliest racist messages she received as a child. In the rest of the chapter, she demonstrates how quiet, self-reflection, and meditation can be a form of action, as it helped her recognize and root out those early messages. By asking herself probing questions and being open to the answers that arose when she did, she developed her framework for the concept of White privilege that has transformed how race is talked about in the twenty-first century. She shares her process of learning, which took place internally and externally, a process she continues to this day.

McIntosh is associate director of the Wellesley Centers for Women and founder of the SEED (Seeking Educational Equity and Diversity) project on Inclusive Curriculum, which she codirected with Emily Style for its first 25 years. She is author of more than 40 articles including "White Privilege: Unpacking the Invisible Knapsack" (McIntosh, 1989), one of the earliest and best-known works that challenges White people to recognize White privilege.

Chapter 2: "The Joy of Antiracism." This chapter gives readers the unique opportunity to know James W. Loewen personally before and after he went to Mississippi, where so much of his worldview became what it is today. We walk in his shoes as he struggles internally with the question of how to demonstrate to an elderly black man that he means no harm, even though in Mississippi in the 1960s, his whiteness would say otherwise. He offers sage advice that stays, including the personal note that he never regrets a time he spoke up, only the times he didn't speak. From a lifetime of battling white supremacy, overtly in Mississippi and more covertly in Vermont, he has learned countless lessons that remain critical today.

Loewen won the first annual Sydney S. Spivack Award of the American Sociological Association for sociological research applied to intergroup relations and was the first white person to win its Cox-Johnson-Frazier Award, named for three famous black sociologists. He taught at perhaps the blackest college in America, Tougaloo, and perhaps the whitest, the University of Vermont. He has been an expert witness in more than 50 civil rights, civil liberties, and employment discrimination cases. His book *Lies My Teacher Told Me: Everything Your American History Textbook Got Wrong* (Loewen, 2007) is the best-selling work by a living sociologist. *Sundown Towns: A Hidden Dimension of American Racism* (Loewen, 2005) showed that entire cities and counties across the United States, especially in the North, kept out African Americans and sometimes other groups; some still do. Loewen continues to work to "out" all these places and help them transcend their racist past.

Chapter 3: "Knapsacks and Baggage: Why the World Needs This Book." If you ever felt confused about the term *intersectionality*, read this chapter. In a uniquely succinct and personal description of intersectionality, Abby L. Ferber shows how a critical lens on gender and religion allowed her to acknowledge and work against racial privilege, from which she benefited. Sharing personal stories to demonstrate the violence of oppression she experienced directly, Ferber clearly demonstrates how the intersectionality of oppressions does damage to everyone. She also shows the converse, how her personal work fighting oppression has been liberating to her on a very personal level with regard to sexism and anti-Semitism.

Ferber is professor of sociology and women's and ethnic studies and associate director of the Matrix Center for the Advancement of Social Equity and Inclusion at the University of Colorado, Colorado Springs. She is the author of *White Man Falling: Race, Gender, and White Supremacy* (Ferber, 1998).

Chapter 4: "The Political Is Personal." Contextualizing his life in key moments of political history, Kevin Jennings demonstrates how the personal is political, and the political is personal. Through family battles over his White brother's marriage to a Black woman, his mother's struggles with sexism, and his uncle's battle to live as a gay man in a homophobic society, Jennings learned about injustice firsthand and was inspired to fight it. He uses his life experiences as a White gay man to show how personal and familial relationships inspire and sustain him to work for social and racial justice. He describes how he became an activist in spite of his upbringing in a family that opposed integration and equal rights.

Jennings is executive director of the Arcus Foundation, which is dedicated to the idea that people can live in harmony with one another and the natural world. He has worked as a high school history teacher; was founding executive director of the Gay, Lesbian, & Straight Education Network (GLSEN), a national education organization focused on making schools safe for lesbian, gay, bisexual, and transgender students, staff, and families; and was assistant deputy secretary for Safe and Drug-Free Schools in the Obama administration. He is the author of six books.

Chapter 5: "Calling Out the Wizard Behind the Curtain." With honesty and humor, Heather W. Hackman describes the painful process of unlearning racism during a college experience where ideas that she took for granted as true were clearly unwelcome. She does not mince words as she describes the coercive pressure she felt early in life to collude with racism to minimize the abuse she experienced at home. In addition to sharing powerful examples that are rooted in her own life, Hackman explains complicated concepts like privilege, whiteness, and the idea of living a racially just life in succinct and incisive ways. Her story demonstrates the expansive possibilities for unlearning oppression and using early experiences of racist training to better know and fight injustice.

Hackman is the founder and president of Hackman Consulting Group. She has taught in higher education for 19 years; consulted nationally and internationally on social justice issues for more than a decade; and has published in the areas of social justice education, racial justice, and climate change and climate justice. Her most current research, writing, and training addresses climate change adaptation and mitigation through a race, class, and gender justice lens.

Chapter 6: "Love, Social Justice, Careers, and Philanthropy." At 87 years old, inspired by the New Deal spirit of their youth, Andrea and Alan Rabinowitz have lived a life dedicated to an ethos of using one's privilege to better the lives of others. Longtime supporters of the WPC, this dynamic couple has worked for incremental change in the United States by supporting small grassroots organizations with money and know-how. Having grown up in a national context that is unfamiliar at best and completely foreign at worst to most readers, they use their chapter to explain the historical influences of the early 1920s and 1930s on their social activism. They learned early that no matter what they do, whether early childhood education or urban planning, people from the communities they plan to have an impact on must be consulted and involved. This wisdom translated into making both effective philanthropists who learned how to make small contributions enormously effective for grassroots groups trying to fundamentally change our society. They also share incredibly valuable—and hard to come by—words of wisdom on managing money in social change organizations.

Andrea and Alan Rabinowitz were both born in Manhattan just before the Great Depression, went to progressive schools and liberal colleges, met after World War II, and married in 1951. Andrea's career has always involved children in her work as a teacher, clinical social worker, and child therapist in Cambridge, Massachusetts, and, after 1971, in Seattle, Washington. Alan moved from the world of finance and economic development to become a university professor, teaching and writing about urban economics. All through these years they have been involved, sometimes individually and sometimes together, with social justice organizations and activities.

Chapter 7: "Learning to Become an Antiracist Racist." Believing that White people will always benefit from racism, no matter how much they work against it, Christine E. Sleeter shares her journey of learning to be an "anti-racist racist" (Katz, 2003). She writes of a segregated childhood and life in her early 20s, demonstrating how race affected every aspect of her life, even though she didn't know it at the time. She shares the different pathways to growth in her life, including her work designing multicultural curricula in multiracial teams. With humility and wisdom, she describes the lessons that antiracist racists might need to be effective allies and collaborators on multiracial teams as well as allies to other Whites working for racial justice.

Sleeter is professor emerita in the College of Professional Studies at California State University Monterey Bay, where she was a founding faculty member. Her research focuses on antiracist multicultural education, ethnic studies, and teacher education. She has published more than 100 articles and 19 books, including *Power, Teaching, and Teacher Education: Confronting Injustice with Critical Research and Action* (Sleeter, 2013) and *Diversifying the Teacher Workforce: Preparing and Retaining Highly Effective Teachers* (Sleeter, Neal, & Kumashiro, 2015).

Chapter 8: "What's a Nice White Girl to Do in an Unjust World Like This? Guideposts on My Social Justice Journey." In this chapter, Diane J. Goodman shares five guideposts for living an antiracist life, providing powerful examples from her life, including her involvement with an anti-incarceration group in her community. In the midst of discussing her guideposts, Goodman demonstrates the joy that living an antiracist life can bring, sharing with readers that the path, while joyful, clearly is not well traveled or straightforward.

Her guideposts make the road less traveled more navigable for those coming behind her.

Goodman has been addressing issues of diversity and social justice for more than 30 years as a trainer, consultant, facilitator, professor, speaker, author, and activist. As a trainer and consultant, she has worked with a wide range of organizations, community groups, schools, and universities. Goodman has been a professor at several universities in education, psychology, social work, and women's studies. She is the author of *Promoting Diversity and Social Justice: Educating People From Privileged Groups* (Goodman, 2001) and other publications. Her website can be found at www.dianegoodman.com.

Chapter 9: "White Water." Using the metaphor of white water, Gary R. Howard takes us through his journey from a *Leave It to Beaver* childhood to a college transformation in which he lived in a Black community and actively participated in the local Civil Rights Movement. He traces his personal transformation from ignorance to a missionary mentality desiring to help the less fortunate to investment in empowering individuals to, finally, the realization that as a White man, he needs to work with White folks. His life experience is replete with powerful lessons that emerge from the risks he took and the relationships he built, which he relates with humility and candor.

Howard has 35 years of experience working on issues of civil rights, social justice, equity, education, and diversity, including 30 years as the founder of the REACH (Respecting Ethnic and Cultural Heritage) Center for Multicultural Education. His book *We Can't Teach What We Don't Know: White Teachers, Multiracial Schools* (Howard, 2006) is considered a groundbreaking work examining issues of privilege, power, and the role of White leaders and educators in a multicultural society. His current work centers on conducting Deep Equity Leadership Institutes, which support schools, universities, and other organizations in strengthening the cultural responsiveness of their practices and building the internal capacity to implement long-term systemic change strategies for achieving greater equity and social justice in their outcomes. This work is documented in his book *We Can't Lead Where We Won't Go: An Educator's Guide to Equity* (Howard, 2014).

Chapter 10: "Looking Back and Moving Forward." Frances E. Kendall paints an intimate and honest portrait of the racism she learned at her family's knees as a child and the process she went through to re-learn and challenge it as she grew up, learning other ways of seeing the world. She describes the resistance she encountered in challenging the racism that mainstream society had come to take for granted, including that of the beloved classic children's book author Roald Dahl. The lessons she shares are clearly borne of a life intimately familiar with the overt racism of the Deep South and the more insidious and normalized aspects of racism that manifests in the North. She provides lessons for tackling both.

Kendall is one of the best-known advocates for racial justice and equity. Her workshops are always standing room only. She is the author of *Understanding White Privilege: Creating Pathways to Authentic Relationships Across Race* (Kendall, 2012) and *Diversity in the Classroom: New Approaches to the Education of Young Children* (Kendall, 1996).

Chapter 11: "Working Within the System to Change the System." When she was a young girl, Julie O'Mara's family had few professional aspirations for her, which motivated her to be successful in her career while also changing the field of business to be more accessible to women and people of color. She comes to the field of racial and social justice through business and uses this chapter to describe the myriad possibilities for creating change in the for-profit sector. O'Mara's contribution is especially valuable to this volume as she demonstrates alternative routes to social change outside academia and the nonprofit world. She gives advice for readers who might not otherwise consider business or politics, two arenas in which White antiracists are very much needed.

O'Mara is president of O'Mara and Associates, an organizational development consulting firm specializing in leadership, facilitation, and the managing diversity process. She is coauthor of *Managing Workforce 2000: Gaining the Diversity Advantage* (Jamieson & O'Mara, 1991) and author of *Diversity Activities and Training Designs* (O'Mara, 1994).

Chapter 12: "Inside and Outside: How Being an Ashkenazi Jew Illuminates and Complicates the Binary of Racial Privilege." "Off White" is how Warren J. Blumenfeld finds himself racialized, not by choice, necessarily, but by all the ways he is seen and responded to as a Jew of European heritage in the United States and in Eastern Europe. In this chapter, Blumenfeld traces the personal and collective experience of being an Ashkenazi Jew in the United States and comes to the conclusion that he is white, but not quite.

Blumenfeld is coeditor of *Readings for Diversity and Social Justice* (Adams et al., 2013), and coeditor of *Investigating Christian Privilege and Religious Oppression in the United States* (Blumenfeld, Joshi, & Fairchild, 2008). He also serves as an editorial blogger for the *Huffington Post*, the Good Men Project, and *Tikkun Daily*.

Chapter 13: "Of White and Hearing Privilege." Growing up deaf in a mixed deaf and hearing family led to a unique identity for Jane K. Fernandes and positioned her as an outsider in both the hearing world and the deaf world. In what she calls "crashing intersectionality," she demonstrates how hearing privilege and White privilege collide in painful and sometimes devastating ways. She teaches hearing people about hearing privilege but doesn't stop there. She challenges the deaf community to see and be responsible for the racism and White privilege that does not stop existing simply because a community is affected by other oppressions. She demonstrates the dangerous ramifications of having a single lens on oppression and the difficult importance of honoring and challenging all oppressions simultaneously.

Fernandes was selected by the board of trustees to serve as the ninth president of Gallaudet University, the second deaf president and the first woman in this role. A national and international protest ensued around deaf identity issues that intersected with race and gender—creating complex dynamics encapsulated in a rallying cry that she was "not deaf enough." As a result of the protest, the board of trustees rescinded her contract before she took office. The next year she began a successful six-year term as provost at the University of North Carolina at Asheville. On July 1, 2014, she became the ninth president of Guilford College in Greensboro, North Carolina. She is the first woman and first deaf person to serve in this role. Her life's work focuses on creating inclusive academic excellence.

Chapter 14: "Hands-On Activism." A master of naming, simplifying, and explaining the complex layers of oppression in U.S. society, Paul Kivel offers wisdom on how to sustain a life focused on activism and change, drawing from his life, which focused on just that. He shows us the process he went through with multiple different projects as he refined his own misconceptions and dug more deeply into webs of intersecting oppressions to address violence and abuse at its very roots. In this last chapter of the book, just as you find yourself asking what you can do to fight racism and how, Kivel demonstrates what action can look like and how to stay involved so that one's engagement continually deepens and becomes more informed and more effective over time. He demonstrates how a person might take action simultaneously on the individual, group, and system levels in a way that is not theoretical or abstract.

Kivel has been a social justice educator, activist, and writer for more than 40 years. His work provides people with the understanding to become involved in social justice work and the tools to become more effective allies in community struggles to end oppression and injustice and to transform organizations and institutions. Kivel is the author of numerous curricula and books, including *Uprooting Racism: How White People Can Work for Racial Justice* (Kivel, 2011) and *Living in the Shadow of the Cross: Understanding and Resisting the Power and Privilege of Christian Hegemony* (Kivel, 2013). His website can be found at www.paulkivel.com.

Afterword: "Resisting Whiteness/Bearing Witness." The book ends with searing, image-rich, illuminating stories—vignette after vignette—of whiteness from Michelle Fine. Using stories from her life, her family, and her research, she paints a complicated picture of the many sides of whiteness. From Ellis Island to Englewood Cliffs, New Jersey, to Morningside Park, New York, from Wedowie, Alabama, to Brooklyn Family Court, she traces the value, power, audacity, and farce of whiteness. She asks again why the world needs this book and answers, "We do," counting herself among the needy, because "it is a self-help manual for recidivist Whites" (p. 168); because "we need to work through all the White muscle memory that has attached to our personal biographies" (p. 163); because "when the question, What do you like about being White? is raised, we have no words" (p. 163); and because we "are repeat offenders of privilege, eager to break the habit, and hungry to engage in antiracist justice movements" (p. 163).

Fine is a founding faculty member of the Public Science Project and professor of critical psychology at the Graduate Center of the City University of New York, which produces critical scholarship for use in social policy debates and for organizing movements for educational equity and human rights. She is well known for her work in community development with an emphasis on urban youth. Her voice is prominent in classrooms across the country as students delve into her honest yet challenging work.

References

Adams, M., Blumenfeld, W. J., Castañeda, C. R., Hackman, H. W., Peters, M. L., & Zúñiga, X. (Eds.). (2013). *Readings for diversity and social justice: An anthology on racism, antisemitism, sexism, heterosexism, ableism, and classism* (3rd ed.). New York, NY: Routledge.

Blumenfeld, W. J., Joshi, K. Y., & Fairchild E. E. (Eds.). (2008). *Investigating Christian privilege and religious oppression in the United States*. Rotterdam, The Netherlands: Sense.

Ferber, A. L. (1998). *White man falling: Race, gender, and white supremacy*. Lanham, MD: Rowman & Littlefield.

Goodman, D. J. (2001). *Promoting diversity and social justice: Educating people from privileged groups*. New York, NY: Routledge.

Howard, G. (2006). *We can't teach what we don't know: White teachers, multiracial schools* (2nd ed.). New York, NY: Teachers College Press.

Howard, G. (2014). *We can't lead where we won't go: An educator's guide to equity*. Thousand Oaks, CA: Sage.

Jamieson, D., & O'Mara, J. (1991). *Managing workforce 2000: Gaining the diversity advantage*. Hoboken, NJ: Jossey-Bass.

Katz, J. H. (2003). *White awareness: Handbook for anti-racism training* (2nd ed.). Norman: University of Oklahoma Press.

Kendall, F. E. (1996). *Diversity in the classroom: New approaches to the education of young children*. New York, NY: Teachers College Press.

Kendall, F. E. (2012). *Understanding white privilege: Creating pathways to authentic relationships across race* (2nd ed.). New York, NY: Routledge.

Kivel, P. (2011). *Uprooting racism: How white people can work for racial justice* (3rd ed.). Gabriola Island, British Columbia, Canada: New Society Publishers.

Kivel, P. (2013). *Living in the shadow of the cross: Understanding and resisting the power and privilege of Christian hegemony.* Gabriola Island, British Columbia, Canada: New Society Publishers.

Loewen, J. (2005). *Sundown towns: A hidden dimension of American racism.* New York, NY: Simon & Schuster.

Loewen, J. (2007). *Lies my teacher told me: Everything your American history textbook got wrong.* New York, NY: Simon & Schuster.

McIntosh, P. (1989, July/August). White privilege: Unpacking the invisible knapsack. *Peace and Freedom,* 10–12.

O'Mara, J. (1994). *Diversity activities and training designs.* San Diego, CA: Pfeiffer.

Sleeter, C. (2013). *Power, teaching, and teacher education.* New York, NY: Peter Lang.

Sleeter, C., Neal, L. I., Kumashiro, K. K. (2015). (Eds.). *Diversifying the teacher workforce: Preparing and retaining highly effective teachers.* New York, NY: Routledge.

1

REAL-IZING PERSONAL AND SYSTEMIC PRIVILEGE

Reflection Becoming Action

Peggy McIntosh

I have found it hard to get out from under the strong training in racism I received as a child. I have come to think of my racist mind and heart as my hard drive, but if I consciously install an alternative software, I can at least temporarily respond to the world with a more whole psyche and sensibility. Doing so has made my life into something more coherent and useful than I ever could have expected. I say to the next generations: Best not to be a good student of all you were taught. What you were taught may be a lot of what got us into the mess the world is in now.

When I was a small girl my grandmother gave me my first clear lesson in racism. I was leaving her big house in Easton, Pennsylvania, after a visit. I realized that I had forgotten to say good-bye to Grandmother and to her cook, Bessie. My mother was idling the car in the street outside, waiting to drive us back to New Jersey. I ran into the kitchen and kissed Bessie and then ran into the front parlor where my grandmother stood and kissed her. She reared back and shrieked at me in a voice I had never heard: "I BET YOU KISSED ME WITH THE SAME L'IL OL' LIP YOU KISSED BESSIE!"

I was terrified. I knew I had done something wrong, but I did not know what it was. I rushed out of the house and got into the car. I was so ashamed of what I must have done to make my grandmother scream at me that I did not tell my mother about it all the way home in two hours of driving. And I kept the secret for another 55 years until my mother died at the age of 98. By the time I was 30 the reason for my silence had changed. I was now so ashamed of my grandmother that I wanted to protect my mother from hearing about her mother's outburst at me and Bessie. Either way, I kept a White silence about racism in the family.

I feel that my grandmother's fury split my world in two, and this probably happens to many wealthy White children, although perhaps in a less violent form, when told that they must separate from people of color who were their caretakers. I was not born looking down on African Americans. I had looked up to Bessie and my grandmother equally as the two stars in the firmament of their household. Now suddenly Bessie's status fell like a sinking balloon, and my grandmother's power rose up, towering. Her fury split off the part of me that was identified upward, toward the White elder, from the lower part, identified with the Black servant.

I never again heard my grandmother use southern slang. She was a polite, "upright" Virginia lady, born just after Emancipation to the owners of a small tobacco plantation. Her family owned two slaves. By marrying a Yankee, she had crossed a South/North line, but her sudden reflex was that of a slaveholder. Her crude speech came roaring out of her when she conceived—who knows?—that I had contaminated her with Bessie's saliva? Bessie's skin? I wonder if she would have tolerated my kissing her good-bye first, and then going out the back door through the kitchen to kiss Bessie good-bye.

This shocking education in racism took five seconds. In a way it worked. I never touched Bessie again, but it did not succeed in wiping away my love of Bessie. In a bundle of letters kept by my mother I am glad, relieved, and proud to see that later on I put Bessie's name before my grandparents' names on an envelope I addressed. The same envelope contains a beautiful Christmas card I made and inscribed for all three of them and a photo, probably taken by my father, of Bessie, a beautiful, queenly woman. But why was the photo still in the envelope? Had they kept the photo from her? Did they not even let her see the card? I wonder—did she ever know how much we children loved her? How could she?

Bessie took my sister Helen to church one Sunday, and there Helen learned this was not "Bessie"; this was Mrs. Elizabeth Jones, a proud, prominent, honored member of the Black congregation. Decades later, I visited one of the cemeteries of the Gullah people on Hilton Head Island, in South Carolina. I visited to honor the memory of Bessie and to mourn what she and her Gullah brothers and sisters suffered at the hands of virtual owners even after Emancipation and right up until the 1940s and to the end of their days. I grieved for myself and her, knowing how she was a friend to us children no matter what she heard my grandmother shriek about her. I hope her Lord sustained her against the violence of an employer who thought of herself as a Christian and could scream out hatred of her servant's body and heart without caring who got hurt.

I never touched Bessie again, but I never willingly touched my grandmother either until she was blind and I would hold her hand to talk with her. A colossal irony of her death is that as she drifted out of this life, hallucinating, she repeatedly took my mother for her childhood companion, a slightly older Black child, whose duty it was to take care of her. She would say, "Effie, let's go down to the springhouse and put our toes in the water, and taste the cream and taste the butter." She would giggle. This was the memory that she was taking with her to the grave. I have visited that springhouse at the edge of a field in Abingdon, Virginia. The clear water is still running through it.

How does the story of Bessie relate to my work on White privilege? One White privilege is to forget one's experiences with racism. For many years after my grandmother died, I forgot Bessie. I chose not to remember this episode or her kindness to us. Such freedom of choice could protect one from bad memories, but I think the memory wounded me, and the wound still impedes my mind and spirit. The example of my southern grandmother allows me to still assume it is appropriate for me to be waited on by those who economically, if not racially, "know their place," and to keep a mostly good image of myself even if I hurt those whose humanity I do not respect. At least I think I have not given my grandchildren lessons in rejecting or fearing people of color. But White privilege makes it easy for me to forget that I am a problem for those I was taught to dominate, to evade my own positioning in racial superiority, and to avoid humbling myself among those Grandmother saw as belonging to a world beneath her. That is, a world beneath her until on her deathbed she unshackled her heart and chose a Black child, her friend and protector, to guide her out of this life.

It was not this childhood training that started my work against racism. The childhood experience was training in fear and hatred, and I felt alone with it and embarrassed by it. It took a whole social movement of resistance to the patriarchal authority of White men to give me strength to observe and act on the racial authority I saw operating in White people. It is characteristic of Eddie Moore Jr. that with initiative, energy, and a driving will for change, he capitalized on the fact that so many people are working publicly for racial justice at this time. He and his White Privilege Conferences have helped to create this groundswell. By asking a group of White people to write down some of the stories of our own commitments, Eddie Moore Jr., with his editorial team, Marguerite Penick-Parks and Ali Michael, is widening still further the understanding of systems of privilege and oppression. I imagine that many of us will be strengthened by testifying about this raw, sobering, and potentially transformative work, and I hope many readers who care about justice will take heart from some of our testimonies, as they take heart from the White Privilege Conferences.

In the 1970s I had the time, space, and professional opportunity to teach in the newly developing field of women's studies and then to bring that experience to the Wellesley College Center for Research on Women in the 1980s. It was then that I began to consciously figure out and emotionally resist male privilege and then White privilege in the curriculum. From 1982 to 1986, men and women in a seminar I was leading for college faculty members had a kind of falling-out three years in a row. The subject of each monthly seminar was how new scholarship on women might potentially change all the liberal arts disciplines. I felt that all the men who participated in these seminars were very nice people and also quite brave to join up for this feminist work. Many people traveled long distances to attend the seminars, from all over New England and from the mid-Atlantic states. There was no drop-off in attendance, but in the spring of each year a certain strain in gender relations developed, and candid conversations between men and women ground to a halt.

I did not want to end the seminar series as it was exciting and oversubscribed, and leading it paid my salary, but I thought I must be doing something wrong as a facilitator to create feelings of male-female alienation. I decided to go back through my notes and find out what I had done wrong so I could apply for further funding. Reviewing the three years of notes I found I had not actually done anything "wrong." Rather, each spring women in the seminar raised a natural question about whether materials from women's scholarship couldn't be put into freshman courses. Each year some men replied with clear reasons why this was not possible, and none of the other men disagreed with them. The curriculum was full, the syllabus was full. A couple of their metaphors, recorded in my notes, opened up a whole world to me. One man said, "When you're trying to lay the foundation blocks for knowledge, you can't put in soft stuff." He had been reading piles and piles of scholarly books and tough-minded articles by and about women, but he was still seeing scholarship on half of the world's population as "soft." The year was 1982. My notes from a different seminar two years later recorded a similar comment: A very nice man said, in good faith, "That first year the students are trying to choose their major. That's their discipline. If you want them to think in a disciplined way you can't put in extras." Like everyone, this man was born of a woman, but something had happened to make her and all other females in his life "extra." I knew these men were "nice," but I was feeling them as oppressive. What were they? At that point in my life, I felt I had to choose either that they were nice or that they were oppressive.

I was rescued from this either/or impasse by remembering 1980 when Black feminist women in the Boston area had published a number of strong pieces that implied or said that White women are oppressive to work with. I remembered my two strong negative reactions to those essays. The first was like a whine: "I can't see why they say that about us. I think we're nice!" My second reaction was outright racist, but this is where I was in 1980: "I especially think we're nice if we work with *them*." Remembering those reactions six years later, I was mortified. I spent a couple of years hoping that my niceness had been so strong that it had covered up my racist assumption that I deserved thanks for working with people I had been taught to look down on. Then I gradually gave up on that hope and concluded that, yes, I was oppressive to work with. Black women probably worked with me because I seemed at least to be *trying*.

I came to a conclusion that I still believe to this day: Niceness has nothing to do with whether or not one is oppressive. These were nice men. But they were very good students of what they (and I) had been taught: Men have knowledge, men make more knowledge, men publish and profess knowledge as professors; men run the university presses and the big research universities; men are knowers; and knowledge is male. Now I knew how they could be both oppressive and nice, but there was no joy for me in this realization. For in a sickening parallel I saw that although I felt nice, I was a very good student of the parallel assumptions I had been taught: White people have knowledge, White people make more knowledge, White people publish and profess knowledge as professors; White people run the university presses and big research universities; White people are knowers; and knowledge is White. Did this make me oppressive to work with? Yes.

It dawned on me with a shock why I could get foundation grants for my work, but my colleagues of color in the same building had such trouble getting grants. I had assumed that I wrote better grant proposals, but now I saw that as a White person, I had the whole knowledge system on my side. And I had the money system on my side too, for Whites ran the foundations I applied to, and I was in the racial group trusted with money. These realities broke apart my sense that I had earned all that I had. I was not as competent as I thought I was, and my colleagues of color were probably more competent than I had thought. But my racial group had the whole system sewn up. I was seeing something huge and inimical to my self-image. But the idea of unearned advantage, as I began to call it, had such a clear explanatory power everywhere I looked that I decided I had to pursue it. I asked myself: What else do I have that I didn't earn besides the knowledge system and the money system working for me?

My conscious mind refused to answer, twice in a row. I am in the habit of asking questions of my mind, and I usually get answers, or at least conversations from whatever other part of my mind I am asking questions of. But twice my mind refused to comment. I obsessed about this and chafed, for I felt I was in a spiritual crisis over the vast world of unfairness I had seen. Finally, I prayed on it; I went to sleep one night demanding an answer. "If I have *anything* I didn't earn, by contrast with my Black colleagues in my building and line of work, except the knowledge system and the money system working for me, *show me!*" In the middle of that night an example swam up. I flicked on the light and wrote it down. I was very disappointed; it seemed trivial. I think I was looking for something big, like The Knowledge System or The Money System. The example that I wrote down was, "I can if I wish arrange to be in the company of people of my race most of the time." It seemed like nothing. Now I think it is huge. The opportunity to choose to be with people of my race most of the time keeps me from being the only, the lonely. My subconscious mind knew its truth and that of all the other 45 examples it gave me over the next three months. I have learned that my conscious mind, with its degrees and credentials, can't be trusted to see the power-related circumstances of my life, for they don't fit with the myths about individual credit for outcomes that I had been taught. But my subconscious mind knew all about what Adrienne Rich (1986) named "the politics of location."

It is interesting to me that I am an English teacher from way back, and all the examples came up fully punctuated and worded well enough so that I did not need to edit them much. This shows me that the whole list was in a fairly shallow place in my subconscious mind all ready to be written but suppressed until I really wanted enlightenment in my heart and demanded it angrily from my mind. It is as though that fund of knowledge said, "All right, if you really want it in your soul, here it is." People often quarrel now with the idea that White people are ignorant of their privilege; some people argue that White people are fully aware of their privilege but do not want to recognize it lest they will lose some of it. I feel two things are true for me: I was taught not to see that my group had unearned advantage, but my subconscious self knew it and had agreed to suppress this knowledge that could (and did) break open my life, confront and injure my sense of virtue and deservedness. And as it happened, my spreading word of this knowledge in me would break open the lives of many others as well. Reflecting on it and seeking answers was for me a kind of action that became social action in raising the awareness of other people as well.

I did have to delete a few of the examples that swam up in the middle of the night. One example was: "I can go all day without thinking about race." This was not true. In my seminar programs for K–12 and college teachers, I was thinking about race often and was frequently hearing my Black colleagues' stories of the way they were being mistreated in the world. I believed them, and empathized, but just *did not connect their stories with mine* and with the ways I was treated in the world. I had put works by Black authors in my university reading lists, but my teaching had focused only on the deficits and affronts suffered by the characters or the authors, never on their strengths and never on my people's unearned social power. So in a way it was true after all; I could go all day, even when teaching Black women's literature, without thinking about my own race. This type of routine White blindness, oblivion, and ignorance must be extremely galling for students of color to endure.

After three months, when the examples stopped coming, a voice in me said, "Peggy, you should publish this. It is probably the most important work you will do in your life." And so it has been. The list is autobiographical, but it has spoken widely to people of color as well as White people, for different reasons. White people often say, "I had never thought about any of this. Your paper gave me a whole new perspective and changed my life." People of color often thank me for showing them they were not crazy. They had known all along that something out there was working against them that was not outright discrimination; my paper gave them names or a systemic framework that validated their experience.

A paradox of this work is that although I was writing only about what I knew as my own experience, it has resonated with the generic experience of huge numbers of other people. Students sometimes tell me that my article titled "White Privilege: Unpacking the Invisible Knapsack" (McIntosh, 1989), an abbreviated version of the paper, mattered to them more than anything else they read in college. Unfortunately, this is easy to believe, since so many college courses are devoid of serious attention to matters of power and inequity. Some readers tell me they can remember just where they were sitting when they first read it, 10, 15, or 26 years ago. I do think learning about the idea of systemic privilege is worth paying tuition for. The paper rests on a combination of remembering my own personal, down-to-earth daily experiences and seeing them systemically as reflecting historical structures and patterns that are both in me and around me in the wider society. From the success of the paper, I learned among other things about the power of using the first-person singular *I* rather than the first-person plural *we*, even when testifying about my experience of huge institutional systems. I learned about the power of giving specific examples from my own life and trying to write in a clear, straightforward way that does not require a reader to have a lot of academic vocabulary. I also learned that following my own trains of thought might make me more useful to others.

After I published the original paper (McIntosh, 1988) as a working paper of what was then called the Wellesley College Center for Research on Women, Roberta Spivek of the Women's International League for Peace and

Freedom in Philadelphia asked to create a three-page excerpt of that original paper. It was she who chose to pull out the lines about White privilege as an "invisible knapsack" and put them in the subtitle of the short paper (McIntosh, 1989). Roberta included only 26 of the 46 original examples. One reason that so many college students love this paper is that it is so short as well as written simply. I think it is less likely than much subsequent writing about privilege to make White people feel guilty, because Roberta kept the crucial lines that clearly say it is about me, not about the readers, that it is limited to a comparison of myself with the African American women in my building and line of work, and that although it focuses on race, race is only one of many dimensions of privilege and oppression.

The original longer paper (McIntosh, 1988) is more useful than the shorter "Knapsack" in a number of ways, for it addresses three forms of privilege—being White, male, and heterosexual—two of which I experience. Although the word *intersectionality* had not been coined yet, I wrote about the intersections of forms of privilege as described by the Black women of the Combahee River Collective in 1977. I know that many readers of my original paper came to realize, through its complexity, that they are privileged in some aspects of their lives and oppressed in others. I believe that all people in the United States have a combination of unearned disadvantage and unearned advantage, and this can become clearer if we remedy the lack that Adrienne Rich (1978) referred to when she said, "No one told us we had to study our lives; make of our lives a study" (p. 77).

Now the Knapsack Institute, held every summer at the University of Colorado, Colorado Springs, and the National SEED (Seeking Educational Equity and Diversity) Project on Inclusive Curriculum, together with thousands of participants in media exchanges, courses, congregations, and conference sessions, build the capacity of people in the United States to think intersectionally and to reflect on how multiple types of privilege and oppression create the structures and circumstances that influence what they see, think, and do in their lives.

As the years went on I learned that colleges and universities were the only major institutions that were taking privilege studies seriously, and that support for such studies was coming from fields like women's studies in which White students could see doubly, for example, as members of a female subordinated group and members of a dominant racial group. But despite the strong support for privilege studies that comes from colleges and universities, all the founding conventions of academic life work against dominant people's ability to learn from people I was taught to look down on. The paradigm of education as learning from the experts keeps power in the hands of the ones who have most if it already. I feel that a teacher who is really committed to social justice will need to be able to expand far beyond what he or she was taught about teaching, teachers, and knowledge itself. He or she must be willing to abandon the roles of always knowing the most, merely tolerating most students' input, and feeling confident in grading. My life was further transformed when I came to see the deficits and paralysis, the unteachability of my White teacher consciousness. As a teacher in a state of re-vision, I needed to turn from mostly being an instructor to being an observer or facilitator of learning, including my own.

In the so-called culture wars, I imagine that many people reading this are trying to survive in climates of argumentation, competition, exclusion, attack, and demonization, and are caught in the midst of fights about the validity of work on privilege systems. I appreciate the educational institutions that have been willing to confront the theme of privilege as well as the theme of oppression and have now awarded degrees to millions of students who may have some understanding that meritocracy and monoculture are myths, and manifest destiny is an ideology that endangers us globally as well as at home. I believe that some of the analyses of privilege that students have read have strengthened their political, sociological, economic, and psychological understandings, and that for many this work has supported their souls as well as their lives as citizens. Often it takes decades before an idea that was sown in college courses, including the idea of privilege systems, comes to make sense to people. I feel that if educators will bravely continue to help students to reflect on systems of oppression and privilege, this will help to mend both the social fabric and the national self-knowledge of the United States. The effects for me of testifying to my understandings have transformed my life and put it on a wider base. It has been such a relief to not feel mistrusted or even hated by people of color. It has been such a relief to be of use to so many readers and people in audiences. It is such a relief to work with scores of other people who have systemic understanding and at the same time have very different experiences from each other. It is moving to be thanked and appreciated by students and their teachers. It is encouraging to turn from a life of feathering my own nest to a life that is expanding, imaginative, social, and connected through SEED and through public presentations to countless other people working for understanding, equity, and justice. The hopeful feelings give some partial relief to the daily grief of seeing again and again the ruinous damage that comes from aggression and dominance in and around us.

My main public action project is the National SEED Project on Inclusive Curriculum, which I founded in 1987 and have codirected with Emily Style for all of its 28 years. The project is for teachers in schools and colleges who wish to form groups of their own colleagues to talk on a monthly basis in interactive and deeply personal ways. The SEED project aims to reduce exclusion, privilege, and oppressiveness in reading lists, teaching methods, and school climates. It aims to reduce damaging assumptions about students and families. It aims to widen assumptions about what schooling is and about what school structures can do to make every student know he or she belongs and is engaged in a curriculum that respects and elicits students' own knowledge from their closely observed daily experience. The very talented and devoted SEED summer staff of 16 teachers, the majority of whom are people of color, creates week-long residential experiences that prepare educators to lead monthly SEED seminars in their own institutions. The New Leaders' Workshops held in the summer teach seminar leaders-to-be what it feels like to be honored, included, respected, and heard during immersion in discussions of one's personal experiences of ethnicity, race, gender, class, sexual orientation, and a host of other variables related to "the politics of location" (Rich, 1986). Those seminar leaders in their turn engage colleagues in monthly school-based seminars that have transforming effects: expanding classroom, curricular, and school atmospheres, and deepening teachers' self-knowledge. Our analytical frames in the SEED project are informed by many other scholars, practitioners, and activists and also invented by us. I urge people in SEED seminars to follow their own trains of thought, no matter where they may lead. I believe the psyche is plural and has many different sources of multicultural knowledge that have been suppressed in most of us. The staff members of the SEED project know the oppressions of schooling and counter them with tremendously imaginative curricula that honor teachers' experience and mine their deep self-knowledge.

I grew up with habits of talking, judging, taking over in conversation among females, and planning to outdo other women. I have needed to control all these habits in order to be effective in social justice work. My main efforts at self-control in racial justice work require a litany of instructions: Thou shalt not preach, not feel self-righteous, not talk too much, not take over; thou shalt say I, not we; thou shalt listen, learn, respect, connect, believe, relate; thou shalt stop always being the speaker, the gatekeeper, the judge, the jury, the expert, the synthesizer, the initiator, the debriefer, the controller, the analyst, and the solution maker. Thou shalt understand that all thee learned about *management* and *leadership* was about how to stay in control. Thou shalt mourn for thyself in this hard learning. Thou shalt study how to be of use to others, and thou shalt keep working on thyself. Thou shalt copresent with people of color. Thou shalt share the time and money and publicity. Thou shalt quiet down, listen, and humbly learn from those thee was taught to look down on. This antique language of "thees" and "thou shalts" comes in part from the Quaker heritage in which I was schooled. But the hard race questions were not really faced in my Quaker high school; it was strong on spiritual reflection but weak on the "politics of location" (Rich, 1986).

Now I know more than Quakerism taught me. I see the injuries done to me and by me in holding both my subordinate and dominant locations in society. I need to face the traumas from racism, sexism, classism, anti-Semitism, militarism, colonialism, heterosexism, and all the other oppressions that damage me and others, though in very different ways. I feel I have to spend my time consciously and carefully in my remaining years. I need to enter the lateral, wordless layer of my mind momentarily and many times a day if possible. I feel that to do work on privilege and disadvantage I need to hesitate and use words ever more carefully. I feel that when people choose to do research on privilege systems they should not ask questions that are less complicated than they themselves are. If a researcher thinks that his or her survey questions are a bit too simple, they probably are, and in the long run will do more harm than good for accumulating understanding. I have learned to try to look for patterns, but not overgeneralize or try to be on top of any of the discussions of race that I face. Being on top of any of this is a ludicrous idea.

I urge the people who are deep into abstruse, theoretical debates over privilege to try to make their statements correspond freshly to actual nuanced experiences. But also for me it is good to keep reading and rereading, being reminded of how power works in human lives: Anzaldúa and Angelou, Baldwin and Boylan, Cajete and Chomsky—but how can I leave out Chodron?—DeGruy and DiAngelo, Ehrenreich and Enloe, Fanon and Freire, Gilman and Guinier, Horton and Hull, and so on through to Zinn. It is good to resee and reabsorb films: *The Color of Fear* (Mun Wah, 1994); *James Baldwin: The Price of the Ticket* (Thorsen, 1990); *Race: The Power of an Illusion* (Adelman & Cheng, 2003); *Cracking the Codes: The System of Racial Inequity* (Butler, 2013).

Our editors have urged us to say some of what we have learned in our work and what we want to pass on. I urge students and teachers in the next generations to take their lives very seriously and ask whatever they think of as ultimate questions sooner rather than later. Because I am a teacher I tend to focus on educational processes when giving advice. I feel that in general, it is important for students to be alert to the fact that education as a field is not asking either teachers or students to take their personal thoughts seriously but is subtly manipulating them into accepting our present social, political, and economic arrangements, which are set up for turning people into winners or losers—and most people lose. I feel it is good for a student to ask of education, Is it respecting me? Is it insulting me? Is it boring me? Is it making an effort to help all of those who enroll, regardless of our sexual, class, and ethnic backgrounds? Do we all belong? If not, what can I do to help teachers improve it or to improve things myself? What can we do to help education create a more accurate picture of us? I feel that most education takes place in an oppressive gray space, between the "lower" knowledge that is deeply personal and the higher knowledge of power systems that teachers are not taught to register on or teach about. I think education as a field unconsciously keeps students and teachers from knowing themselves and knowing how power works in, around, and above them. I also think it is time to protest an outrageous but taken-for-granted form of adultism (adult privilege) in teacher training. It is possible to get a whole PhD in education without reading a single thing said by a child about his or her experiences in school. So who is education for? Who is education serving if children are not considered sources of knowledge about the experience of school? I feel that teacher and student self-knowledge are worth putting high on a list of ideals to be worked for, and I feel we need to be ready to face what such self-knowledge reveals. It will bring every kind of power relation into the picture and humanize the teacher to be more than an instrument of instruction and the student to be more of an authority on schooling. In the SEED project, a teacher becomes a person who knows that he or she can be in a continual process of growth and development, being a student of one's life, and that this can change all of his or her actions for the better. One of the gratifying opportunities of my life has been the chance to experience how such deep work by educators can transform us and the children of the next generation into workers for social change and racial justice, despite the grim political realities in and around all of us.

References

Adelman, L. (Executive Producer), & Cheng, J. (Coproducer). (2003). *Race: The power of an illusion* [DVD]. United States: California Newsreel.

Butler, S. (Producer/Director). (2013). *Cracking the codes: The system of racial inequity* [DVD]. United States: World Trust.

McIntosh, P. (1988). *White privilege and male privilege: A personal account of coming to see correspondences through work in women's studies* (Working paper no. 189). Wellesley, MA: Wellesley College Center for Research on Women.

McIntosh, P. (1989, July/August). White privilege: Unpacking the invisible knapsack. *Peace and Freedom*, 10–12.

Mun Wah, L. (Director). (1994). *The color of fear* [Video]. United States: Stirfry Seminars.

Rich, A. (1978). Transcendental etude. In *The Dream of a Common Language: Poems 1974–1979* (p. 77). New York: Norton.

Rich, A. (1986). Notes toward a politics of location. In *Blood, Bread, and Poetry: Collected Essays, 1979–1985* (pp. 210–31). New York, NY: Norton.

Thorsen, K. (Producer/Director). (1990). *James Baldwin: The price of the ticket* [DVD]. United States: American Masters & Maysles Films.

2

THE JOY OF ANTIRACISM

James W. Loewen

In a democracy, there can be but one fundamental test of citizenship, namely: Are you using such gifts as you possess . . . for or against the people? (Louis Sullivan, 1918/1979, p. 151)

I have to start with a disclaimer. I have worked hard on this chapter, but I know it will not be good enough. *Good enough* would describe a piece that would leave us all in tears. *Good enough* would describe a message that would convince you that we in America still live, as we have always lived, in a society that especially disadvantages African Americans, Mexican Americans, and Native Americans. *Good enough* would describe a chapter that would motivate you to go out and change your home community or your college today, to make it distinct from that white supremacist culture.

How did I get to the place where I spend so much of my life exposing and opposing racism? Let me explain by telling something about the story of my life.

I enjoyed an ordinary childhood in the ordinary town of Decatur in central Illinois. Decatur was a city of about 75,000 people. About 5,000 were African American. There were a couple of Chinese American families, a couple of Japanese American families, and some ethnic variety among the white folks. Only whites lived in my part of town, the west end. Hence, my elementary school was all white and upper-middle class. Most working-class neighborhoods were somewhat integrated, however. When I went off to junior high school, about five blocks from my house, my path crossed the railroad tracks, and there I passed some black residences. So then I had black classmates.

I remember little snippets about race relations while growing up. For example, in junior high school, the two main choirs—girls' choir and mixed chorus—were all white. Even though we white kids didn't necessarily think that African Americans were equal to whites in mental abilities, we did not consider them inferior in singing. After all, we had heard of the blues, had sung spirituals in church choirs, and admired performers like Fats Domino and Billie Holiday. We whispered that Miss Lancaster, who had ruled these choirs for decades, was *racist*, though we probably didn't use that word.

I remember overhearing a conversation between my parents and their best friends, the Staffords. The Staffords admitted that "Negroes" (the term everyone used then) didn't have equal opportunity in America, including in Decatur. "Nevertheless," said Mrs. Stafford, "they're not going to move next door to me—we won't have it! I don't care if he's Ralph Bunche!" Ralph Bunche had recently received the Nobel Peace Prize for trying to mediate peace in the Middle East. Mr. Stafford's job was negotiating with farmers to buy the right to paint insurance ads on the roof of their barns. I was only 10 but old enough to understand that his occupation was hardly in the same league with an international diplomat like Ralph Bunche.

I did not understand then that the Staffords were right: That is, Ralph Bunche in fact *could not* live next door to them. Indeed, I was 59 years old, and it was 2001, when I first learned that almost every little town around Decatur was a "sundown town," where Ralph Bunche could not even have safely spent the night.

My parents did not argue with Mrs. Stafford. Indeed, my father, a medical doctor who ran the Macon County Tuberculosis Sanatorium, sometimes said vaguely anti-Semitic things, such as Jews were more likely to be Communist.[1] I need to say one thing on behalf of my father, however. In about 1955, he hired a black woman, Clemmie Howard, to be one of two receptionists in the front office of the "San." That might not seem important; receptionist is not that great a job. But when he hired her, she was the first African American ever to be a receptionist in *any* white office in Decatur. Before then, African Americans could not be receptionists. They could not be secretaries. They could not be salesclerks in department stores. They could not even be industrial workers in most factories in the North, including Decatur. They could not brew beer in Milwaukee. They could not be engineers who ran railroad locomotives. Labor unions shut them out from being electricians, plumbers, or carpenters. In short, they were not only excluded from middle-class jobs, they were also kept out of the working class, except for low-level jobs like janitor and part-time seasonal work like sweeping out boxcars. For that matter, in many towns and cities, African Americans *still* are rarely hired as receptionists, especially if they are dark skinned (e.g., see Maxwell, 2003; Samuels, 2008).

I went off to a virtually all-white college, Carleton, in a small town in Minnesota, in 1960. After I learned what sociology was, I chose to major in it. Then in my junior year, I did something a bit unusual. My friends who were French majors were going off to France. Political science majors were taking a semester in Washington, DC. Meanwhile I, a sociology major, had never lived outside the Midwest. I did not think that was competent. So I took a "semester abroad" in Mississippi, which in 1963 was the closest thing the United States had to a foreign country. I enrolled at Mississippi State University, at the time the largest all-white university outside South Africa. I wanted to see segregation firsthand. I also spent time as a visiting student at Tuskegee Institute in Alabama and at Tougaloo College in Mississippi, both historically black colleges. I suggest you do the same: Live in a milieu where you are the minority. Fit in. (That does not mean to agree with everything.) Learn. You will find that living in the black world will change your view of the white world.

What should I tell you about Mississippi? I must explain that racial segregation was a system of norms. It worked to label African Americans as inferior and keep them locked into subordinate positions. Every interaction between blacks and whites was prescribed—or proscribed. An African American who violated a norm—even a minor one like looking a white person in the eye while talking with him or her—risked punishment, such as getting fired, hurt, or even killed. When whites harmed blacks, victims typically had no recourse.

To help you see this, I present the following stories. As part of my plan to learn about Mississippi, I called the office of Dr. Douglas Conner, the only physician for the black community in Oktibbeha County or any adjoining county. He was known to be a member of the National Association for the Advancement of Colored People, a fact that in itself showed considerable courage. I told his secretary why I wanted to talk with him, and she made an appointment for me at the end of the following workday. Late that afternoon, I went to his office. Seated in the waiting room was an attractive 30-year-old black woman; her 3-year-old daughter was playing with some toys on the floor just to the right of the secretary's window. I walked toward that window to tell the secretary that I had arrived. As I did, the mother called to her child, "*Elizabeth*, come *here*." I heard the grave tension in her voice and realized she was afraid of what I might do to her little girl if I thought she was the least bit in my way. I felt terrible.

What would you have done?

Then there was the late afternoon when I was walking back to my dormitory. The edge of campus was just beyond Dugger Hall, and just beyond that were two African American households. Getting to Dugger or those homes meant walking on a narrow dirt path or following the paved road, which took twice as long. It had rained for most of the past two days, and the path was about eight inches wide of compacted clay that was okay to walk on, while stepping off the clay meant walking in mud deep enough to ooze over your shoe tops. Ahead of me on the path walked an old black man.[2] Even though I was maybe 50 feet behind him, he immediately stepped off the path upon hearing my steps and trudged along in the mud. At first I almost stopped, trying to signal that I did not plan to pass. Then I realized he would simply walk in the mud all the way, so I sped up to pass him as quickly as possible. I wanted to say to him, "You didn't have to walk in the mud for *me*!" But I realized there was no reply he could make that might not endanger him, as far as he could know. So instead, as I passed I said, "Terrible weather we've been having!" He replied, "Sho 'nuff" and was able to get back onto the path. I felt terrible.

What would you have done?

My final story comes from my final day in Mississippi, March 31, 1963. I went to the Illinois Central Railroad station in downtown Jackson, the state capital, to take the train back home to Illinois. I have said that segregation is a system of norms. It forced every person to take sides. I had to choose: Do I go into the "White Waiting Room" or the "Colored Waiting Room"? Indeed, this was part of the power of the segregation system: It forced everyone in the society to be complicit with it. If I went into the White Waiting Room, then I was part of the problem. If I went into the Colored Waiting Room, I was not, but who knew what might happen to me? The clerk might refuse to sell me a ticket. He might call the police on me. He might call Ku Klux Klan friends to come and beat me up. Or he might sell me a ticket. No way to know.

What would you have done?

I chose the Colored Waiting Room. The clerk scowled at me and made a point of waiting on every white passenger and every black passenger, including those who came in after me, before selling me a ticket. He then did sell me my ticket. I sat down to wait. The train was due in 20 minutes. Had he called the police? Had he called the KKK? Would I get arrested? Beaten up? No way of knowing. It was the longest 20 minutes of my life to that point. In the end, nothing happened; the train came; I got on.

I went to Harvard for my PhD in sociology. Again, Mississippi beckoned. I had to research and write a dissertation. During my experience at Mississippi State, I had learned that the school was not really all white. Chinese could attend, including Chinese Americans from the Mississippi Delta. The Delta stretches down northwest Mississippi from Memphis to Vicksburg. It was perhaps the most racist place in the most racist state in the most racist region in the United States. Yet it was home to about 1,300 Chinese immigrants, more than in any other southern state. Chinese people opened grocery stores there, even though for decades whites kept them out of such institutions as hospitals, the white public schools, and, of course, churches and social clubs. In the late 1950s, as the Civil Rights Movement got started (and the timing was no coincidence), whites began to allow Chinese Americans into "white" institutions like hospitals, churches, and Mississippi State. By 1967 Chinese Americans were becoming "white."

My research led to a book that is still in print, *The Mississippi Chinese: Between Black and White* (Loewen, 1971), which also became a movie and has been called a classic. You can read it yourself, which you should, because it has enduring antiracist elements for the reader to take away. Everyone "knows" that Asian Americans do better than European Americans in school, while whites do better than African Americans. That just seems natural. But by *natural*, a sociologist does not mean that a practice is natural at all, but rather it lies so deep in our culture that we neither notice nor question it.

Studying the Mississippi Delta clarified for me why Chinese grocers rose in the social structure. Except for a handful of competing white grocers, white interests were not hurt as the Chinese rose. On the contrary, some whites profited from the Chinese Americans' good fortune: food wholesalers, the Buick dealer, home builders, and the like.

For African Americans, it was exactly the opposite. White plantation owners depended upon cheap black labor—first slaves, then sharecroppers, and later tractor drivers. Whites used their political power to keep agricultural workers from being covered by federal minimum wage laws. If African Americans did better, whites reasoned, whites would do worse.[3] This thinking also affected schooling. After 1890, when white supremacists in Mississippi managed to pass a new state constitution that removed blacks from citizenship, whites then systematically deprived African Americans of educational opportunity as well. On the eve of the 1954 *Brown v. Board of Education* decision that made segregated schools illegal, Mississippi was paying $117.43 for the education of each white student and $35.27 for each black child (Lowen & Sallis, 1982). For these and other sociological reasons, Chinese Americans rose, while African Americans did not.

After Harvard, I returned to Mississippi to teach at Tougaloo. I went to Mississippi because I thought that race relations was the most important social problem in the United States as I began my adult life, and Mississippi manifested the issues more severely than anywhere else. In short, I went where I thought my life and work might make the most difference. I suggest you do the same. For some of you, even for some readers who are African American, race relations may *not* loom as the most pressing problem facing the United States. Fine. Work on what does. Or perhaps work on whatever problem or project gives you the most "bliss," using the term Joseph Campbell (1991, p. 113) made famous. In that case, maybe you can spend some time on the side—a creative hour each week?—working on improving race relations. Certainly my work on racism has made me more sensitive to other issues, such as sexism, classism, and environmental problems, and more effective in working on them.

I taught at Tougaloo for seven years. During those years, I also participated as an expert witness in several important civil rights cases and spearheaded the creation of a new kind of textbook for Mississippi history that led to a path-breaking First Amendment lawsuit, *Loewen v. Turnipseed* (1980). Then I moved to the University of Vermont (UVM).

I don't really want to write more about race relations in Mississippi, because most readers will find it easy to agree that Mississippi was racist. In some ways, however, Vermont was more difficult. I had gone from the blackest to the whitest state in America. Therefore, it just seemed natural to Vermonters that its main university would be overwhelmingly white. When I arrived in 1975, the student population totaled about 11,000, including the medical school, but had just 76 African Americans, or 0.7%.

This small number was *not* natural. More than half of all students at UVM came from the metropolitan areas of Boston, New York City, New Jersey, Philadelphia, and Washington, DC—areas of considerable racial diversity. Moreover, even 76 was a big jump from the six black students of just five years earlier, caused by one person who cared, Richard Steele, director of admissions from about 1970 through 1975. In short, *people* made a difference—people who set policies in place at the institution. Unfortunately, Steele's successors had no interest in racial diversity. Indeed, one told me about the black male she had hired supposedly to increase the recruitment of African American students, "I only hired him because they made me." She then told him to recruit black students by going to overwhelmingly white suburban high schools like Bethesda-Chevy Chase outside Washington, DC. Her rationale was that African Americans who do well at places like that show they can do well at overwhelmingly white UVM. There were two problems with this. First, the black students Steele had recruited, some from a black Catholic high school in Newark, New Jersey, mostly did fine at UVM, proving there was no need to limit recruitment to white milieux. Second, the students that UVM recruited at overwhelmingly white suburban schools were of course overwhelmingly white. By the early 1980s, the number of African Americans in the student body fell to fewer than 30.

Yet racism was hard to discuss at UVM. Most people "knew" they were not racist. Therefore, they were not very willing to question the policies that made the school—including its faculty—so white. When I brought things up, sometimes I got marginalized. One solution I did learn was to be sure to have friends who are not white, because they will not marginalize you for speaking out about race.

During my 20 years in Vermont, I came to question what became the usual race relations workshop in America. This was a meeting or series of meetings whose purpose is to get white people to see and question their white privilege, still-racist attitudes, and ways in which they still oppress or ignore people of color. There is nothing wrong with doing so. But it is not enough, and sometimes it can even distract us from what we need to be doing. Some professional workshop leaders even declare, "We have to change ourselves before we can change society." That sounds plausible but isn't. If we wait until we are ready, until we have eradicated every shred of prejudice and have taught ourselves to be suitably ashamed of our white privilege, we may wind up old and feeble before we ever *do* anything. Conversely, getting out there and trying to change society can teach us some things and wind up changing ourselves.

Many people are afraid to act to change society. They would rather assure themselves that they have correct attitudes about race relations than do something to improve them. I think this unwillingness to act stems from two problems: shyness and decorum. It can be hard to bring up a substantive problem in many social settings, especially a problem that demands action, not merely discussion. The answer to this problem is simply to *do* it, once, for example, saying out loud, "Our faculty had three African Americans out of 50 people way back in 1980. Today, we have just one. That's a problem. I suggest we can change it." Or whatever. Bringing something up once makes it easier to do again. Yes, I have felt awkward. Yes, I have been put down. But those times that I have done nothing about racism rankle me more. I still regret, at a meeting of the Mississippi Historical Society in 1974, hearing the plenary speaker say "nigger" in his talk and not interrupting him. Yes, I was seated toward the back. Yes, it was a luncheon speech, not really part of the intellectual part of the society. I still wish I had done something. I still recall, at a National Park Service workshop on teaching slavery, hearing a ranger say we should defer to black authors on slavery rather than white. I should have pointed out how that's too simple, how one's racial group membership does not inoculate one against doing inferior history. I still rue not publishing a book showing how the SAT (and similar tests) are biased against nonwhite, nonrich, nonsuburban students. But I don't regret any antiracist action I have ever taken, including those that embarrassed me at the time.

We live in interesting times. Calhoun County, Illinois, votes for Barack Obama for president, yet not one black family lives there—and for good reason. It remains a sundown county; whites tell me black households would likely still be harassed today. The most widely distributed catalog in America, *Skymall*, in front of us on every airplane seat, contains almost no illustrations of people of color, yet no one at *Skymall* excluded them on purpose. Our textbooks still give worshipful treatments to people like Vasco da Gama and Woodrow Wilson, whose actions embodied the most horrific racism. Meanwhile, antiracist whites like Bartolomé de Las Casas and Elizabeth Van Lew lie forgotten. So we have much to do.

Yet we can have the country we dream of. We can build the beloved community. *You* can right these wrongs. Act. Engage. You will find that the fray can actually be fun. Sure, you will take some knocks. You will also reap some rewards.

I remember stopping to see the huge Confederate monument in Texarkana, Texas. While I was photographing it, a young Mexican American couple also stopped by. "What do you make of this?" I asked them. The male replied, "They were not exactly on the side of human potentiality, were they?" I agreed: Confederates seceded and fought for slavery. When *you* die, may people say of you: This person acted on the side of human potentiality.

Notes

1. That turns out to have been true, but saying it nevertheless was anti-Semitic. Moreover, even if Jewish Americans were five times likelier to be Communist, that would only mean that maybe 2% of Jews were Communist, compared to maybe 0.4% of non-Jews. Thus, most Jews were *not* Communists.
2. He was about 60. I'm 72. He no longer seems so old.
3. Whites were not necessarily right. A more progressive approach to race relations might have led to economic growth and better education for all, hence a bigger pie to divide.

References

Brown v. Board of Education, 347 U.S. 483 (1954).

Campbell, J., with Moyers, B. (1991). *The power of myth*. New York, NY: Anchor.

Loewen, J. L. (1971). *The Mississippi Chinese: Between black and white*. Long Grove, IL: Waveland Press.

Loewen, J. W., & Sallis, C. (Eds.). (1980). *Mississippi: Conflict and change*. New York, NY: Pantheon.

Loewen v. Turnipseed, 488 F. Supp. 1138 (N.D. Miss. 1980).

Maxwell, B. (2003, August 31). The paper bag test. *St. Petersburg Times*. Retrieved from http://www.sptimes.com/2003/08/31/Columns/The_paper_bag_test.shtml

Samuels, A. P. (2008, February). Do light-skinned black people have an advantage? *Ebony*. Retrieved from http://books.google.com/books?id=PdMDAAAAMBA J&pg=PA165&lpg=PA165&dq=%22Do+Light-Skinned+Black+People+Hav e+An+Advantage?%22&source=bl&ots=bQxtGT0yPs&sig=7l1jm5rWDVLYj 68g5lJKpmTVRGs&hl=en&sa=X&ei=T382VKm6LoaZyASqxoGADA&ved =0CDIQ6AEwAw#v=onepage&q=%22Do%20Light-Skinned%20Black%20 People%20Have%20An%20Advantage%3F%22&f=false

Sullivan, L. H. (1979). *Kindergarten chats and other writings*. New York, NY: Dover. (Original work published 1918.)

3

KNAPSACKS AND BAGGAGE

Why the World Needs This Book

Abby L. Ferber

The chapters by Peggy McIntosh and Paul Kivel highlight the origins of their own antiracism work in their efforts to fight patriarchy and anti-Semitism. My own story is similar. My passion for social justice came out of my Jewish cultural upbringing and my identity as a woman, both of which made me acutely aware of the operations of oppression and the extreme forms it takes.

While much of the time we focus on White resistance to recognizing White privilege, I do not recall ever feeling anything like resistance (however, that does not mean I did not display resistant attitudes and behaviors that I was not conscious of). In fact, there is often an assumption that White people will be resistant to recognizing their White privilege. We need a more nuanced approach to understanding the multitude of sources of the resistance we do encounter. What factors make it more difficult and what factors facilitate different White people's ability to see, acknowledge, and work to eliminate White privilege? Thus, the title of this chapter, "Knapsacks and Baggage." The knapsack has become a wonderful metaphor for describing the many privileges that we benefit from, that we carry with us every day, wherever we go. But we each bring a lot of baggage with us. My own story is about some of my baggage that has indelibly shaped my own experience and understanding of White privilege. Our baggage is complex; it is the sum of all our life experiences, identities, socialization, messages from the media, family and educators, and more. This baggage invariably has an impact on how we respond to the concept of White privilege. The process of writing this chapter has been extremely helpful in allowing me to stop and examine a few pieces of the baggage I bring with me into my relationships, learning, and sense of who I am today. I encourage readers to spend some time examining their own baggage.

I am White. I grew up in a White, mostly Jewish, upper-middle-class suburb of Cleveland, Ohio (one of the most segregated cities in the United States). I never had reason to think about race; instead, throughout my childhood, my Jewish identity was much more salient.[1] My family was not very religious, but we were "cultural Jews." Like many nonreligious Jews, we felt an obligation to carry on our Jewish cultural and religious traditions because they have always been threatened. My own personal interpretation of these practices was that I felt I was publicly practicing and claiming my freedom of religion, remembering that throughout much of history, in many different contexts, Jews had been killed for doing so. I attended religious school on Sunday mornings and synagogue services on the High Holy Days. I was raised with the awareness that we were part of a historically persecuted minority group. I learned about the six million Jews killed in the Holocaust (although it was not until I was older that I learned about the other groups that were also targeted by the Nazis, including gays and lesbians). I learned about the Inquisition and pogroms. The history of the Jewish people that I learned was largely a history of surviving historical trauma, persecution, and genocide. The message I internalized was that Jews were the universal scapegoat, and even when fully assimilated and successful, as they were in Germany prior to the rise of the Nazis, their safety was never secure. So even though I have never considered myself religious, I have learned that what often matters more is whether other people see me as Jewish. My Jewish identity is not simply a religious designation I can choose or discard (Ferber, 1999).

I learned this lesson from my family's personal experiences as well. My great-grandparents, all from Eastern Europe, lost most of their relatives in the Nazi Holocaust. My great-grandmother Anna, for whom I am named, fled a small Russian village at the age of 16 to avoid an arranged marriage. She came to the United States to seek out a cousin who had immigrated earlier. Her parents disowned her, and she never spoke to them again; she later learned that her entire family perished in Nazi concentration camps. I realize how precarious my own existence is; were it not for random actions such as those by each of my great-grandparents, I would not be here today.

In the United States, my family members have all experienced incidents of anti-Semitism. My grandmother recounts tales of growing up in a Catholic community where her family was ostracized and she was labeled a "Christ killer." When my mother went to college at Ohio State University, her roommate asked her if she could see her horns. Recently, on a family vacation with my adolescent daughter, another member in our tour group took the guide's microphone and entertained the group with anti-Semitic jokes.

Social psychological research on objectification theory, microaggression, and stereotype threat argues that cues experienced by subjugated group members that remind them of their marginal status can reinforce and contribute to the experience of oppression (Moradi & Huang, 2008; Steele, 2010; Sue, 2010). According to Claude Steele (2010), these cues often take the form of identity threats. Identity threats can be very minimal, incidental, and even unconscious passing cues that refer to one's marginality. Yet research shows they can powerfully influence one's emotions, behavior, performance, and sense of self.

According to Steele (2010),

> The kind of contingency most likely to press [a social] identity on you is a threatening one, the threat of something *bad* happening to you because you have the identity. You don't have to be sure it will happen. It's enough that it *could* happen. It's the possibility that requires vigilance and that makes the identity preoccupying. (p. 74)

Certainly the degrees of anti-Semitism we have faced in the United States are minimal. Nevertheless, for my family, and many members of the American Jewish community, we experience race and class privilege, *and* live with the knowledge that there is no guarantee of safety.

This knowledge nurtured my awareness of other systems of oppression as well. I had trouble understanding how members of my own family could exhibit racist behaviors, given their own connections to oppression. I challenged my grandmother every time she used the word *schwartze*. While family members always responded that it was nothing more than the word for *Black* in Yiddish, I always sensed a negative connotation. I always responded the same way: "Why don't you just say Black, then? Why is it the only Yiddish word you are using in this conversation?" Like Mark Naison (2009), I never heard the term used to refer to Black people in a positive way.

I also grew up with a Black Jamaican maid. She worked in our home a couple of days a week. When my mother decided to return to school to get her master's in education and then became a teacher, Cynthia fed us when we came home from school for lunch and was there when we would get home at the end of the day until my mother returned. Cynthia was a wonderful woman who took great care of us. We felt secure with her. She had two children of her own who were close in age to my siblings and me. It wasn't until I was a teenager that I wondered if anyone was at home for them. I felt more and more uncomfortable as I recognized that my mother's own independence was predicated on the subordination of a Black woman.

Gender inequality continued to become more and more visible for me when I went to college. I learned the language to describe the multiple experiences of attempted rape and frequent sexual harassment I experienced as a teenager. At the time, they just seemed like normal life occurrences—that was the way things were. My first job was at a Burger King, where I worked for more than five years and was repeatedly groped by male employees every time I had to enter the walk-in cooler. The saddest part of this was that while this behavior made me uncomfortable, I did not see it as wrong. It never occurred to me to report it. I had internalized the message that it was simply normal for males to try to force themselves on women, and worse, that I should feel good about it because it was a sign of my attractiveness to men. As Edwin Schur (2007) puts it, "Intimidation, coercion, and violence are key features of sexual life in America today. We may profess to view coercive sexuality as deviant. But, actually, it is in many respects the norm" (p. 80). It was not until college that I was able to see my experiences in a broader context and to understand that this was not the way things had to be. ˙

I also began to understand the sources of my disordered eating. I grew up with a mother and grandmother obsessed with appearance and weight. I was put on a diet starting at age two, and my mother constantly monitored my weight. I often heard what a shame it was that I had not inherited my mom's "good nose." For my family, beauty was tied up with White images of ideal beauty. A big Jewish-looking nose could only be seen as ugly. Still today my mother and grandmother discuss publicly at family gatherings how fortunate it is that all of my mother's granddaughters inherited her good nose. When I explain the dynamics of internalized oppression, I am dismissed as taking things too seriously.

As a college student I became a feminist and began to recognize the ways in which my own life and that of those around me was shaped by gender inequity. I worked for more than four years in a homeless shelter during the Reagan era and saw firsthand the impact of the growing wealth inequality and the elimination of much of our social safety net. One of our clients, Barbara, was murdered by a serial killer targeting prostitutes. My commitment to gender and class equity grew. So did my feelings of anger, depression, and helplessness. These feelings are constantly reinforced by endless cues reminding us that women's lives are disposable. Countless television shows and movies

display women's violently murdered bodies to titillate heterosexual male view-
ers. Violence against women is sexualized; it is offered as entertainment. These
cues often serve as an identity threat, reminding women that they are targeted
for violence simply because they are women. In Jill Filipovic's (2008) words,
"The threat of rape holds women—all women—hostage. . . . The emphasis on
rape as a pervasive and constant threat is crucial to maintaining female vulner-
ability and male power" (p. 12, p. 24). I had to stop watching *Law & Order*.

So it was within this context of a life steeped in knowledge of my own
oppression that I first discovered I was privileged. It was not until I began
graduate school that I began to learn about White privilege and the real extent
of White supremacy that our nation has been founded upon. Two classes I
took were key: One was a course focused on race and the construction of
whiteness that included readings from the foundational works of David Roediger, Alexander Saxton, and Noel Ignatiev. Around the same time I took a
life-changing class called Black Feminist Thought, taught by visiting professor Rose Brewer. I learned from amazing feminist sociologists of color like
Patricia Hill Collins, Mary Romero, and Elizabeth Higginbotham, and read
the works of Angela Davis, Audre Lorde, bell hooks, and Gloria Anzaldúa.
Thus, my introduction to White privilege was immersed in a feminist intersectional framework where we examined the ways in which gender oppression does not affect all women in the same way. While the White women's
movement was fighting for women's right to abortion, women of color were
fighting for the right to give birth and keep their children (sterilization campaigns throughout the past century had targeted women of color and poor
women, sterilizing them without their consent). I learned from the work of
W. E. B. Du Bois and Peggy McIntosh that race also shaped my own life. I
began to see that I experience White privilege every day. My introduction to
White privilege as essential to feminism and the women's movement was key
to my immediate sense of urgency in examining whiteness. From women of
color I learned that we would never significantly advance equity for women if
we did not examine racial oppression and privilege at the same time.

As I worked to examine my privilege, I don't recall experiencing guilt or
shame. As a graduate student in sociology, I had learned to look at the world
through a sociological lens that emphasizes institutions, structures, and contexts. Through this sociological lens, I recognized that I often had no control
over the privileges I received, yet at the same time knew that institutional
structures of White supremacy are reproduced on a daily basis by individuals,
including myself. Thus, I have a responsibility to work toward dismantling
these systems.

When I discovered the large archive of White supremacist literature at
the University of Oregon, where I was a student, I knew immediately this

would be the focus of my dissertation, which led to my book *White Man Falling: Race, Gender, and White Supremacy* (Ferber, 1998). My intersectional feminist and privilege-focused perspective prepared me to examine the White supremacist movement in new ways. First, while all the previous literature had focused on the movement as strictly about hatred aimed at non-Whites, I argued that the movement was just as much, or more so, about the construction of whiteness and the maintenance of White privilege. Second, I saw the centrality of gender and the reassertion of male privilege as central to the movement. The only research at the time that examined gender in the White supremacist movement focused on women's involvement and roles within White supremacist organizations and communities. My burgeoning understanding of privilege revealed a different story: The White supremacist movement was largely a male movement, about reasserting masculinity and male privilege. In the context of the visibility and successes of the Civil Rights and women's movements, the White supremacist movement at that time was about reestablishing White male supremacy by White men who saw their privilege under attack.

Researching the White supremacist movement made me even more cognizant of my White privilege, ironically, because for White supremacists I am not White. They see Jews as non-Whites and as their ultimate nemesis. They construct Jews as the masterminds behind all movements for race, gender, and sexual equity, all reframed as attempts to eliminate the White race. Conducting this research helped me to make sense of my Jewish upbringing and to recognize that I grew up in a family and community striving to achieve safety in whiteness. While my great-grandparents were not seen as White when they first immigrated to the United States (this was also the case for the Irish, Italians, Greeks, and other groups), over time, restrictions against Jews at universities and workplaces were lifted, and Jews were the beneficiaries of the same benefits other whitened people received thanks to the GI Bill. Today, as a result, Jews are accepted as White in the United States, yet each time the news highlights the latest anti-Semitic hate crime, we are reminded how fragile that acceptance is.[2] I see that ever-present fear shaping some American Jews' uncritical support of Israel. As a friend said to me just the other day, "But Israel is all we have. It will always be there for us if we need it."

My own life is now about striving to maintain a both/and approach (Collins, 2008). Jews have been historically oppressed and often experience anti-Semitism today, *and* Ashkenazi Jews in the United States also benefit tremendously from White privilege. I am a member of *both* oppressed *and* privileged groups. I am *both* a Jewish woman *and* a White, upper-middle-class, heterosexual, temporarily able-bodied U.S. citizen.

Warren (2010) identifies cross-racial relationships as one of the keys to sustaining antiracist commitment. That has certainly been the case for me. My greatest growth has occurred in the context of working with people of color. While my commitment to antiracist work was strong, it was not until I began working closely with Eddie Moore Jr. on the national planning team for the White Privilege Conference that I learned to see the myriad ways in which every aspect of our lives is imbued with White supremacy. My learning ranges from numerous experiences of meeting with conference participants or hotel managers who address their questions directly to me when Eddie and I are standing there together, and they know *he* is the founder and director of the conference, to our ongoing relationship-building work over the past decade where I have learned to "trust a brother," as Eddie would put it. This has been the most significant working relationship of my life. It has also made me realize the importance of working in cross-racial teams in everything I do. That has led to other significant cross-racial working relationships in my teaching and research. It is only through these relationships that I have learned to see the countless microaggressions that people of color experience every day and that simultaneously reveal the depth of my privilege.

Embracing my whiteness has continued to be empowering for me. In the classroom, students are less likely to dismiss me when I teach about racism than when gender inequality is my subject. I found that I had a voice when it came to whiteness. I also found a way to work for social justice that was more personally and emotionally sustainable for me. I need to live my life working toward social justice, and the way I have the most power to make change is in focusing my efforts more directly on White privilege and White supremacy (from an intersectional perspective). I see now that I did not resist examining my own privilege because I saw it as essential to advancing my commitment to gender justice. Two key pieces of baggage, my feminism and my upbringing as a Jew and a woman, significantly shaped my ability to see my White privilege and recognize its significance. Thus, I do not see antiracist work as something separate and distinct from work for other forms of equity and liberation. They are and need to be recognized as all bound together in the movement for social justice (Ferber, 2012).

Perhaps the best example I can offer is the current backlash against the White Privilege Conference. I and many other folks involved have been the focus of right-wing media stories, blogs, White supremacist website articles, and so on. The attacks run the gamut from organizations such as the *Weekly Standard*, to FOX News, to Stormfront.[3] In the hate mail I receive, and in the various YouTube videos about me, the misogyny and anti-Semitism are striking. They attack me for working against White privilege, but they do so by reducing me to my nonprivileged status as a Jewish woman. Those who wish to stop us are not just doing so to defend whiteness but to defend other systems of privilege as well. *Those who wish to silence us are working from an intersectional worldview; shouldn't we be as well?*

For me, the only viable answer can be for all of us, White people and people of color, to speak and act, as often as possible, for an inclusive social justice. Every oppressed person also likely benefits from some form of privilege, and I believe we all need to start speaking from our positions of privilege. *There is no system of ism that will be destroyed without the involvement of the privileged, and there is no system of ism that will be destroyed alone.* When we look at advancing antiracism work within the context of also dismantling sexism, heterosexism, ableism, and so on, *every* voice is needed.

Why the World Needs This Book

I would like to offer an alternative perspective to that of my friend Paul Gorski in his beautiful foreword for this volume. He raises important points for White folks to consider, and they are all worthy of further dialogue. From my own perspective, the very simple reason we need this book is *because* we live in a White supremacist society. The conditions that give rise to why we are doing this work in the first place are the same conditions that create a need for a book like this. The following facts about White privilege and White supremacy help explain just why I believe this work is so desperately needed. I offer them as a contribution to Paul's discussion about the role of White folks in racial justice work, and I invite readers to continue the dialogue.

1. White people are more likely to listen to other White people. Because of White privilege and the normalization of White experience as universal and neutral, Whites are seen as less biased and more objective. That is the unfortunate reality. Books like this, then, can play an important role in encouraging White people to begin looking at their own privilege and to ask readers to examine where this assumption comes from. To reach people, we must begin where *they* are.

2. Because of the normalization of whiteness, White people's lives are often assumed to be unshaped by race and racism. It is essential that White people work to reveal otherwise. This book does not aim to teach readers about racism or the experiences of people of color, but it does examine how race operates to shape the lives of and benefit White people, and reveals a variety of paths that have moved White people to action.

3. White people must teach White people about whiteness and racism. People of color deal with racism on a daily basis; they cannot be held

responsible for educating the world about racism. We as White people have the obligation to speak up and act and write and make our voices heard in any and every way possible. *People of color are dying from racism every day.* White supremacy will not end without the active involvement of White people. White supremacy was created and is maintained and advanced by White people. We are the problem; we must be a significant part of the solution.

4. This book's title emphasizes that the contributors are not exceptional in any way. Hopefully, White readers will see aspects of themselves in some of the stories shared here. In demonstrating how just average White folks can work for racial justice, we implore White readers to join us. What are *you* doing to understand and dismantle White privilege?

5. In the foreword for this book, Gorski worries that White readers may seek "safety and comfort" (p. xii), rather than read the work of people of color. I suggest we reframe the issue in both/and terms, rather than see it as either/or. While it is far easier for White people to write and teach about White privilege, that does not mean it is easy and safe. It requires commitment and work, maintained over a lifetime. I say this not to ask for sympathy for White antiracists, but to be realistic. White people making this commitment must be prepared to lose friends, risk family relationships, risk jobs in some cases, and more. We are not guaranteed "institutional likeability" (Gorski, 2015, p. xiii). These are all risks White people *must* take, but we also should do a better job of mentoring young White social justice activists about the obstacles and resistance they *will* face in order to sustain this work. I have found Mark Warren's (2010) book *Fire in the Heart: How White Activists Embrace Racial Justice* extremely helpful in this respect.

6. We can learn a great deal from the rise in vicious attacks on the national White Privilege Conference and educators engaging in work on White privilege (e.g., see Ferber, 2003). Right-wing and Tea Party media have built coordinated, concerted, well-funded attacks on the conference over the past few years, including conducting hate mail and phone call campaigns targeting conference sponsors and speakers. They have broken copyright laws by secretly recording and videotaping conference sessions and then taking bits and pieces out of context to distort their meaning. Speakers' employers, grant sources, and such are being contacted in an attempt to cut off people's livelihood. This attack campaign is part of a larger campaign against public education and is one of many ways teaching for social justice has come under attack across the country. One important lesson to take away, however, is that there are vested powers

that feel very threatened by the work we are doing as White people to fight White privilege and White supremacy. If people are going to such great lengths to silence these voices, we must be doing something right.

7. This book also reveals the ways doing antiracist work has become essential to the authors' lives. I have become more fully human through this work. White people need to understand that their own lives are limited in so many ways, and our own self-understanding of who we are in this world is curtailed without a racial analysis. We also need to recognize that our leisure in unlearning racism comes at great peril to ourselves. Much of my own writing has focused on the need for an intersectional approach to understanding privileged and oppressed identities, but, even more important, on the need for intersectional responses and social movements (Ferber, 2012; Kimmel & Ferber, 2013). Our lives are all bound up together; as long as any group is oppressed, we are all at risk of becoming targets of oppression. Every system of oppression and privilege reinforces other systems of oppression and privilege (e.g., sexism, heterosexism, ableism, class inequality, etc.) We *all* need to be working for an inclusive social justice together.

Notes

1. I find it highly ironic how central my Jewish identity is to this story, given that I lead a secular life and personally see religion and religious institutions as more dangerous and damaging than helpful in the historic struggle for social justice. Yet, this is a result of not having the Christian privilege to choose whether to have a religious identity.
2. Just Google "hate crimes against Jews" for the latest examples; the Southern Poverty Law Center is also a great resource that tracks hate crimes and White supremacist groups.
3. Tellingly, the stories usually begin with outlets that define themselves as more moderate, such as the *Weekly Standard*, and then immediately get picked up and circulated by websites ranging from FOX News, Watchdog, and The Blaze to Stormfront and Expel the Parasite.

References and Recommended Readings

Albrecht, L., & Brewer, R. M. (1990). *Bridges of power: Women's multicultural alliances*. Santa Cruz, CA: New Society Publishers.

Anzaldúa, G., Cantu, N., & Hurtado, A. (2012). *Borderlands/La frontera: The new mestiza*. San Francisco, CA: Aunt Lute Books.

Collins, P. H. (2005). *Black sexual politics: African Americans, gender, and the new racism*. New York, NY: Routledge.

Collins, P. H. (2008). *Black feminist thought: Knowledge, consciousness, and the politics of empowerment*. New York, NY: Routledge.

Davis, A. (1983). *Women, race, & class.* New York, NY: Vintage.

Du Bois, W. E. B. (1994). *The souls of Black folk.* New York, NY: Dover. (Original work published 1903)

Ferber, A. L. (1998). *White man falling: Race, gender, and white supremacy.* Lanham, MD: Rowman & Littlefield.

Ferber, A. L. (1999, May 7). White/Jewish/other: What White supremacists taught a Jewish scholar about identity. *The Chronicle of Higher Education,* B6–B7.

Ferber, A. L. (2003, October 1). Increasing synergy between the conservative movement and the far right [Web log post]. Retrieved from http://mobilizingideas. wordpress.com/2013/10/01/increasing-synergy-between-the-conservative-movement-and-the-far-right/

Ferber, A. L. (2012). The culture of privilege: Color-blindness, post-feminism and Christonormativity. *Journal of Social Issues, 68*(1), 63–77.

Filipovic, J. (2008). Offensive feminism: The conservative gender norms that perpetuate rape culture, and how feminists can fight back. In Friedman, J. & Valenti, J. (Eds.) *Yes means yes! Visions of female sexual power and a world without rape* (pp. 13–28). Berkeley, CA: Seal Press.

Friedman, J. & Valenti , J. (2008). *Yes means yes! Visions of female sexual power & a world without rape.* Berkeley, CA: Seal Press.

Gorski, P. C. (2015). Foreward. In E. Moore Jr., M. W. Penick-Parks, & A. Michael. *Everyday white people confront racial and social injustice* (pp. ix-xiv). Sterling, VA: Stylus Publishing.

Higginbotham, E. (2001). *Too much to ask: Black women in the era of integration.* Chapel Hill: University of North Carolina Press.

hooks, b. (1999). *Ain't I a woman: Black women and feminism.* Boston, MA: South End Press.

Hull, G. T., Scott, P. B., & Smith, B. (Eds.). (1993). *All the women are White, all the Blacks are men, but some of us are brave: Black women's studies.* New York, NY: The Feminist Press at the City University of New York.

Ignatiev, N. (2008). *How the Irish became White.* New York, NY: Routledge.

Ignatiev, N., & Garvey, J. (1996). *Race traitor.* New York, NY: Routledge.

Kimmel, M., & Ferber, A. (Eds.). (2013). *Privilege: A reader* (3rd ed.). Boulder, CO: Westview Press.

Lorde, A. (2007). *Sister outsider: Essays and speeches.* Berkeley, CA: Crossing Press.

McIntosh, P. (1988). *White privilege and male privilege: A personal account of coming to see correspondences through work in women's studies* (working paper no. 189). Wellesley, MA: Wellesley College Center for Research on Women.

Moradi, B., & Huang, Y. (2008). Objectification theory and psychology of women: A decade of advances and future directions. *Psychology of Women Quarterly, 32*(4), 377–398.

Morraga, C., & Anzaldúa, G. (1984). *This bridge called my back: Writings by radical women of color.* New York, NY: Kitchen Table/Women of Color Press.

Naison, M. (2009, March 17). Is "Schwartze" a racial slur? Reflections on Jackie Mason's comedy and Yiddish vernacular speech [Web log post]. Retrieved from http://withabrooklynaccent.blogspot.com/2009/03/is-schwartze-racial-slur-reflections-on.html

Roediger, D. R. (2007). *The wages of whiteness: Race and the making of the American working class*. London, UK: Verso.

Romero, M. (2002). *Maid in the USA* (10th anniversary ed.). New York, NY: Routledge.

Saxton, A. (2003). *The rise and fall of the White republic: Class politics and mass culture in nineteenth century America*. London, UK: Verso.

Schur, E. (2007). Sexual coercion in American life. In L. O'Toole, J. Schiffman, & M. Edwards (Eds.), *Gender violence: Interdisciplinary perspectives* (2nd ed., pp. 86–98). New York: New York University Press.

Steele, C. M. (2010). *Whistling Vivaldi: And other clues to how stereotypes affect us*. New York, NY: Norton.

Sue, D. W. (2010). *Microaggressions in everyday life: Race, gender, and sexual orientation*. Hoboken, NJ: Wiley.

Warren, M. R. (2010). *Fire in the heart: How White activists embrace racial justice*. Oxford, UK: Oxford University Press.

Zinn, M. B., Cannon, L. W., Higginbotham, E., & Dill, B. T. (1986). The costs of exclusionary practices in women's studies. *Signs, 11*(2), 290–303.

4

THE POLITICAL IS PERSONAL

Kevin Jennings

I was born May 8, 1963. While my parents' eyes were on the delivery room at Broward County General Hospital in Fort Lauderdale, Florida, that day, the world's eyes were on Birmingham, Alabama.

In 1963 Birmingham was probably the most thoroughly segregated city in the nation, according to none other than Martin Luther King Jr. Local leaders decided to challenge this injustice in early 1963 in what became known as the Birmingham Campaign. Using nonviolent means like sit-ins and protests, they directly confronted White authorities.

The White authorities, led by a notoriously vicious police chief known as "Bull" Connor, decided to crush the movement, even putting King himself in jail. Having run out of adult volunteers and bail money and pretty much any other option, the leaders of the campaign agreed to let the thousands of young people who were clamoring to join in the protests take to the streets in early May.

Bull Connor launched a wave of violent terror in response. Turning fire hoses and attack dogs on the teenage protesters, he horrified the nation as TV networks broadcast footage of children being slammed against walls by high-powered streams of water and bitten by snarling German shepherds.

On the day I was born, the nation was particularly stunned by the image of a prim and proper female high school student being hosed against a wall by members of the Birmingham fire department. During the first week of my life, federal troops were deployed to restore order, and business authorities, whose commerce was choked off by the protests, agreed to desegregate. The protesters won.

The events of the 1963 spring in Birmingham not only led to the desegregation of that city's public institutions but also provided fuel for the movements that led to the passage of the Civil Rights Act (1964) and the Voting Rights Act (1965), which struck down legalized segregation and the disenfranchisement of Black voters, changing the course of American history forever.

Personally, I was too busy nursing and teething to notice. These movements didn't in fact affect my life too much at first. Segregation was all I'd ever known, so I didn't find it odd to start first grade in 1969 in an all-White class. (When the Supreme Court ordered the desegregation of schools to proceed "with all deliberate speed" in the landmark 1954 *Brown v. Board of Education* decision, most southern school boards took the court at its word when it said "deliberate," and many did not fully desegregate until two decades later.) My parents were not big fans of these social changes. Having grown up in the South as a descendant of Confederate veterans and the daughter of a father who was an active Ku Klux Klan member, my mom thought segregation was the natural and right order of things. As for my dad, on more than one occasion I saw him react to news footage of Civil Rights protests by muttering, "Go back to Africa!" Nobody in the Jennings family was a fan of integration.

Or so we thought—until 1971.

In the late winter of 1971, when I was nearly eight years old, my older brother Alan took leave from the Marines to come home from the base where he was stationed in Newport News, Virginia. One evening during his visit I was awakened by Mom yelling at Alan. Sleepy and alarmed, I came out of the bedroom I shared with my two brothers in the three-room trailer where we lived in Lewisville, North Carolina, and watched silently as the fight unfolded. I didn't understand exactly what was going on but could gather from Mom's near hysterics and Dad's stern countenance that Alan was in some kind of trouble. I would learn why: Alan had just told them that he had fallen in love with and was planning to marry an African American woman, my future sister-in-law, Claudette.

This was a bold and stunning turn of events. It had only been four years since interracial marriage was legalized in Virginia, thanks to the deliciously named *Loving v. Virginia* (1967) Supreme Court case (yes, when I was born, my brother's and my adult relationships—my partner is a man—were not legally recognized in the states where we grew up). The court's decision was made even bolder by how it flew in the face of the beliefs we had been raised with. Alan's decision literally came out of nowhere. Our family was baffled—and largely furious. At age eight I was mainly confused. Alan was my hero, the beloved older brother who had given me the cherished nickname "Champ"; why were Mom and Dad yelling at him?

We had no way of knowing it at the time, but this would be the last time my brother ever saw our father. On May 8, 1971 (my eighth birthday), Dad suffered a massive heart attack and died at the age of 47. At the funeral, one of our relatives told Alan that Dad had died of a broken heart caused by Alan's decision to marry a "n__."

Soon, word of Alan's marriage got out at school. Because my brother was married to a Black woman, I automatically was labeled an *n__ lover*. I was confused and horrified. The last thing any White boy growing up in the volatile days of desegregation wanted, when racial loyalty was at a premium, was to be known as an n__ lover. I was already considered weird because I liked books and not NASCAR (the synonym for *weird* being *queer*—a loaded term for a young boy just coming to terms with his same-sex sexual orientation), and now this. But I adored and hero-worshipped my brother, so I stood by his marriage when other White boys (it was always boys) mocked me for being related to a race traitor.

I learned an important lesson as a kid. Standing up for what is right will rarely (if ever) make you popular. Being an ally to a disenfranchised group is often severely punished by those with whom you share privilege, whether based on your race, religion, gender, sexual orientation, ability, or any of a host of other categories I could name. Bigots reserve a special fury and hatred for "their kind" who defect to the other side. My queerness, literal because I was gay, and metaphorical because I was the poor child of a single mother with a Black sister-in-law, indelibly marked me as *other* as a child.

Being the *other* turned out to be a gift. It started me down a path of working for social justice, which has shaped the course of my life and helped me be part of some momentous changes in society. In fact, the world we inhabit today would be unrecognizable in many ways to those alive (but not nursing) in 1963. Marriages like my brother's, which were illegal in 1963, are today increasingly unremarkable, and feelings toward marriages like mine are headed that way too. The America I was born into in 1963 did not allow most Black people to vote; today we have a Black president. My family celebrated our engagement with the Klan in 1963 as a badge of honor; today it is one of shame (and one that some in my family try to deny, as people are wont to do with histories that have become inconvenient). The world has changed, not because time has passed, but because, as Martin Luther

King Jr. (1968) put it, "Change does not roll in on the wheels of inevitability but comes through continuous struggle."

As they say, however, in human rights there are no final victories, and there are no final defeats. When the Voting Rights Act passed in 1965, few envisioned that five decades later the Supreme Court would void the federal role in guaranteeing the right of people to vote and that new efforts at disenfranchisement would surge as a result. When the 1973 *Roe v. Wade* ruling gave women the right to control their own bodies, few would have expected that four decades later this right would be increasingly curtailed by a concerted attack from opponents to a woman's right to choose. When U.S. Representative Bella Abzug proposed the first congressional Gay Rights Bill in 1974, few foresaw that four decades later it would still be legal to fire lesbian, gay, bisexual, and transgender people from their jobs in 29 states. When the Americans with Disabilities Act was passed in 1990, few would have predicted a quarter of a century later that unemployment among people with disabilities would still be more than twice the rate of those without disabilities. The need for continuous struggle is ongoing. Victories are still to be won as well as victories to be protected and preserved.

It's important to recognize the need for continuous struggle and to understand one's proper role in that struggle. Depending on where you sit in relationship to the issue of privilege, that role can either be the one of the disenfranchised making a *courageous push* against oppression or that of the person with privilege who uses his or her position to give a *compassionate pull* to those pushing against the very system of privilege. If you lack privilege because you are a person of color; a lesbian, gay, bisexual, or transgender person; a woman; one who practices a faith that is not Christian (or has no faith at all); a person with a disability; or for any other reason, you have to push back against the forces of oppression. Whatever degree of freedom you have today was won for you by previous generations that fought in much darker times against much worse conditions so that you could be freer than they were, and you owe it to them to continue the struggle so the next generation will be freer than you are.

I owe a personal debt to my Uncle Mickey. I never met Uncle Mickey, who was my grandmother's youngest brother, born in 1915, but I grew up hearing all about him. My dad's people were poor Massachusetts millworkers, and there was rarely money left over for luxuries like Christmas presents and, all too often, not enough for necessities like food. Uncle Mickey always showed up on the birthdays of his nephew, Chet (my father), and his nieces, Doris, Arlene, and Merlyn (my aunts), with bags full of gifts, and when supplies were running low, he showed up to hand his sister (my grandmother, Merilda) bags of groceries. My father so adored Uncle Mickey he named one of my older brothers after him. I learned all about Uncle Mickey, who died when I was five years old, as a child.

Everything, that is, except the fact that he was gay, something Aunt Merlyn told me three decades after he died.

It couldn't have been easy for Uncle Mickey to be gay, not in an era when same-sex sexual activity was a criminal offense, when being outed would cost you your job, when being gay was deemed a mental illness. But he lived his truth as best he could, never marrying, refusing to live a lie. But his courage came at a cost.

My Aunt Merlyn found Uncle Mickey dead on April 14, 1968. He'd been dead for several days when she found his body. His death certificate said he died of "portal cirrhosis of the liver." My Uncle Mickey drank himself to death, just two months before the Stonewall riots in New York and the beginning of gay liberation. He left his small estate to Aunt Merlyn, and she was able to buy a house with it, becoming the first member of our family to ever own her own home. Even in death, Uncle Mickey looked after his family.

Rarely a day goes by that I don't think of Uncle Mickey and how lucky I am that I was born in 1963 and not 1915, how I benefit daily from freedoms that previous generations won for me, freedoms that might have saved my uncle's life. I consider it my duty to make sure that the next generation has it even better than I do. I owe it to him.

If you have privilege because you were born a man, a Christian, a White person, a straight person, an able-bodied person, or for any other reason, I believe you are obligated to use that privilege to put your hand out and give a compassionate pull to those seeking to dismantle the system of injustice that gives privileges to some over others. I did nothing to earn the privileges I have because I am White, male, able-bodied, and Christian, and I have no right to benefit from them. That's called cheating, and my momma taught me never to cheat. I believe I have a moral obligation to use my privileges for good instead of for self-aggrandizement. I don't get to sit one out because it's not my issue. Silence is not neutrality; it's complicity.

I didn't learn this in a theory class. I learned it from my family. I saw my mom being paid less than men who did the exact same work as she did simply because she was a woman. I saw my brother having to abandon our hometown because his wife was Black. I saw many of my best friends from college die from AIDS because they had a virus, a disability, that I was lucky enough not to catch. And I learned that as the Black lesbian poet Audre Lorde put it, "There is no hierarchy of oppression. . . . I cannot afford the luxury of fighting one form of oppression only" (Byrd, Betsch Cole, & Guy-Sheftall, 2009, p. 220). To imagine that any human rights issue is not *my issue* is to live in a place of delusion and folly. My family and friends are made up of humans (and animals, I might add!), and any issue of theirs has to be an issue of mine. I can't be free if they aren't. I love them too much.

It's funny how easy it is for haters to understand this when it seems so hard for so many who profess to care about a specific group's rights to broaden their view to include all living beings. Like the 1970s commercial for Lay's potato chips, bigots can't stop at just one. They have bought into a system of thinking that says some people are better than others simply because of who they are. If you think you are somehow protected from this mind-set because your issue is not under attack at the moment, remember the fateful words of the Rev. Martin Niemöller (2014) about the Nazis:

> First they came for the Socialists, and I did not speak out—Because I was not a Socialist.
> Then they came for the Trade Unionists, and I did not speak out—Because I was not a Trade Unionist.
> Then they came for the Jews, and I did not speak out—Because I was not a Jew.
> Then they came for me—and there was no one left to speak for me.

When I look back over the half century that has passed since I was born, I see enormous cause for optimism and hope, for as the legendary civil rights leader and congressman John Lewis (as cited by Eversley, 2012) put it, "If you're not hopeful and optimistic, then you just give up." Just as Audre Lorde did not allow herself the luxury of fighting only one form of oppression, social justice activists, especially those of us who occupy positions of privilege in our deeply unjust society, cannot allow themselves the luxury of pessimism and defeatism. It's too easy to give up when you have only White skin in the game (or straight or Christian or able-bodied or male skin, for that matter). Our allies don't get to quit, because they can't escape back into privilege. Neither should we.

Personally, I'm in it for the long haul, because I share John Lewis's hope and optimism. I'm not saying I don't get discouraged; I do. But when I get tired, I think of my mom's struggle against sexism and my brother's struggle against racism and my uncle's struggle against homophobia and how hard these fights were for them, and I know I can fight on, too. I owe it to them. And I remember what my momma always told me as a child: "Kevin, the truth will set you free." The truth is that every person has worth and value and deserves to be treated with dignity and respect. I must continue to speak that truth as long as I live, and I truly believe it will help set us all free.

With 50 years now in my rearview mirror, I look forward to being 100, I hope, and to a new wave of progress occurring in my second half century of life. But I know that won't happen unless people not only my age but also those younger than I fight for it. As the gay White artist Andy Warhol (1975) once put it, "People will tell you that time changes things, but actually you have to change them yourself" (p. 111).

References

Americans with Disabilities Act, 42 U.S.C.A. § 12101 *et seq.* (1990).

Brown v. Board of Education, 347 U.S. 483 (1954).

Byrd, R. P., Betsch Cole, J., & Guy-Sheftall, B. (Eds.). (2009). There is no hierarchy of oppression. In *I am your sister: Collected and unpublished writings of Audre Lorde* (pp. 219–220). Oxford, UK: Oxford University Press.

Civil Rights Act, Pub. L. No. 88-352, 78 Stat. 241 (1964).

Equality Act, H. R. 14752, 93d Cong. (1973–1974).

Eversley, M. (2012, July 7). Rep. John Lewis shares life lessons. *USA Today.* Retrieved from http://usatoday30.usatoday.com/news/nation/story/2012-07-08/john-lewis-book/56067554/1

King, M. L., Jr. (1968). *I see the Promised Land.* Retrieved from http://www.seto.org/king3.html

Loving v. Virginia, 388 U.S. 1 (1967).

Martin Niemöller: "First they came for the socialists . . ." (2014). Retrieved from U.S. Holocaust Memorial Museum website: http://www.ushmm.org/wlc/en/article.php?ModuleId=10007392

Roe v. Wade, 410 U.S. 113 (1973).

Voting Rights Act, Pub. L. No. 89-110, 79 Stat. 437 (1965).

Warhol, A. (1975). *The philosophy of Andy Warhol: From A to B and back again.* New York, NY: Harcourt Brace Jovanovich.

5

CALLING OUT THE WIZARD BEHIND THE CURTAIN

Heather W. Hackman

Truth be told, I never had any intention of becoming a professor, trainer, or consultant whose focus was racial justice issues. Quite the contrary, I was actually a science major as an undergrad and planned to go to medical school and then live a very comfortable, middle-class life as a physician in Southern California. The time I took off between undergraduate and medical school, however, exposed me to social justice issues in ways I had never experienced before, and in the end it changed me in much the same way I have heard undergrads in my classes say that a social justice course or experience changed them. There's something about this content that speaks so deeply to our core human values that despite my lack of initial intention, I can think of nothing I would rather be doing than committing my life to social justice work and contributing what I can to make the world a better place. Sounds like a cliché, I know, but it's my truth. I want to do more than just work for social justice; I want to be *living a socially just* life, and to do that means I commit to growth and learning and change for the rest of my life. And so when folks ask what my path toward racial justice work has been, I typically say, "While this was not the plan, I've been doing this work for 23 years, I absolutely love it, and it has been an *incredibly imperfect* process." To better explain, I'll break down this last bit throughout this chapter: What is the *doing* of racial justice work? For that matter, what is racial justice *work*? What have the *23 years* been like? And finally, why has it been *incredibly imperfect*? Answering that last question, of course, answers the others, and so I will begin there.

Incredibly Imperfect

I first started leading racial diversity workshops in my work as a student affairs professional in 1991. In all honesty, I was a little overconfident, and so it did not occur to me then to explicitly say that I did not identify myself as an expert. Today I think there are obvious reasons why, as a White person, I would never claim expertise regarding racial issues, but just to be clear: I have never experienced racism directly, and thus how would I be able to lay claim to any lived expertise regarding racial oppression? Yes, I have spent the last 23 years studying it and its complicated presence in this society, but to claim expertise insidiously buttresses my White privilege even while I am working for racial justice. Thus, the slippery nature of whiteness and the incessant seduction of White privilege demand that I maintain a level of critical self-reflection and accountability as I do this work (at times, even my saying "I'm no expert" was an unconscious attempt to buffer a sort of false humility and gain racial justice credibility). For me this process of looking deeply and critically at my whiteness did not come easily or gracefully. In fact, I often share the arc of my development around these issues as a way to make it clear that my disclaimer of expertise is not me saying "Aw shucks, I'm just a humble White person trying to help out," but rather an honest effort to make my whiteness visible and checked. And so . . .

I grew up in Las Vegas. I was not born there (I was born in northern Michigan), but from the ages of 6 to 18 I lived in Vegas, a city I did not like and could not wait to leave. I did not have words for it at the time, but there was something about that place that made me feel lost and on the outside looking in. Today I know that it was my early sensitivity to sexism/gender oppression and heterosexism/homophobia that made Vegas a tough place to find myself and feel like home. I could not stand examples of sexism on television (and would often walk out of the room), in the movies, or in society in general, and was desperate for images of strong, powerful, intelligent, and independent women who did not cleave to the demands this sexist society placed on them. Needless to say, Vegas in the 1970s and 1980s was not replete with such images. Despite this dearth, a burgeoning feminist consciousness took root, and it would serve me well in my pursuit of science and my desire to do social justice work.

From the ages of 6 to 10 I had a stepfather who was not skilled at managing his anger and would often take it out on others. Being an only child, I frequently caught the brunt of his explosive fury. Though he mostly personalized his violence, on occasion he would engage in sexist and racist rants toward certain groups or society as a whole. In these moments I learned that one way to mitigate his gendered violence toward me was to go along with his racist comments and jokes. And while cognitively I knew that was wrong, my survival instincts completely trumped any sense of reason or fairness, and I would sidle up to his racism if only to find some moment of respite from his rage. Even when he was no longer in my life, the lesson of how to leverage racism and privilege to avoid my own oppression stayed with me, and I used it to the same effect through the end of high school.

As a high school student I looked very good on paper and had all the accomplishments that the structure of education values and rewards. My test scores and grades made me seem like I was very well educated and destined for success. In terms of the real world, however, the combination of my early racist socialization and an education full of lies, omissions, and obfuscations about race made for a hugely problematic combination as I headed off to Los Angeles for my undergrad degree. Being a biology major, I was not encouraged to take social sciences or humanities courses and instead learned in my general education the prominence, indeed the sole presence, of Western ways of thinking and knowing (the general education curricula was even titled European Cultures, or EC for short). This came to a head my first semester when in a seminar course about who knows what I blurted out some absurdly ignorant and racist comment. The room froze. I was not sure what the problem was, but I could sense something was wrong. In an instant a number of my peers basically tore me to shreds while the professor slowly rolled his chair away from the table as if to say, "Feast on her." Perhaps for most people this experience would have been humiliating enough to foster a new attitude regarding race. For me, however, the power of White supremacist thinking and the leveraging of White privilege I had learned a decade before meant it would take another year of making racist mistakes before I was willing to move in my thinking.

Unfortunately, my movement was incremental. I now just wanted people to stop calling me racist, and so I went to a few talks on campus, had a few book titles in my head, a few lines from speeches memorized, and took in just enough information to make it seem like I was on board with racial issues. But if one were to scratch beneath the surface, one would see that I had no real *knowledge* of racial issues, and worse, I had no real *desire* to know. And here is why working with White folks at this developmental stage is so difficult: I could not see *why* I should care about it because I could not see myself in this country's story of race. To Whites in this stage, caring about racial issues is tantamount to disrupting the natural social order. Endemic to this developmental space is the disaffection brought about by the disconnected, disembodied, and ultimately disassociated state that whiteness creates, supports, and propagates for its survival. How else could a White family in the early twentieth century go to church in the morning and a lynching in the afternoon *with no cognitive, emotional, or spiritual dissonance?* The answer is disassociation. To a lesser degree, how else could I have been so insensitive, callous, and victim blaming my first year or so in college? The answer again: a profound disconnection from myself and from others brought about by the system of racial oppression. For me this system had such an impenetrable hold on my mind that I truly could not see that *our* common humanity was the currency the system traded on and that I indeed had a place in the conversation.

And so there I was with my tokenized knowledge of racial issues, content in my ignorance and happy to be out of the direct line of fire for being racist. But something was percolating in me that made this ignorance untenable for much longer. My identity as a feminist, coming out as a lesbian, and learning how the systems of oppression associated with those identities worked were beginning to make it impossible for me to persist in my racial delusions. My last two years of college were filled with moment after moment, lesson after lesson, and conversation after conversation that helped me to see that learning about racial issues in earnest and then speaking out about racial oppression was deeply connected to my speaking out about gender and queer oppression and that I could not advocate for the latter without addressing the former. I would love to say that I was working from a critical race framework, but the deep roots of whiteness are not often dislodged so easily, and it would be a few more years before I was aware of what a critical race framework even was.

Twenty-Three Years

In my early 20s I built off this growing knowledge of racial issues and for the first time began to address them specifically and concretely. Unfortunately, I did so from a White liberal perspective that resulted in my wanting to "save People of Color." Awful, I know, but it's where I was at, and as I look back I can have some compassion for the me who was in that space while still being able to see how problematic that perspective was. The toxicity of this saving attitude came to a head while I was working at a private college in a very liberal and progressive town in the Northeast. I was attending a program for students of color, and I must have said something glaringly White liberal because immediately afterward a woman of color asked me what I was doing there. I told her I was there "to empower her." With palpable anger and frustration she looked at me and said, "I do not need you to 'empower' me. I need you to get out of the way." It was a pivotal moment because my White liberal mind-set was dislodged just enough for me to see how utterly insulting, dehumanizing, and racist my attitude was. In the two years that followed I learned how this idea of saving People of Color is one of the preferred weapons of whiteness. First, it tricks White people into thinking that we have actually done something to stem the tide of racial oppression in this country when in reality we have just appeased our own guilt. Second, when People of Color/Native People are not sufficiently grateful for *our* saving *them*, it allows Whites to feel as if they tried and are thus justified in giving up and walking away. And most important, this approach ends up leaving the system of racial oppression completely intact because the power dynamic of saving someone solidifies the idea that Whites are the superior group, while the perceived need to be saved supports the pathologizing of People of Color/Native People. I knew none of this when I began my work on racial issues, but I was quite clear that men saving women actually made sexism and gender oppression worse for me, and so it was not too difficult a connection to make once I was clued in.

With this information I was able to move from saving to what is typically referred to as being antiracist. More specifically, I carried the right signs, went to the right marches, supported the right groups, and while I still dropped names, this time I had actually read the books and even understood them. I was also able to discuss intersectionality and more definitively bring feminist, gender liberation, and queer liberation frameworks into the discussion of antiracism. I was sure I had arrived at the place all White people needed to be and was overly confident in my ability to engage in my work on racial issues. What I did not know was that simply being antiracist did not mean that I was looking at the countless ways I am privileged as a White person in this society. I was giving a cursory nod to my whiteness (I had read Peggy McIntosh's 1988 article on White privilege) but did not *really* know what it meant to be White. This is a common occurrence for multigenerational White U.S.-ers like myself.[1] In training sessions I often ask folks to write down the first time they knew what their racial identity was or is in the United States. Invariably People of Color/Native People will identify a racist incident, while Whites almost exclusively talk about the first time they met a Person of Color/Native Person or witnessed racism targeting them. These White folks do not notice they are focusing on others, even though the question specified *your* racial identity. When I press this point, they are startled to realize that they have never thought about what it means to be White as a stand-alone experience. Privilege and White normativity have made their lives seem racially neutral, and thus they have never had to consider what it means to be White. That was certainly the case for me, and it is what made it so frustrating for People of Color/Native People to work with me. I was still pretty clueless about what it meant to be White (and specifically the benefits and advantages that came with it), and as a result it was running unchecked in everything I did.

Thankfully, about 18 years ago I came to understand in deeper ways how my whiteness was playing out in my work, in my education, and, most important, within myself. I cannot identify a specific moment or a single conversation that did it, I just know that a corner was finally turned, and I started learning, feeling, and sharing more about the meaning of my whiteness and the critical importance of dismantling it to fully achieve racial justice. While most of this process happened in my work life, it manifested itself most poignantly in my personal relationships because I realized how White my life had been up to that point, having almost all White friends, engaging in activities and interests that White normative society valued (I played competitive tennis from ages 6 to 20 and easily fell into its class- and race-dominant framework), and not seeing myself as deeply affected when racial incidents took place in my community. As I gained clarity on how my values were compromised by consciously or unconsciously going along with my whiteness, I wasn't sure what surprised me more, that the cost was so incredibly high or that I had never noticed it before. As I looked back, the lost friendships with students of color in elementary school; the ignorance I displayed because I knew only a particular version of history; and, most important, the contradiction I lived between who I said I was (based on moral, spiritual, and even intellectual values) and how I was really living all came at the hands of whiteness.

Please don't misunderstand; I am in no way equalizing the price White people pay to that of People of Color/Native People. The sampling of costs I list here in no way compares to the utter devastation caused by colonization and genocide, the institution of slavery, the Japanese internment camps, or the treatment historically and currently of Latinos in relation to the establishment and maintenance of the U.S. border with Mexico. Instead I simply want to draw attention to the essential truth I became aware of at that time: The oppressor is also profoundly dehumanized by systems of oppression, and there cannot be racial equity unless we are all freed of this system. In his classic piece *Pedagogy of the Oppressed* (1970), Paulo Freire described in great detail how one's role as a member of the dominant group or as the oppressor destroys one's capacity to feel, to love, to understand human connection, and to live the values of compassion, justice, or freedom. The slow and steady degradation of a dominant group's humanity is as inevitable as the erosion of rock by water. It may not be obvious day to day, but over years, and in the case of whiteness over four centuries, the devastation is astonishing. I'm not a victim of this—it is by my own hand—but I am certainly caught up in the system and experience deep loss as a result. For these reasons I began to turn my attention slightly away from antiracism and slightly more toward talking about whiteness and its constituent parts. In so doing I came upon mentors, role models, and dear friends who offered me a more comprehensive, contemplative, and lived understanding of the minute-to-minute ways the White imperial gaze is policing behavior, restricting lives, and ultimately going against the reality of the interconnected web of life of which we are all a part. Leaning into this with a community of committed friends, family, and colleagues (People of Color/Native People and White people) I came to continually see more clearly the wizard behind the curtain of whiteness in my life and in my work and have striven to end this system ever since.

This Work

The evolution of how I define *racial justice work* has grown and changed in chorus with the personal path previously described. It is not just about stopping overtly racist acts, saving People of Color/Native People, or simply ending racism; for while the latter does interrupt the systemic dynamics that impact People of Color/Native People, it does not address the core driver of the system of racial oppression: whiteness. I define *whiteness* as the combination of White privilege (the system that grants concrete and life-sustaining advantages and benefits to Whites) and White supremacy (the ideology that says we deserve them because we are superior). I define *whiteness* this way because these two parts need each other to survive. If the system merely benefitted Whites with no supremacist justification explaining it away, many good-hearted White folks would see the unfairness of it. Similarly, if there was an ideology that professed the superiority of Whites in all areas of life but no system of unearned benefits and advantages to prove it, the ideology would fall away. But when taken in combination, the system of advantages and the ideology of deserving them, whiteness becomes almost invisible to most Whites, thereby ensuring our inaction against it.

The implications of this for racial justice work are significant. For me it means I must shift my focus to a much more critical analysis of whiteness in all its manifestations and make a firm commitment to end it in radical and profound ways. This means more than just *acknowledging* White privilege but actually *doing something about it* in terms that are concrete and proportional to the degree of its influence. For example, it is one thing to acknowledge that my home in Minneapolis sits on land stolen from the Dakota. It is another to pay reparations to the Dakota Nation for such a theft. Thus, understanding that home ownership is one of the key ways everyday multigenerational White U.S.-ers have accumulated and passed on wealth, and also understanding that the possession of individual parcels of property buttresses one of the core ideologies of colonizing whiteness ("rugged individualism"), *and* being serious about dismantling whiteness, I have come to see my relationship to this land differently. I have chosen to make reparations in the form of regular payments to the Dakota Nation and to funds specifically established for land reclamation. Taking this action, and others like it, helps me move from being a White person who decries the system of racial oppression or even calling out my White privilege to someone who wants to make amends for the privileges and benefits obtained at the direct expense of People of Color/Native People. Amends are not made out of guilt or shame or trying to be a good White person, but rather from a place that really wants to set right what has come before and heal this deep and old wound in our society. For this reason, I believe that at its core, this work is about us White people coming to terms with the fact that the privileges and benefits Whites get from this system are the *sole reason* for its existence. Once we do, we must then respond not with strong words or intellectualizing but with actual resource redistribution and systemic change.

From Doing to Living

As stated previously, my road to being someone who works for racial justice has been a bumpy one and is still in progress. Lately I have been up against paying closer attention to the internal work needed to move from being someone who *does racial justice work* to someone who *lives a racially just life*. This is not semantics nor is it simply a matter of perspective. Moving from *doing* to *living* is exactly what the system does not want me to do, for once I am on the path of living a racially just life, not only will I be striving to embody racial justice in everything I do, but also I will have made the final connection of racial justice to my core humanity and, thus, will have taken my commitment to a level that has the capacity to overthrow the system. White identity development theories help us understand that at the latter stages, White people actually can and do stop pledging allegiance to whiteness and replace it with a lifelong commitment to racial justice and the eradication of whiteness as a system. Once that transition has been undertaken, there is really no way to stop the march of White people in collaboration with People of Color toward racial justice and its attainment in our society.

So much of this is easier said than done, though, and it begs a few questions: (a) How can we help more White folks become aware of not only race and racism but also of their whiteness? (b) How do we take right action against racial oppression without reinforcing White privilege and supremacy? and (c) How do we actually live racially just lives when this society is so completely saturated with racialized dynamics? Is it even possible?

To the first question, the typical answer is education, but if you have sat in a class about these issues, or taught one, you know that simply conveying information about whiteness does not seem to do the trick. I think that is because whiteness runs so much deeper emotionally, socially, psychologically, economically, and politically than most Whites even know and thus requires more than education. What felt particularly poignant in my own learning about it was to see not just how I benefitted from White privilege but to also *feel* in real-life terms the price I pay for it. Reading Paulo Freire (1970) in my early 20s tapped into my deep-seated feelings about right and wrong, fairness, and being a person who cared about others. I agreed so strongly with him (and others I read after him like bell hooks [1999], and Cornell West [1993]) regarding the fundamental power of love and collective care that by the time I got to his conversation about the oppressor and dominance, I was very open to learning more about how my privilege was eroding my deepest values. And although it seems like I am contradicting myself by saying I was moved by information, what I am referring to here is the way these authors spoke to my heart, to the emotional side of my life, and to the vision of a world I wanted to live in. Similarly, we can help White folks who are having a hard time with this content not by throwing more information at them (although sometimes that does help) but by touching their humanity, their hearts, the best of who they are, and gently but consistently helping them see the price they pay for it.

Once awake, or at least more awake, to whiteness, how do White folks take the right action even while their privilege and supremacy are invariably operating in their thinking and actions? Of course, whole books have been written about this, but let me throw out a few basics that were presented to me and I believe have served me well. First, I had to realize that almost like a meme, whiteness will seek to survive by constantly situating itself in the center of my life at all times. Attuning to this helped me remember that attending to racial justice is a 24/7 commitment and helped me more effectively incorporate it into the subtleties of my daily life. Second, I had to develop the ability to "read the race of a space" and in particular read the presence of the White racial narrative. In everyday practice this means understanding the story we tell about who White people are and what it means to be White (e.g., on time, a rugged individual, a real American, hardworking, honest, responsible, civilized, smart, innovative) and then looking for it in mine and others' actions. Reading the race of a space gave me a better chance of consistently noticing, naming, and then challenging whiteness. A final general point for White racial justice advocates was to make manifest the foregrounding of whiteness in my internal lens *but not always* in my commentary. In my experience, People of Color/Native People were not interested in listening to me identify my whiteness every time it came up (because it was a lot). In majority White groups, this plays out differently, and it was actually quite important for me to name my whiteness and its privilege and supremacy. Using myself as an example of missteps and subtle goofs around this has often been a way to enter into a conversation with other White folks without bringing up a lot of defensiveness on their part.

What's Next?

While I will never purport to be done learning about the history, systemic realities, and structural impacts of racial oppression in the United States, over the last handful of years my attention has been drawn less to those areas and increasingly to that of historical trauma and deep healing on racial issues. Just as there are external realities of racial oppression manifesting themselves in the systems and structures that favor White people over People of Color/Native People at every turn, there are also internal realities that land on and in the bodies (DeGruy, 2005) of People of Color/Native People and White people in this society. And this actually makes sense when we remember that race was created to further British colonial ends, and one of the key components of such colonization is for the colonizer to colonize the mind, spirit, and body of the colonized. In this way racism and whiteness, as tools of colonization, are literally meant to take root within the bodies and minds of everyone in the society to make the system seem natural.

As I have studied the ways racial oppression has landed in my own heart, mind, and body via the examples I have shared, I have come to understand that any framework of racial justice that does not include this internal component will inevitably fail. We have seen this throughout U.S. history: Policies are enacted to redress systemic inequalities, but because there is no corresponding *internal* transformation across this society, the desired result is not fully achieved. Therefore, any structural change we seek must correspond with some degree of internal change, and the literature on trauma and racial healing advocates for just this type of approach. In recent years a colleague and I have developed a three-day intensive institute for White folks where we specifically work to get underneath the *head* aspects of being White and attend to the deep, internal processes that either block or nurture White U.S.-ers in becoming people who live racially just lives. In some academic circles this content has received criticism for being too touchy-feely or not critical enough. In truth, however, it gets to the heart of the matter with respect to the subtle ways whiteness operates. That is why it is poo-pooed—not because it is *not* powerful, but precisely because *it is so powerful*. Whiteness knows (if you will allow me to anthropomorphize it for a moment) that if White U.S.-ers actually got in touch with their whole emotional, psychosocial selves and truly came to know how deadly this system is, most of us (perhaps a strong majority of us) would never stand for it and would be compelled to join our friends and family of color in ending it. As a result, my racial justice focus today is on digging more deeply than I ever have, looking more closely than I thought possible, and leaning farther in than ever before to more rigorously challenge the wizard behind the curtain and try to live a racially just life. It has been a long journey, and I certainly do not claim to be done, but what I know is that nothing less than my very humanity is at stake, and as such I will be walking this path for the rest of my days.

Note

1. I use the term *multigenerational* as part of my description of being White in this society because it sheds light on how long ago my ancestors made the trade of their culture (German, Irish, etc.) for the moniker at first and then later the identity of White. In general, the farther back the trade, the less connection a person has to his or her cultural identity, and, thus, the more central White becomes as the only identity the person has left. As a result, Whites whose ancestry dates from a long time often have a stronger resistance to dismantling whiteness because they so deeply identify with it. And so, when I describe myself in training sessions, workshops, or even in everyday conversation I always say "multigenerational, White U.S.-er" as a way to make it very clear where whiteness exists in my life and history.

References

DeGruy, J. (2005). *Post traumatic slave syndrome.* Portland, OR: Uptone Press.
Freire, P. (1970). *Pedagogy of the oppressed.* New York, NY: Continuum.
hooks, b. (1999). *All about love: New visions.* New York, NY: HarperCollins.
McIntosh, P. (1988). *White privilege and male privilege: A personal account of coming to see correspondences through work in women's studies* (Working paper no. 189). Wellesley, MA: Wellesley College Center for Research on Women.
West, C. (1993). *Race matters.* Boston, MA: Beacon Press.

6

LOVE, SOCIAL JUSTICE, CAREERS, AND PHILANTHROPY

Andrea Rabinowitz and Alan Rabinowitz

Reader, you may have noticed that we are the only couple writing a chapter in this collection about white people learning lessons about how to work for social justice. We are a married couple, we have four children and six grandchildren, and we have lived together for 63 years of marriage. And yet we each have had professional lives in different fields. We have our own separate, modest bank accounts, and our own set of social justice activities and donations. We also sometimes work together on boards or fund-raisers. We are unfailingly interested in each others' work. For us, there is nothing better than a cause that excites, inspires, and attracts others, a cause that justifies taking time away from family and warrants making a significant financial contribution. Fund-raising for such a cause is a necessary part of anybody's activism, and securing a major gift from a prospective donor is always a source of great satisfaction, especially when it brings our world one step closer to social justice.

In our lives as activists and philanthropists, we've worked with scores of advocacy and grassroots organizing groups as donors, advisers, or board members. Our joint or individual work for social justice has been honored or given special recognition by the Association of Fundraising Professionals, the American Civil Liberties Union of Washington, Social Venture Partners, Powerful Schools, A Territory Resource (now Social Justice Fund for the Northwest), and now this book chapter on what we've learned from all these years of seeking justice.

With this as an introduction to our lives, we turn to our separate stories of what we have learned through our involvement with social justice causes—first Andrea's story, then Alan's, with our hopes for the generations that follow.

Andrea

My life and work have focused on the importance of early childhood education because I believe that we cannot achieve racial or social justice without giving children a sense of being valued and enjoyed so that they will enjoy others. I structure my writing, as I have my life, around stories of childhood, describing four ways that experiences in childhood have an impact on a person's capacity to work for racial social justice. First, I share my own early experiences that shaped the person I am today. Second, I illustrate the importance of teaching all children about difference at a young age, even white children and class-privileged children. This is important because children in early childhood are in the process of creating the foundation for how they see the world, and the more they are exposed to difference as youngsters, the better they are able to live and work across difference without judgment as adults. Third, I describe why meeting the education and care needs all children have is a basic requirement for creating a world that is fair and just. Finally, I share the critical lessons I learned with and from Alan about how to fund this important work.

Lunch in the dark front hall by the radio. Why? I wondered. My parents explained that the new president, Franklin D. Roosevelt, was to make his inaugural speech. My questions as a six-year-old persisted, and I wondered why this was so important. I often saw people lined up waiting for food, living in tumbledown shacks, and many knocked on our apartment door in Greenwich Village asking for food. My parents always found something to give them. No matter how little we had, it was more than some people had. They showed me it was important to share, even with strangers.

It was 1933, the Great Depression was at its height. My mother worked as a counselor to parents and wrote books and articles to help parents understand the development of their children. My father worked sporadically, as executive jobs were hard to find. I knew he worried about money and pinned his hopes on this new president. Perhaps his policies would pull us out of the mire and help business thrive. In fact, FDR created the milieu that I internalized, that government was "of the people, by the people, *for* the people" as Lincoln said at Gettysburg, meaning that we all must help people when people need help ("The Gettysburg Address," 2014). This philosophy has atrophied as a national philosophy over my lifetime, but it remains true for me.

My mother came from a long line of Philadelphia Quakers, and the Quaker belief that "there is that of God" (however *God* is defined) in every person was the underlying message I got from my parents. My father, as a nonreligious Jew, held this belief close to his heart. It was also stressed that men and women were equal, as were people from all cultures and races. Before and after marriage, my mother worked and always kept her own bank account. Life had gone quite well for my parents until the crash of 1929. My father lost his Wall Street job, and in 1930, with the financial help of my mother's aunt, we moved to Vienna, Austria where life was cheaper, and hoped the Depression would soon be over. I was distressed to leave home, be in a strange place, and hear ominous conversations about disturbing events in Germany. However, I learned to live in a different culture and spoke a new language. We returned to the States in 1931. Nothing had improved, but my mother was able to go back to work.

Growing up during the war to defeat Hitler, I became increasingly conscious of my Jewish heritage and the effects of anti-Semitism. A few of the Jews who escaped from Austria came to our house to be tutored in English by my parents. They also worked with some New York psychoanalysts to bring colleagues out of Vienna to the United States. From the conversations I overheard I became aware of how Jews in Vienna were being persecuted, snatched from their homes never to be seen again. I knew that had we stayed in Vienna, as a half Jew, that would have been my fate. How could there be such cruelty? How could I and my friends do anything to win this war against evil? We knitted socks, scarves, sleeveless sweaters, and fingerless gloves, which were sent to the war effort.

When I was in eighth grade someone came to my school and said volunteers were needed to teach very young children in a settlement house in Harlem, a few blocks from my school. I had often walked on the edge of Harlem and seen how crowded and dilapidated the houses looked. So I jumped at the chance to get to know the neighborhood and the children better. Children took to me, but I wondered why their clothes were shabby and their shoes didn't fit. It was hard for me to put together the history of slavery, which seemed something out of the Dark Ages, and the condition of black people as I was experiencing it in New York City 80 years later. Had anything changed since the world I read about in *Gone With the Wind* (Mitchell, 1936)? All through my childhood I had heard stories about my great-great-grandmother Deborah Fisher Wharton, who had helped slaves from the South travel north to Canada. Her house in Philadelphia was a station on the Underground Railroad. This was dangerous work, and I marveled at her courage.

All of these early experiences taught me the importance of helping others and questioning inequality. When I got to college, I had built relationships with black children in Harlem and Jewish refugees from Vienna. I had discovered my own capacity and resources for helping others while learning about the dignity and self-efficacy of those I helped. As a young child, the idea that people should have relationships with those they seek to help was simply obvious. I took for granted that we all have a duty to create a society in which all people have a chance. These lessons were part of the fiber of who I was, shaping my instincts and intuition, as well as my social networks and my choices about how to spend my time for the next 70 years. In college I helped start a race relations committee. It was hard to believe that Swarthmore College, a Quaker college founded in the mid-1860s, had had no black students until after World War II. In the spring of 1947 a number of us joined with other colleges to found the Intercollegiate League for Educational Democracy. Our aim was to get pictures and religious affiliation questions removed from college applications. This was a time when there was a quota on the number of Jews colleges would accept, and there were only a handful of blacks in the Ivy League colleges. The GI Bill (Servicemen's Readjustment Act, 1944), which made it possible for millions of veterans of World War II to go to college, did not work for blacks. Our intercollegiate group organized a conference at Princeton with 20 to 30 colleges sending delegates. Bayard Rustin was our inspirational speaker. My father had worked with him on the Citizens Committee on Harlem and took me to his tiny office on Broadway. I explained that we at Swarthmore College, along with other colleges, were trying to open up admission policies. I asked if he would be our lead speaker and describe the obstacles blacks faced in getting a college education. He agreed! Little did I know what a force he would turn out to be during the Civil Rights Movement. He was instrumental in guiding the work of Martin Luther King Jr. and others. He helped orchestrate many of the marches and gatherings that awakened millions to the blight that segregation was on our democratic ideals. The conference was a success, and I was elected president of the organization. Because of my connections through my father and the passion that he and I shared, I began to feel that I could be effective in creating change with people less fortunate than I.

"What do you have all over your face?": Children discovering difference. I took my passion for civil rights and applied it to giving small children the foundation they need. An early experience helped me see the importance of creating opportunities for privileged children to be exposed to children who are different from them. After college I was a teaching intern for four- and

five-year-olds at Shady Hill School in Cambridge, Massachusetts. My focus was always on the very young child, those all-important formative years. In the summer after my first year of teaching I drove a van picking up children who were coming to the summer playgroup at Shady Hill. Children came from inner-city Boston and the suburbs. At one stop a child was helped into the van by her black nanny. Four-year-old Nell, who was sitting next to me on the bus, looked at the nanny and asked her, "What do you have all over your face?" The woman smiled at me. I told Nell that people come in many colors; we are not all white. I realized in that moment how important it was for this wide-eyed child to see people different from herself. Children need to have opportunities to have relationships and interactions with people who are different from them so that they can learn not to be threatened by or judgmental of those differences.

"More is caught than taught." The vast majority of my career focused on providing services for children and family. I earned a master's degree in clinical social work, writing my thesis on interracial adoption, which in 1968 was relatively new. It raised many important questions for me about the value of growing up with people who look like you and the extent to which that matters if you are loved. It was a big question then, and it remains a big question today. I worked at the Cambridge Guidance Center, Children's Hospital in Seattle, and eventually I established the Seattle Child Guidance Center. In my view it was critical for any guidance center to have a community aspect where people from around the city could get support raising their children. Unlike on the East Coast, the idea of getting support to raise your children was anathema in this individualistic, western city. Even the strong and healthy could learn more about being effective parents and work together with teachers to ensure their child's well-being.

In 1988 my life and work changed when I met Sophia Bracy Harris. I had decided to spend time in the South to learn what was happening to southern children since desegregation. I made the Highlander Research and Education Center in Tennessee my base. Rosa Parks and Martin Luther King Jr. received training at Highlander in nonviolent civil disobedience in the late 1940s and during the 1950s. But with the advice of the director of Highlander, I saw that if I wanted to know about children, I needed to work with Sophia. She had created an organization to support child care workers in Montgomery, Alabama. Most important was teaching black women to value their work, to have dreams and ambitions for themselves and the children in their care. She knew that unless people valued themselves they would send subliminal messages to children that they were not valued. Sophia believed and often said that "more is caught than taught," and that children would pick up on the beliefs and actions of their caregivers.

Sophia got me thinking about internalized oppression and internalized superiority in a new way. Her work inspired a book titled *More Is Caught Than Taught: A Guide to Quality Child Care* (Guillebeaux, 1998) that described the ways our society is built on a racial hierarchy of superiority and inferiority. She helped me to see the damaging ways that an internalized sense of oppression could hold people back and spread easily to the children in their care. She made me conscious of the internalized superiority I had been taught. Sophia explained that so many poor black women have no concept of a dream, no concept that there could ever be change in their day-to-day lives. Sophia knew that change was possible; she had been one of several children who desegregated the local white high school when she was a teenager.

Sophia's story inspired me and connected us. She has been one of my greatest teachers, paving the way for my continuing education at White Privilege Conferences and the work I do with other organizations. My connection to philanthropy has made it possible for us to work together on raising funds for her organization, the Federation of Childcare Centers of Alabama, and thinking together about its future. Our relationship is interdependent, as we both have something to bring. I think it is this interdependence, the mutual sense of admiration and the different assets we each bring, that makes our relationship strong.

"Spurn not the nobly born with wealth afflicted" (my mother, misquoting a ballad from Gilbert [1882], *"Spurn not the nobly born with love affected."*). When I first married Alan, I was horrified by the idea of marrying someone who came from a family with money. It took a number of years of knowing him before I realized that we had mutual interests, and together we could put money to good use. I didn't have to fear a life with stuffy rich people, as I previously thought. I continued to be very independent even after we married. To this day I still have my own bank account, just like my mother had. If we had more money than we need to live on, I say, "Let's give it all away." But in marrying somebody from such a different world, I also learned a tremendous amount. When I founded the Seattle Child Guidance Center, Alan helped me realize that I was running a business. And although the goal was to do good for people of all racial and economic backgrounds to access support in raising their children, we could not accomplish our mission if we could not stay afloat financially.

In my work with Alan, we became part of A Territory Resource (ATR), a collective of people with money looking for ways to support grassroots organizations run by people working to improve their life circumstances. I learned many new concepts, including community organizing and social change. I had to learn to read proposals written by the groups and go on site visits to hear the stories of the people doing the work. This put me in touch with farmworkers, Native American tribes, gay and lesbian groups, and many others who were organizing in five northwestern states. As a result of working directly with people from the communities our foundation supported, many of us began to feel that they should be able to be members of the foundation. We wanted to diversify by race and class. This meant lowering the membership fee and greatly expanding the number of members. There was a real upheaval and split among the old members. One director left, as did many members. Those of us who stayed tried to step back in our leadership roles to make room for new members. One longtime white board member noticed that the people of color on the board felt that white board members were leaving because of them. So at that point, she and I decided to go back on the board. This required facing our white privilege and demonstrating that we could work together to make good decisions for the community. The shift was not easy or straightforward; however, over several years we had a much more diverse board and a much larger membership that was more representative of the region.

Alan and I also worked together to use our knowledge about money to support children. About 10 years ago we established a small foundation of our own that focused on supporting grassroots organizations in low-income communities that was devoted to improving the lives of children and the parents and educators who cared for them. This foundation has been successful because of the long-term, committed relationships we have built over our lifetime with people of color who now sit on our board. It is a racially diverse board, and the members of the board trust one another and trust us because we had preexisting relationships with them before they joined the board. One of our board members was the director of Highlander when I was living there.

My hope is that younger generations will always see possibilities for improving life for people in disadvantaged communities, venture into unfamiliar places, and get to know people different from themselves. They must never see themselves as helpers but as collaborators, a lesson I learned from the American Friends Service Committee, and the Highlander Center. Both of those organizations work alongside people, and together they find the solutions to their problems. It is important to look inside ourselves, face our biases and prejudices—including, perhaps, our internalized sense of superiority—and how they influence our choices. We must acknowledge the systemic flaws in our culture that we often overlook because we are used to them. Most of all, we must make our homes and schools places where children feel respected and enjoyed. Children must have opportunities to build relationships across differences. I fear that with our test-driven education system, the emotional and social development of children, which should be front and center, is receding into the background. Children should be seen and heard so they will feel included and want to participate in our democracy.

Alan

Each chapter in this book is supposed to have inspirational lessons for readers, especially raw recruits to the complex field of social and racial justice and equity, so let's begin with a big caveat and end with a few lessons I have learned. The caveat is that the thoughts of someone (me) who has lived for almost nine decades were developed in contexts of depressions and prosperous times and various kinds of wars—hot, cold, political, racial, ideological (socialism in America being symbiotic with capitalism), and sexual/gendered—so, let's face it, the so-called lessons I dig out from my life's stories may or may not be relevant for you and your life.

There are three parts to my life's story in this chapter. The first takes place from my birth in 1927 to my 18th birthday and going into the U.S. Navy. The second part is about my years in business, academia, and government for the following four or five decades, and the third part, somewhat overlapping with the second part, deals with my experiences with activist participatory philanthropy, making grants to grassroots and progressive organizations; the second and third parts provide some opportunities for lesson making.

It's obvious that the Great Depression and the New Deal shaped my thinking about social justice, with much emphasis on helping disadvantaged people. My understanding of the deep-seatedness of racism in America was cultivated in my early professional years. A concern with racism was virtually ubiquitous when I was active professionally in the fields of land economics, city planning, real estate investment, housing, and state-local finance. For example, in 1948 just as I started my career, the U.S. Supreme Court in *Shelley v. Kraemer* (1948) ruled that restrictive (anti-black and anti-Jewish) covenants in housing developments were not enforceable. In 1950 came the National Committee Against Discrimination in Housing and its work to get the Federal Housing Authority to stop creating segregated housing developments in the suburbs, and shortly after the American Housing Act of 1949 created redevelopments in inner cities on a massive scale, I was working with the antiracist Planners for Equal Opportunity. In the early 1970s, I testified in Congress on behalf of the American Institute of Planners against federal revenue sharing, which put federal funds in the hands of state officials (mostly from the suburbs) rather than directly into the control of local inner-city elected officials. Note that the term *inner city* often had become shorthand for places with large numbers of nonwhite people, while *suburban* often became shorthand for communities with restrictive zoning and other regulations that were designed to keep such racial diversity out. In short, antiracism was instinct in all my professional work, reflected in all the reports and books I wrote and the courses I taught.

A few biographical notes before thinking about some lessons from my and our work in philanthropy. I was born in Manhattan into a secular Reform-German-Jewish family that treasured the tribe's heritage of survival, economic savvy, and personal rectitude. In my youth I followed the script as well as I could, was always a pretty good student in school, was in college during much of World War II, and found myself in the top 1% of the class of 1950 at Harvard Business School. I had been programmed all my life to enter my father's business.

All the while I had the feeling I had to do something positive to make the world a better place. This began soon after I became aware of how privileged my family was in the middle of the Great Depression, for my father had a good salary and we had a nice house to live in, food on the table, and an automobile. I began to see that the people who lived in the shacks we passed by (known as Hoovervilles), the black kids who had razors in their shoe-shine kits and threatened me and my classmates on our way to our private school in Harlem, the organ grinder playing the "Marseillaise" on the corner picking up the pennies we were taught to give him all represented people who were not privileged at that time in our society.

It was an era of social responsibility created by the New Deal's ideas and ideals that pervaded everything, especially the private schools I attended; President Franklin Delano Roosevelt and his wife, Eleanor, were our icons who epitomized their New Deal's focus on programs to help the unemployed get back on their feet and to help a drought-stricken land return to productivity. In my case, I had no impetus to think about alternatives to a life as an ardent *New Dealer*, defined as someone who believed government was a tool for citizens to use in making society fairer and more prosperous for everyone.

When I married, I was a confirmed New-Deal-and-civil-liberties kind of person with my career in front of me. My basic sense of social and racial justice, much enhanced by the far more developed ideas of my new wife, Andrea, had become a part of me but was untested in the field. My father had been mentored and helped into the real estate business by the liberal reformer Lillian D. Wald at her Henry Street Settlement on the Lower East Side, but, slightly ironically but not surprisingly (given the pro-business environment he found himself in at the end of the nineteenth century), he was never pleased with my liberal leanings, particularly with regard to antiracist desegregation in housing markets. After graduation from business school, I worked for my father's real estate management company but was most uncomfortable with his reluctance to allow "Negroes" to rent space in the developments he was managing. As a result, after being recalled into service for the Korean War, I went to work for some nonprofit organizations that promoted desegregation in housing and did regional planning for the New York area. Over the years, there was a very profound change in the attitude of the development community, which had previously been extremely top down in terms of federal money and urban planning. It started to become obvious that unless you started working with the people you were moving around or wanted to move in, the project couldn't succeed. It started to require advocacy activities and community organizing. This was different from my father's world of real estate. And this notion of working with people and communities to create fairness and equity in systems like housing or philanthropy became the foundation of all my work. The following are some of the lessons I learned in my life and work.

Lesson: The realization that social justice is necessary for me and you (and everyone) is probably inculcated in the first few years of life and grows and grows over the years. I learned early in life that my real (white) privileged status was balanced by inescapable responsibilities for those without real privileges in our competitive society. The Golden Rule is truly operational: Do unto others . . .

Lesson: Even though I enjoyed a great education, fine health, and access to good jobs because of starting with privilege, I had been taught an important lesson: I had to prove myself capable in the real world, earning professional credentials. In my case, I had a master's degree from Harvard Business School, majored in finance, before I ventured into the private business world and later earned experiential and academic credentials in the public realm of city and regional planning and economic development. As you can imagine, the ethics and sensitivity to social or racial justice can be dramatically different in these two fields. The idea of social justice linked with grassroots organizing was not even on the horizon when I was at the Harvard Business School in 1948–1950 but was central to the ethos of the Department of Urban Planning at Massachusetts Institute of Technology when I received my doctorate in city and regional planning in 1969.

Lesson: I had to learn to be a minority in each of these combat fields, too critical of unregulated capitalism to be wholly accepted by the moguls of business, too burdened with the details of finance to be wholly accepted by either the activist community organizers or the design fraternity. I had, of course, learned that I was a member of a minority, Jews, who until decades after World War II, which ironically was fought under the banners of democracy and freedom, were not noticeably being employed in the major corporations or law firms of the day, nor were they being admitted to medical schools or the nonpolitical part of the federal government such as the State Department or the armed forces.

Lesson: I learned that having a foot in two dissimilar worlds that actually needed each other had its advantages. I may have had to forego dreaming of highest achievements within the boundaries of one or another profession, but I found I was appreciated on many occasions for my ability to translate the language and apply the techniques of one field to the language and techniques of another. For example, many of my professional articles and books on state-local finance and housing finance were used extensively in the planning field, and my knowledge of business administration and finance proved important to start-ups in the community development, advocacy, and philanthropic worlds.

Lesson: A wise person once said that if you give a man a fish, you feed him for a day, but if you teach him how to fish, he can feed himself for a lifetime. This truism helps describe the difference between what I call *real philanthropy*—which leads to systemic change—and *charity*, which often amounts to Band-Aids that help people simply get by day to day without changing the structures that contribute to their oppression.

Real philanthropists give something without expecting the gift to benefit themselves but intend the gift to help others or even humanity itself. Real philanthropy implies you're doing something that needs to be done, but there's no direct benefit from it. Corporate philanthropy is not real; it's wonderful public relations and good for keeping the working force happy, but it's too self-serving. Corporations get tax deductions for philanthropic donations counted as business expenditures. They rarely ruffle feathers or do anything risky.

Charity implies gifts that ameliorate life for needy people but do not seek to change the basic conditions that create large inequities among people. Charity is useful and necessary, but it doesn't change the system. We do need soup kitchens, I'm sorry to say, but we also need to be changing the system at the same time so we don't permanently need soup kitchens. It's a different mind-set to move things around so that you don't need the soup kitchens, so that people have their own homes and can feed themselves. Other important forms of charity include gifts to local community chests, Boy and Girl Scout troops, and school PTAs from individuals and businesses. Hundreds of individuals and corporations in each community contribute charity to the arts, musical and dance productions, and operas. Again, financing these types of endeavors is valuable. But charity in the arts is often self-serving; those who give enjoy the status of being part of the elite and being invited to elegant parties, but none of this is system changing.

We learned to avoid the charms of such forms of charity; that is, we elected to spend our time and money on activities that would change lives for the better. I found it embarrassing that so many multimillionaires report giving rather piddling amounts to charity, and I regret that so much attention is given to the foundations established by superbillionaires such as Bill Gates and Warren Buffett and so little to the variegated foundation world that Andrea and I came into in our midlives that features very small foundations giving small but meaningful gifts to small but worthy organizations.

Lesson: One must learn the difference between social change philanthropy and social and racial justice philanthropy. Social justice philanthropy (which includes racial justice) attempts to tackle the really sticky problems in society that are screwing people up. It is focused work that is sustained over time, dealing with the realities and the disparities in our society. With our involvement in the ATR foundation, we helped give some of the first grants to early feminist organizations, to the emerging environmental justice movements to protect farmworkers from the chemicals used in the fields, and to gay and lesbian organizations working to shift the culture and the law on gay rights. We funded organizations on Native American reservations. There was so much to do. And it made us feel good, I have to admit. But they were changing the system, and we were helping.

When you talk about changing white privilege, you are dealing with something that is so deeply embedded. Changing white privilege requires getting into the hard stuff that is built into the system and undermining the very structures of oppression in our society. It means dealing with the intractable problems.

Lesson: In discovering that racial justice is the larger part of social justice, we also began to realize how little we actually knew about how poor people and non-white people viewed the world (perhaps blinded by our white privilege), and thus how important it was to listen to the wisdom of the grassroots workers and the organizers in these communities. Whatever definitions of *racial justice* we had been using on the East Coast before moving to the state of Washington in 1971 expanded as we came in touch with Native American tribes; Hispanic farmworkers; lesbian, gay, bisexual, and transgender groups fighting AIDS and hostile laws; and Japanese families that had been sent to concentration camps early during World War II. The challenge was to find ways of working creatively in sync with other small-size funders on problems of racial and social injustice.

About that time, when so much was changing in society, David Hunter began a campaign to interest the major philanthropic foundations in what became known as social change philanthropy. In the end he did not make as much progress in getting foundations to fund the grassroots and progressive groups as he had hoped, perhaps because of the elitist and presumably class-based prejudices of foundation trustees then and still; it remains difficult to get these foundations to support progressive system-changing programs and to get them to diversify their staffs and boards.

Lesson: Andrea has described how in 1979–1980 we joined ATR, a group that was being mentored by David Hunter. Lessons we learned from that wonderful experience include the following:

- You can make a difference even if you don't have a billion dollars, but sometimes it doesn't feel that way.
- Why give money when it's not very much? A little goes a long way with grassroots organizations.
- Community organizing is the basic organizational technique to be encouraged with grants and training (including attention to unconscious racist and class-based policies).
- It is important that grantees with progressive objectives hire people from disenfranchised and racially affected communities to work on their staffs and to sit on their boards—the same holds true for foundations—and it is important to support these individuals with the training and financial resources needed for them to be successful in their work.
- Donors and donees need to be conscious of their mutual and interlocking forms of oppression and privilege, as well as the necessity of turning over power and resources to the donees.

Not so obvious to us at the time was the hard work involved in making group decisions about grants and in finding ways to get to know and understand many types of people we had no prior experience with (as we were from a different world), hoping that they would get to know us and collaborate with us. The creation of strong, enduring relationships, even friendships, far more than the monetary value of the grants, is at the heart of this work.

Lesson: Practically all the advocacy and social justice instruments we work with are merely little corporations, such as 501(c)(3) tax-exempt organizations with .org in their URLs, family foundations, and community foundations. Certainly (my) business training and experience is useful from the time these groups are formed and chartered to the time they are in full operation and looking for grants. In 1970 there were relatively few such grassroots organizations; by 2000 there were hundreds of thousands. Officials of each one needed to learn that orderly and understandable procedures and strict attention to tax laws and banking regulations were essential ingredients, no matter how radical the subject matter or how upsetting to the existing system. It's not so surprising that I ended up as treasurer or on the finance committee of many of the groups I or we worked with (and sometime gave money to).

Lesson: Learning how to take care of money is as important as learning how to earn it or how to get grants for a cause. Indeed, the young people at the White Privilege Conference 14 in Seattle pleaded with their elders to teach them the fundamentals of finance and even capitalism so that they and their social justice endeavors would not make mistakes that could have been avoided. As an example of such a mistake, consider how one of the fundamental rules of the game (never use restricted funds given for a specific purpose for general operations) was tragically violated by some leading antiracist nonprofits, leading to their threatened or actual demise. Their administrators had foolishly assumed unrestricted revenues would be available from some other source to pay back the monies taken from the restricted accounts.

Lesson: We discovered that we had to explain to our four children what we were up to with all these little nonprofits and little charitable foundations that we spent our time with (and gave our family money to). About that time, in the 1990s, a small foundation started by my father was being broken up into three pieces to hand over to his three children to manage, so Andrea and I became the trustees for the new smaller foundation that we could use for any philanthropic purpose we chose. What we chose was a system of making our offspring and grandchildren advisers who would each have a vote about each proposed grant and would have the privilege of suggesting a grant to some progressive organization that had taken their fancy. But to make it a proper teaching situation, anyone proposing a grant had to create a full dossier on the group, show that it had federal tax-exempt status and a decent financial record of revenues and expenses, and give reasons why we as a group should use our limited resources for it. Such training has been useful to all of them, especially when they are fund-raising for one cause or another, including nonprofits they have helped start.

Lesson: The biggest lesson I have learned is that money is nothing without someone to put it to work, and the job of the fund-raiser is to give the donor confidence that his or her contribution will be properly cared for and put to good use. I have spent much time as a fund-raiser for progressive and otherwise antiracist groups that I have given some money to; my background in finance and my willingness to part with some of my own money is always appreciated by donors. It is always fun to raise money for just causes, and I hope you are engaged in such a socially valuable activity.

Thus endeth the lessons, with my thanks to the reader. The choir will now sing the closing hymn.

References

American Housing Act. Title V of Pub. L. No. 81-171 (1949).
The Gettysburg Address. (2014). Retrieved from http://www.abrahamlincolnonline.org/lincoln/speeches/gettysburg.htm

Gilbert, W. S. (1882). Spurn not the nobly born. *Iolanthe,* act 1.

Guillebeaux, A. J. (1998). *More is caught than taught: A guide to quality child care.* Montgomery, AL: Federation of Child Care Centers of Alabama.

Mitchell, M. (1936). *Gone with the wind.* New York, NY: Macmillan.

Servicemen's Readjustment Act, Pub. L. No. 78-346, 58 Stat. 284m (1944).

Shelley v. Kraemer, 334 U.S. 1 (1948).

7

LEARNING TO BECOME AN ANTIRACIST RACIST

Christine E. Sleeter

In order to learn to work against racism, White people must first recognize its everyday existence. Further, White people learning to work against racism must come to grips with their own position as ongoing participants in and beneficiaries of racist systems that shield us from awareness of racism. As Katz (2003) put it, although White people cannot escape participation in a racist system, we can learn to become "anti-racist racists" (p. 179).

In this chapter, I cannot recount how I learned not to be racist, because I continue to benefit from racism. I can, however, share my learning to struggle against White complicity with racism—to become an antiracist racist. The chapter is organized into four parts that readers may recognize as paralleling research on White racial identity development theory (Helms, 2007): growing up segregated, learning to listen, visualizing antiracist White people, and developing commitment and resilience. While these parallels are no accident, my emphasis has always been less on identity than action, less on what it means to *be* White and more on what it means to act while White.

Growing Up Segregated

"Segregation is not neutral; it is lived and, as such, is socializing us in every moment" (DiAngelo, 2012, p. 186). I grew up in the 1950s and early 1960s in what was then a small town in southern Oregon, a documented sundown town (Loewen, 2005). With the exception of a Chinese American family that owned a restaurant, the town was all White. I have two recollections of being aware of racism while growing up. The first is when I was about six. My mother mentioned that a meteorologist who had been assigned to work there was pressured to leave after only about six months because he and his family were Black. Many years later I learned that the pressure took the form of a cross burning in his yard. In the second recollection, I was in the car visiting family in California when I heard my aunt make disparaging comments about Black people as we passed them. When I told her she shouldn't say such things about people she doesn't know, she replied that she lived near those people, and that I didn't know what I was talking about.

Before congratulating me for having tried at an early age to interrupt racism, consider this: Having only two recollections of awareness of racism over a span of 18 years living in a town that actively excluded almost all people of color—years that included the Supreme Court decision *Brown v. Board of Education* (1954), the arrest of Rosa Parks, the murder of Emmett Till, and the many other incidents that sparked and expanded the Civil Rights Movement—is astounding. This fact illustrates the tremendous power of segregated settings in obscuring racism, working in tandem with the dominant ideology that denies racism's existence. As Applebaum (2010) puts it, "One of the ways whites *actively* perpetuate systemic injustice is when they are privileged in ways that give them permission to be ignorant, oblivious, arrogant and destructive" (p. 33). As a young child I, like other children, perceived my everyday life as representative of everyone's life. But with the burgeoning systems of mass communication and transportation during the 1950s and 1960s, I now ask myself what kind of work it took on the part of my family, my teachers, my community, and myself to shut out glaring evidence of the racism that was part of the fabric of where I lived and quite visible in the media.

Learning to Listen

Until my early 20s, I tacitly perceived racism as something happening "over there" but not within my sphere. By then I had seen many, many images of civil rights protests on TV and in newspapers, and had heard speakers such as Julian Bond talk passionately about the wrongs of racism in this country.

And yet, I had grown up learning to distance myself from it. White ignorance of racism helps maintain the idea that racism is only a matter of individual prejudice rather than directing us toward interrogation of systemic racism. Such ignorance sustains the status quo and "white moral innocence" (Applebaum, 2010, p. 40), or the illusion that individual "good" White people do not necessarily participate in racism.

Although I came into the learning process perceiving myself as one of the good Whites, I acquired a different perspective in the context of interpersonal relationships in which I gradually learned to listen to people of color. While White people are used to listening to other White people, as Leonardo (2004) points out, "critical analysis begins from the objective experiences of the oppressed in order to understand the dynamics of structural power relations" (p. 141). In other words, those who are victimized most by racism—people of color—understand it best, having to navigate racism on a daily basis. White people who want to understand racism need to shift from listening to other White people to learning to hear people of color.

After graduating from college without a plan for the future, I enrolled in a teacher certification program based in inner-city Seattle designed to prepare urban teachers. In that program, I participated in an eight-month field experience in a very diverse high school located in a working-class neighborhood, completing most of my education courses in late afternoons. One such course was taught by a local Black sociologist and civil rights activist, my first experience being taught by an African American teacher. I was probably resistant to the structural analysis of racism he most surely taught (which I was not ready to hear), although I remember cautiously interviewing homeless Black people for one of his assignments.

In the high school where I was placed, however, I began having many conversations with my racially diverse students. The most lasting lesson for me was that if I showed interest in listening, the students talked freely about a wide range of things. Sometimes they deliberately played on my ignorance, such as when a few African American girls, trying to get a rise out of me, brought their birth control pills to class during a lesson about population growth. But as I picked up on ways to support the students (such as volunteering to supervise the gym during lunch so students could play basketball), students began to volunteer pieces of their lives that were personal to them and new to me, such as what it meant to be of multiracial descent.

Students of color are easier for White teachers to listen to than adults of color, especially on issues of race, likely because of the bureaucratic power teachers hold over students and, at younger grades, the smaller sizes of children. Yet gradually, I began forming personal relationships with a few teachers of color (primarily African American), allowing myself to learn about racism through conversations with them. In retrospect, I believe I was able to make myself vulnerable partly because by nature I listen before interjecting my opinion. For example, I commonly heard African American friends debrief the day with each other, in which experiences navigating racism were an overt part of the discussion. Rather than arguing, I just listened. At times when I ventured an opinion that reflected ignorance (such as my belief that the Civil Rights Movement had solved housing segregation), African American friends patiently explained to me how things actually worked. I believe that the power of personal relationships on both sides enabled me to listen and learn, while it enabled my African American friends to decide it was worth attempting to educate me.

Relying solely on friends to reeducate oneself, however, would reflect a shallow understanding of racism, an even shallower commitment to learning about it, and a minimization of the harm racism brings to those friends every day. I began to realize that I needed to read more about race in the United States. Having become aware that most White versions of U.S. history and race relations would "obscure racial processes" (Leonardo, 2004, p. 144), I began what became a lifelong commitment to reading works in ethnic studies, starting with Ralph Ellison, Richard Wright, and Malcolm X, connecting what I was able to comprehend with the stories told by my students and friends of color.

Visualizing Antiracist White People

As I gradually began to grasp the systemic nature of racism, its deep intransigence in U.S. society, and the complicity of White people in maintaining it, like many other White people, I wanted to figure out what to do about it. As Applebaum (2010) points out, however, the common question asked by Whites just learning about racism—"What can we do?"—has the effect of distancing ourselves from the problem by assuming that we stand outside of racism rather than being complicit with it (p. 183). Understanding the systemic nature of racism, which cannot be challenged through individual actions alone, is important to visualizing antiracist White action. DiAngelo (2012) explains that racism is hard for White people to see partly because Whites learn to see through an individual ideology, thereby equating racism with racist individuals rather than systems. Applebaum (2010) proposes that beginning with the principle of complicity in maintaining racist systems rather than White privilege alone "is the starting point for White engagement with systemic racial injustice" (p. 180). This principle holds that racism is best challenged through collective action in which Whites learn to become allies. Being an ally, which requires learning to listen to people of color, also requires maintaining vigilance of the impact of participation in White supremacy.

In my case, a beginning awareness of White complicity confounded me: I was aware that not becoming involved meant condoning racism. However, I also knew that White people, on becoming involved, would tend to take over, then rearticulate the work to fit White understandings and interests. We have a long history of doing just that. As I put it in a letter I wrote to Carl Grant (before I met him, while I was still a teacher in Seattle): Is there a constructive role for White people in multicultural education?

At the time I wrote to Carl, embedded in my memory was a model of White people working as allies, although it was only later that I recognized it as such. I had experienced this model as a teacher attending workshops conducted by Seattle Public Schools' Rainbow Program, which helped teachers work with desegregated student populations. The creator and director of the program, Mako Nakagawa, an educator who had been incarcerated along with other Japanese Americans during World War II, assembled over a dozen team members to create a multicultural curriculum for elementary schools and provide workshops for teachers.[1] The team was very ethnically and racially diverse and included a couple of White people who seemed to understand racism in ways similar to their teammates of color and contributed to the team effort without dominating it. Impressed by the team effort, I created a small racially diverse committee at my high school to try to bring the Rainbow concept there. But I gradually realized I didn't yet have the background to go beyond the superficial.

So I went to Wisconsin, where I earned my doctorate working with Carl Grant and his teams of Teacher Corps teachers and graduate students. Then, as an assistant professor at the University of Wisconsin–Parkside, in one of the nation's first faculty positions designated for multicultural education, I was given several opportunities to learn to work as a White person in a multiracial team addressing racism. One was serving as my campus representative to the Wisconsin State Human Relations Association (still in existence), formed in 1979 to help teacher education programs prepare teachers in multicultural education. The racially diverse group, led by an African American woman, met periodically and sponsored an annual conference. A second opportunity was serving as campus representative to the University of Wisconsin System Institute on Race and Ethnicity, another multiracial group that met periodically, held an annual conference, and published a series of books about issues related to race and ethnicity. At the time I was active, the director was Afro-Caribbean, and the publications managing editor was White. In both organizations, I not only learned to define and frame issues collaboratively with a multiracial group of colleagues but also to take on active roles (such as in connection with conference planning) that facilitated the work of the group as a whole.

Another opportunity to learn to work as a White person in a multiracial team grew from coordinating a community-based field experience that was part of a multicultural education course I taught. I assembled a network of leaders of grassroots community organizations serving mainly African American and Latino communities, where my students completed field experiences. Periodically I brought the directors together, initially to inform them about the field experience. At one such meeting, I was thinking out loud about future meetings when one of the directors said, "Christine, we appreciate what you are doing, but let us help you." They gently suggested that the directors (all of color) might have ideas to offer that I was not hearing. After that, we shifted the location of meetings out of the university and into the community centers, then reworked the student placement process according to community center needs. With this group, I learned to share authority with people of color in what began as an administrative meeting based on university needs but became a collaborative network linking university needs with the needs of communities of color.

Antiracist White people can learn to work collaboratively as allies, without dominating, on agendas that address racism primarily as people of color experience and analyze it. But since White people are socialized to take their dominance for granted, learning to work as a collaborative ally usually does not come naturally, even when they are trying, such as when I assembled the network of community center directors. It was important for me that there were groups, networks, and organizations already in existence that I could become part of, learning through processes similar to communities of practice (Wenger, 1998) how to collaborate across racial lines on addressing racism.

Learning to work as an ally in multiracial contexts is ongoing for me. Especially tricky is leading an effort, which I have done from time to time, most notably for two years as president of the National Association for Multicultural Education. I will not pretend that there were no conflicts and tensions, or that my being White was never an issue. Previous experiences, however, had taught me two very important lessons. The first was to involve the multiracial board as often as possible in making decisions rather than going it alone. This did not mean abdicating responsibility or leadership but rather collaborating in that effort. The second lesson was to make difficult decisions in relationship to their probable impact on the organization, always keeping its health and well-being at the center. Conflicts happen(ed), some having more to do with race and racism than others. But having been an active member of the organization for almost two decades, I found prioritizing the well-being of the group as a whole—the organization—a useful touchstone, a worthwhile and useful lesson.

Developing Commitment and Resilience

"In the dominant position, whites are almost always racially comfortable and thus have developed an unchallenged expectation to remain so" (DiAngelo, 2012, p. 179). Working against racism is messy and frequently uncomfortable, even when you can't imagine yourself doing anything else. The often tacitly assumed expectation of comfort needs to be questioned, particularly since White people never stop benefiting from racist systems in ways that are not always visible to us. In other words, we need to learn not to avoid discomfort but to grow through it, as the following illustrates.

During my first year at California State University, Monterey Bay (the university's first year in existence), I agreed to teach a freshman seminar that was being collaboratively planned by a racially diverse group of faculty and staff simultaneously as we taught it. One of our goals was to help our racially and ethnically diverse freshman students develop a sense of community while deepening their understanding of racism. (I overestimated how my long-past experience teaching high school and my more recent experience teaching similar concepts with upper-division university students would prepare me for teaching freshmen.) As a culminating activity, the various sections produced a theater event in which each section put on an original skit.

As my students began their performance, I briefly tuned out their voices while I checked to make sure the PowerPoint slides in English, projected from one computer, coordinated with the slides in Spanish, projected from another computer. Suddenly I felt a chill in the air. As my attention flashed back to the performance and the auditorium, I wasn't able to identify what might have happened. It wasn't until the event concluded that an African American colleague angrily demanded why I had done nothing in response to one of my White student's use of the term *colored people* rather than *people of color*. He pointed out that despite the work the campus purported to do to create a welcoming climate for students of color, not only had a White student uttered an unwelcoming term but also more disturbing was the fact that I had done nothing about it. He said that this incident, coming after other ways in which he saw me as acting White (he didn't elaborate on specifics), let him know that I was not to be trusted and should rethink my engagement with antiracist multicultural education.

I tell this story because I suspect that most White people engaged in antiracist work have had similar experiences. The issue is what the experience might reveal and what to do next. Initially deeply shaken, I briefly considered getting out and doing something altogether different, whatever that might be. Had I become the kind of White person who got in the way of significant work challenging racism? I decided to check out this question with two other African American colleagues whom I knew fairly well and who had attended the event. Both appreciated the question; both also told me to keep doing the work. In addition, both helped me see how race is always present. I will never be a perfect antiracist White person; indeed, there is no such thing. And my African American colleagues will never be certain exactly how race matters in particular instances. With respect to the skit, they advised me to talk one-on-one with the White student to help her see why the phrase "colored people" was upsetting, which I did. With respect to the larger issue of my stepping back, neither entertained that as a possibility; instead, both supported my checking out my Whiteness by talking with them, which they understood as part of the process of growing and learning.

Commitment and resilience require self-forgiveness as well as staying focused on why one engages in antiracist work. Perhaps the biggest reason for me is that racism harms people I know and care about, such as the colleagues of color who are routinely denigrated by White students and White colleagues, the African American with a PhD who experiences difficulty finding a job because he is "too" focused on race, the grandchildren of friends who dislike school because their teachers cannot relate to them, the Black mother whose son's White first-grade teacher thinks he should be referred to special education because he is "too active," the Asian immigrant colleague who went through school getting beat up because he was "different," and the Latino colleague whose contributions to professional discussion are routinely ignored by White committee members because they seem "irrelevant." By extension, racism harms millions of people of color I don't know personally in the same ways it harms people I do know.

Racism also harms those of us who are White in many ways. It limits who we can have personal relationships with; it leads us to act in ways we know are morally wrong; it fools us into thinking we deserve benefits (jobs, awards, attention, and so forth) when often we have them because others were shut out (Jealous & Haskell, 2013). Further, racism robs us of our own history. Recently I have been digging into my family history and have realized there is much I didn't know, partly because of racism and xenophobia. My German American ancestors, whom I discovered used to live in bilingual, bicultural communities in the Midwest during the 1800s, were forced under violent pressure during the two World Wars to give up not only their German language and culture but also stories about their very existence. My ancestors descend from European immigrants who participated actively in the conquest of indigenous peoples by becoming the first private owners of land indigenous peoples had been expelled from. Profit from the land, as well as escalation of its monetary value, continue to benefit me as these have been passed down through inheritance, but the whole system of Whites benefitting from conquest continues to be ignored (Sleeter, 2014). As these examples illustrate, while some memories may be celebratory, others show how we have become complicit in today's racism through actions of the past. I believe that the lack of historical memory contributes to White ignorance of racism and ambiguity about who we are culturally.

Cultivating Antiracist Racist Allies

I have learned to do the kind of work I have been doing in antiracist multicultural teacher education largely through experiences and relationships with people of color but also through experiences with White antiracist allies. The White members of the Rainbow program in Seattle, for example, first gave me a vision of White allies. As people of color point out regularly, and I gradually came to realize, White people can engage in a form of antiracist work that is particularly suited to our experiences: We can help other White people learn to stand up to racism. As a teacher educator, I engaged in this work for many years before retiring from the university (see Sleeter, 1995, 2000).

But there are many other ways I and others like me can continue to cultivate White antiracist racist allies. Remembering the importance to me of learning to work in multiracial groups, whenever I have an opportunity to construct a committee to work on something, it is always a multiracial group that includes but is not necessarily led by White people. Wishing I had been exposed to White people talking about their engagement with racism earlier than I was, I don't miss an opportunity to do so now, for example, as a guest speaker in a class. Remembering struggles I and my former teacher education students worked through in an effort to understand ourselves as potentially antiracist White people in a racist society, I am currently writing fiction in an attempt to educate a broader, general audience of readers.

There are myriad opportunities in everyone's life space to help cultivate White allies in struggles against racism. It is a healing journey worth committing to.

Note

1. *Incarceration* is the term that Nakagawa uses to describe her unjust imprisonment with over 110,000 other people of Japanese ancestry in concentration camps in the United States during World War II. Nakagawa is part of a movement to end the use of euphemistic language to describe injustice. For more details, go to http://blog.manzanarcommittee.org.

References

Applebaum, B. (2010). *Being white, being good.* Lanham, MD: Rowman & Littlefield.

Brown v. Board of Education, 347 U.S. 483 (1954).

DiAngelo, R. J. (2012). *What does it mean to be white?* New York, NY: Peter Lang.

Helms, J. E. (2007). *A race is a nice thing to have* (2nd ed.). Hanover, MA: Microtraining Associates.

Jealous, A. T., & Haskell, C. T. (2013). *Combined destinies: Whites sharing grief about racism.* Washington, DC: Potomac Books.

Katz, J. H. (2003). *White awareness: Handbook for anti-racism training* (2nd ed.). Norman: University of Oklahoma Press.

Leonardo, Z. (2004). The color of supremacy: Beyond the discourse of "White privilege." *Educational Philosophy and Theory, 36*(2), 137–152.

Loewen, J. W. (2005). *Sundown towns: A hidden dimension of American racism.* New York, NY: The New Press.

Sleeter, C. E. (1995). Teaching Whites about racism. In R. J. Martin (Ed.), *Practicing what we teach: Confronting diversity in teacher education* (pp. 117–130). Albany, NY: SUNY Press.

Sleeter, C. E. (2000). Strengthening multicultural education with community-based service learning. In C. O'Grady (Ed.), *Integrating service learning and multicultural education in colleges and universities* (pp. 263–276). Mahwah, NJ: Erlbaum.

Sleeter, C. E. (2014). Inheriting footholds and cushions: Family legacies and institutional racism. In K. Luschen & J. Flores Carmona (Eds.), *Crafting critical stories: Toward pedagogies and methodologies of collaboration, inclusion, and voice* (pp. 11–26). New York, NY: Peter Lang.

Wenger, E. (1998). *Communities of practice: Learning, meaning, identity.* Cambridge, UK: Cambridge University Press.

8

WHAT'S A NICE WHITE GIRL TO DO IN AN UNJUST WORLD LIKE THIS?

Guideposts on My Social Justice Journey

Diane J. Goodman

When I am asked what led me to do social justice work, the best answer I can give is that I feel this is what I have always been called to do. For as long as I can remember, I have been concerned about issues of equity and fairness. As a child, I would often speak up when I felt things were unjust. For example, as a sixth grader, in about 1969, I helped organize a sit-in to protest the fact that girls could not wear pants to school. (Yes, I know that policy seems unbelievably archaic now.) Many of the girls wore pants to school that day in a form of civil disobedience. I had to sneak out of my house so my parents would not see me. We won. I can now appreciate the significance of my being a "nice" white middle-class girl who did well academically. In this situation, and many others, these characteristics contributed to how I as a person and my challenges to the status quo were generally perceived in a positive light.

I grew up in a family that was not particularly political in an almost all-white working- and middle-class suburb in northern New Jersey. While I was in high school, we moved to a more affluent and slightly more racially diverse community on Long Island, New York. One message I heard repeatedly as a child was to stand up for what I believed in. I am not sure my parents realized

---

I would take it as literally as I did. While my parents thought I would make a good lawyer since I liked to argue, I always felt drawn to education. I wanted to raise people's consciousness, help them shift how they thought about the world and what was possible. This felt more enduring to me than changing particular laws or policies. While I have come to deeply appreciate all the ways people work for social justice (and I have participated in many kinds of efforts), I have always felt my niche was in the realm of education, in the broadest sense of the word.

My social justice work has taken different forms over the years. I've been a faculty member, an Affirmative Action officer, a trainer and consultant, a community educator, an activist, a speaker, and a writer. Regardless of the role, my passion and pull for wanting to foster individual and social change to create a world with greater love and justice has never waned. At times I focus specifically on racism; frequently, I look more broadly at systems of oppression and the interconnections among them. There have been countless influences on my evolution as a social justice educator and activist, but here I highlight a few significant experiences and then discuss some of my key learnings that still guide me today.

My early political involvement and consciousness-raising experiences were through feminism. The works of Audre Lorde, bell hooks, Patricia Hill Collins, Gloria Anzaldúa, Cherríe Moraga, Marilyn Frye, Alice Walker, Carol Gilligan, and Barbara Smith, among many others, lined my bookshelves. Their writings and lectures moved, taught, and inspired me. I participated in many women's gatherings, political events, and conferences. It was particularly through these experiences and the lens of being a woman that I began to explore racism, homophobia, classism, and other forms of oppression.

My graduate work was also critical to my growth as a social justice activist. In my early 20s I did not have the language or concept of doing social justice education, particularly with adults. Yet, the minute I walked into the first meeting of the Social Justice Training Project at the School of Education at the University of Massachusetts Amherst, I knew I was home. I found kindred spirits in this diverse group of graduate students committed to social change. This network of people supports and sustains me to this day.

Guideposts

I have learned and continue to learn more than I can possibly recount or convey. My journey has been less about particular transformative moments and more a steady stream of experiences that has continued to deepen and widen my understanding of racism and white privilege. The following are five guideposts (with interconnected themes) that help keep me on my path.

I am particularly speaking as a white woman to other white educators/activists, although I hope these perspectives are helpful to social justice activists more generally, especially when dealing with issues as a member of a privileged group.

"We can't teach what we don't know and we can't lead where we won't go."[1] Good intentions go only so far. My ability to be an effective educator, role model, activist, or leader is tied to the degree of consciousness and competence I myself have developed. Gaining the needed awareness, knowledge, and skills is not only an intellectual process but also one that involves deep personal and emotional work as well, and these aspects complement each other.

Understanding racism and other systems of inequality is, of course, critical. Facts, theories, history, critical analysis, alternative visions, and strategies for change are all necessary. Since issues evolve and there is always more to learn, I need to stay current and curious.

My self-development has also been essential—exploring how my racial (and other) identities and socialization shape how I view, act, and experience the world. A powerful experience during my years in graduate school was my involvement in a small antiracism group for white women. We spent a couple of years doing intense emotional work unlearning racism, confronting our racist conditioning, and working through myriad feelings. I know from this and many other experiences since that personal growth and learning involve a willingness to take risks, make mistakes, sit with discomfort, and find ways to deal with feelings to stay engaged.

Particularly challenging is the task of becoming ever more conscious of how I enact my sense of internalized superiority: Do I more readily give white people the benefit of the doubt on being competent? Do I feel the same degree of empathy and urgency to act when people don't look like me? I also keep learning about my sense of entitlement and how my white privilege allows me to take things for granted and be oblivious to the challenges faced by people of color. I remember when I was facilitating a workshop and I first told the story about how I would open up a bag of snacks in a store to taste them so I could decide if my kids would like them and how many I should buy. (I would always pay for whatever I opened.) Seeing the look of shock on the faces of the people of color, it dawned on me that my unconscious assumption that I could just sample food with impunity, because no one ever suspects me of any wrongdoing, was an expression of my white (and class and gender) privilege and sense of entitlement—of being a "nice white girl."

Recognizing that I am always a work in progress helps me develop and maintain humility and check my self-righteousness and arrogance. An ability and willingness to listen—deeply listen—to the needs, perspectives, experiences, ideas, and feedback from people of color, even if it's not expressed in the way I would like, is a central piece of personal growth. White people in multiracial groups need to learn how *not* to be in charge and in control. Especially as I engage in antiracism work, I try to navigate how to support and follow the lead of people of color while also contributing the knowledge, skills, and resources I have to offer.

It takes courage to be a leader, to speak up, challenge the status quo, try new initiatives, put oneself out there. I struggle with this frequently, doubting the importance of what I have to say, worrying I will get it wrong, fearing judgment and ridicule. But if I expect others to take risks, I can expect no less of myself. "We can't teach what we don't know, and we can't lead where we won't go."

Everything is about relationships. I increasingly believe that everything comes down to relationships. What I care about, how I learn, my motivation to stay engaged, my ability to engage others, the support I get on my journey, opportunities for work, and the effectiveness of my change efforts are all connected to relationships with others. The more I do my own work (see previous guidepost), the stronger and more authentic those relationships can be.

Relationships of many sorts have been critical to my learning and evolution as a social justice activist, and doing this work has created many openings for personal connections. In graduate school we formed a community that worked and played together, endlessly discussing theory and our personal experiences related to our social identities and systemic inequalities. In addition, since I often work with diverse co-trainers and colleagues, we have opportunities to talk about how our social identities inform how we collaborate and think about social issues. Every time I am in a setting where people share who they are and how they experience the world, it is a privilege and a gift, and some of my most powerful learning. Hearing these stories not only gives me insight into other people's realities but also helps me reflect on my own. I clearly remember a dinner at a conference many years ago where for the first time I heard black women share their worries and strategies to keep their black sons safe as these boys went out into the world, especially if they engaged with police. (I have since heard similar stories many times.) It struck me how different it was from my experience as a "nice white girl" and the jingle I learned as a child about "Officer Friendly" if I ever needed any help.

When developing relationships with people of color, I always expect that I will have to earn their trust; I never expect that I will be given the benefit of the doubt that I am one of the "good" white people who "gets it." A black student told me that he assumed when I was first hired that I would just be another "white lady administrator." It is usually only after I have demonstrated and continue to demonstrate my authentic and ongoing commitment to racial justice that relationships with people of color can become more honest and open.

I often think about and refer to the words of Pat Parker (1990) from her poem "For the White Person Who Wants to Know How to Be My Friend": "The first thing you do is forget that I'm black. / Second, you must never forget that I'm black" (p. 297). This seeming paradox highlights the importance of seeing people's full humanity, including the significance of their race, if we are to have meaningful interracial relationships.

Relationships with other white people are also indispensable. We can nurture and challenge each other in ways that take the burden off people of color to educate or take care of us. I regularly look to other white people to be role models, providing inspiration and examples of what solidarity and effective action look like.

White people and people of color provide essential support and accountability. I could not do this work without people to encourage and challenge me intellectually, politically, professionally, and emotionally. I need people to check in with when I feel confused, to provide reality checks, give me hugs, let me know if I am being an effective ally, push me to think and write more critically, reassure me when I doubt my abilities, and give me feedback to help me grow. One extremely valuable piece of advice came from a friend of color after I was obsessing about how I inadequately facilitated a racial discussion. She finally said, "Get over yourself! Learn what you need to learn from this and move on. We need you out there doing this work." Relationships with people of color and other white people committed to racial justice help ensure that I, especially as a white person, am acting in ways that are responsible and in solidarity with the efforts of people of color. I cannot (and should not) do this work alone. Moreover, when I enjoy the people with whom I am working, it helps me persevere through the inevitable challenges and disappointments. Since social change requires collective action, I need to be able to forge bonds and work collaboratively.

"*Can you love them enough to help them learn?*" (Romney, 2000, p. 71). Whether in formal educational contexts or casual conversations, in front of the classroom or across the kitchen table, this question reminds me of the importance of relating to people with compassion and respect. This can be especially challenging when working with white people (and others from privileged groups) on social justice issues. Yet, I believe I am most effective as an educator and activist when I can employ "critical humility" (Barlas et al., 2012) and when I can recognize individuals' full humanity and not just see them as their social identity or some stereotype. I try hard to empathize with how they are feeling and how they see the world. People shut down when they feel judged, blamed, shamed, or attacked; they do not want to engage if they feel they're being told they are a bad or racist person. While we may be quick to call people out when they do something we find racist, I suggest we think more about how to call people in to the community of people concerned with racial justice.

By "loving them enough" I am not referring to being nice or keeping people comfortable but creating meaningful connections with individuals that can promote growth and learning, responsibility, and accountability (Goodman, 2015). When I am able to love them enough, I feel more confident that I will not be acting from a place of anger and judgment and that my humor (which tends to be a bit sarcastic—a cultural style) will not be mean-spirited. I can constructively challenge people and trust that my actions more likely will be received as they are intended. When I do this work rooted in love, the process and outcomes are enhanced.

Think structurally and intersectionally. Looking at racial issues structurally and intersectionally (Collins, 1990; Crenshaw, 1993) is central to how I approach social justice work. These forms of analysis have not only expanded my own thinking but also have provided me with invaluable perspectives to help others understand and address racism and other forms of social inequality.

Over the years I have repeatedly heard variations on the following questions from white people: If my immigrant family could make it in America, why can't they (referring to black or brown people)? or, Why do they have to be so . . . (angry, violent, uninvolved, lazy, etc.)? I have found that providing a historical and structural analysis is one of the most effective ways to help people change how they interpret the racial disparities they see and to develop strategies for change. This lens enables people to see that racial and other inequalities are not simply a result of individual behavior but the consequences of deeply embedded structures, policies, practices, and belief systems that create, maintain, and perpetuate inequities (Katznelson, 2005; Lui, Robles, Leondar-Wright, Brewer, & Adamson, 2006). A structural perspective helps challenge assumptions of meritocracy and equal opportunity. This approach reminds me to ask, What are the historical, social, economic, and political realities that are affecting this person or situation? What toll have these factors had on people's body, mind, and spirit? When I and others can recognize the larger societal forces that affect people's experiences, opportunities, and access to resources, there is less victim blaming and often more empathy.

A systemic analysis also leads to systemic change. Changing the hearts, minds, and behaviors of individuals is critical. Yet, that approach needs to be joined with people working together to make changes in the institutions, structures, and ideologies that foster inequality.

Intersectionality at the institutional and structural levels builds on the importance of using a systemic analysis by looking at how different forms of oppression simultaneously interplay with racism. For example, in the grass-roots group I am part of that addresses the mass incarceration of people of color (which I'll discuss more later), our focus has been on the experiences of black males (as has most of the research). However, when we only use the lens of race, we miss differences because of gender (and other social categories). In particular, in the school-to-prison pipeline, black females are more likely to face harsh exclusionary discipline for "being unladylike" (rather than being a perceived threat to public safety) and may have different pathways to incarceration (e.g., being a perceived coconspirator to a partner's criminal behavior; Morris, 2012). Unless we take these differences into account, our analysis and change strategies will be limited in their effectiveness. An intersectional perspective helps me consider how policies, laws, programs, and practices may have a different impact on people of the same racial group depending on the other forms of privilege or oppression they experience.

At the level of the individual or group, intersectionality underscores how various axes of identity interrelate. An intersectional approach allows me to explore how my own and others' social identities shape our racial realities, perspectives, and experiences. My multiple social locations, being a member of privileged and marginalized groups, increases or mitigates my racial advantage. My class privilege clearly enhances my white privilege, for instance, by increasing my access to employment and by benefiting from others' positive assumptions of my intelligence. As a white woman, sexism often diminishes my perceived authority relative to a white man when I walk into a classroom or a meeting of administrators. Being Jewish shapes my experience of whiteness in ways that are different from those of an Anglo-Saxon Protestant, such as not feeling part of the traditional white power structure or not sharing some of the communication norms. When I am collaborating with people of color, we need to navigate not only culture and power related to our racial differences but also the impact of our other social identities as well. For example, when I co-facilitate with males of color, I try to be conscious of how I enact my white privilege (e.g., thinking I know best how to do something), yet I may also experience their unconscious sexism (e.g., their assumption that I'll do the administrative tasks).

An intersectional perspective need not dilute or shift the focus from race and racism. It can provide a more complex, nuanced, and multifaceted understanding of racial issues. As Audre Lorde (2007) cautioned, "There is no such thing as a single-issue struggle because we do not live single-issue lives" (p. 138).

This is about liberation—for everyone. Unlearning racism and doing social justice work is deeply liberating for me. For starters, I am more comfortable in my own (white) skin, more at ease and authentic with people of color, feel less stupid in conversations about racial issues, am a more effective educator and advocate, have a much more meaningful and interesting life, and can live more aligned with my values. There is real joy in shedding layers of destructive conditioning and working with kindred spirits who share my passion and commitment to justice. I have never questioned that I am a healthier, more capable, and more compassionate person because of my involvement in efforts for social justice. I know these feelings are shared by other white antiracist activists (Goodman, 2011; Warren, 2010). By staying rooted in the fact that this is about my liberation too, it helps avoid patronizing helping (just doing it for *them*) and helps sustain my long-term commitment to social change.

I also find it deeply, deeply painful to witness, participate in, and benefit from the oppression of other people and experience disconnections from other human beings. As Nelson Mandela (1994) observed, "The oppressed and oppressor alike are robbed of their humanity" (p. 7). This is not to say that the ways I and other white people are dehumanized or harmed are equal to the ways people of color are oppressed; the experiences are not the same nor comparable. However, this recognition highlights that eliminating racism and all forms of social inequality holds benefits for everyone, individually and as a society. Dismantling racism is not only about personal liberation but also our collective liberation and well-being. Justice frees us all.

The Guideposts in Action

To illustrate how I currently use these guideposts, I briefly discuss my involvement in a local volunteer grassroots group that examines and addresses the ways mass incarcerations and the criminal justice system are used in the United States to maintain white supremacy. I became familiar with this fledgling group when I was invited by a colleague to co-facilitate one of several study groups around the county on Michelle Alexander's book (2010) *The New Jim Crow: Mass Incarceration in the Age of Colorblindness.* I decided to become involved because I knew and liked some members of the group, it was multiracial, it focused on systemic racism (not just social services), it would expand my circle of relationships, and it would deepen my understanding of racism. As the group struggled to find its footing, I became one of the six core members—three white and three people of color, two of whom were formerly incarcerated—who temporarily took on some of the leadership for the group. As we tried to clarify our specific actions, I was vocal, along with others, about ensuring we were working collaboratively with people who were most directly impacted and were developing our goals and campaigns based on their needs and priorities. I was clear that as a white middle-class woman who had no criminal history I was not the one to be setting the agenda for the group. Yet, we acknowledged that having a multiracial team reinforced the idea that these issues matter for all people. We also talked about how those of us with certain skills and experiences could best help develop the leadership of people who were formerly incarcerated, especially those recently released. One of our major campaigns has been to get our county legislature to "ban the box," the question on employment applications that asks if one has a criminal record. Once the box is checked, employers rarely pursue that applicant. We highlight the benefits of having formerly incarcerated people employed, not only to those individuals but also to the community at large.

I try to practice critical humility, compassion, and respect as I talk with predominantly white community members to educate them, address their stereotypes and misconceptions, and enlist their support and involvement. It has been challenging to maintain that approach as we deal with our own internal power (and personality) dynamics, and name and address ways white, male, and class privilege and dominance get played out in our group. However, it is the commitment to this work and bonds that we have been building that I hope will help us move through these tensions.

Conclusion

As I reflect on my social justice journey as a "nice white girl," a few things stand out. First, I see how intertwined my whiteness is with my other social identities (especially class and gender). These intersections of identity shape how I experience being white and the opportunities it grants me. Second, I realize how often I am seen as nonthreatening and credible (something I have never heard from a person of color). This perception allows me to move relatively easily through the world and reap not only material benefits but also psychological freedom. I continually think about how to appropriately use these privileges to advance social justice, knowing that I will often be seen and heard differently than a person of color. Last, I realize how easy it is to be oblivious to the realities of people of color and how much persistence and vigilance it takes to learn, notice, and act.

So, even though I have been engaged with social justice work for many years, I am acutely aware of how my personal journey is far from over. I continue to see how much I do not know and need to learn, uncover ways I have absorbed and act out my internalized dominance, grapple with the many contradictions in how I live my life, and notice how much I still need to do to be the smart, skilled, compassionate, and courageous person I seek to be. I continue to be immensely humbled by and grateful to the amazing people who have come before me and who currently do this work in all sorts of ways and places far more skillfully and extensively than I. They serve as my beacons. So this "nice white girl" (now middle-aged woman) will continue to work to create the world I want to live in, rooted in love and justice.

Note

1. The quote is generally attributed to Malcolm X.

References

Alexander, M. (2010). *The new Jim Crow: Mass incarceration in the age of colorblindness*. New York, NY: The New Press.

Barlas, C., Kasl, E., Macleod, A., Paxton, D., Rosenwasser, P., & Sartor, L. (2012). White on white: Communicating about race and white privilege with critical humility. *Understanding and Dismantling Privilege, 2*(1). Retrieved from http://www.wpcjournal.com/article/view/10106/White%20on%20White%3A%20%20Communicating%20about%20Race%20and%20White%20Privilege%20with%20Critical%20Humility

Collins, P. (1990). *Black feminist thought: Knowledge, consciousness, and the politics of empowerment*. New York, NY: Routledge.

Crenshaw, K. (1993). Mapping the margins: Intersectionality, identity politics, and violence against women. *Stanford Law Review, 43*, 1241–1299.

Goodman, D. (2011). *Promoting diversity and social justice: Educating people from privileged groups* (2nd ed.). New York, NY: Routledge.

Goodman, D. (2015). Can you love them enough to help them learn? Reflections of a social justice educator on addressing resistance from White students to anti-racism education. *Understanding and Dismantling Privilege; 5*(1).

Katznelson, I. (2005). *When Affirmative Action was white: The untold story of racial inequality in twentieth-century America*. New York, NY: Norton.

Lorde, A. (2007). *Sister outsider: Essays and speeches*. Berkeley, CA: Crossing Press.

Lui, M., Robles, B., Leondar-Wright, B., Brewer, R., & Adamson, R. (2006). *The color of wealth: The story behind the U.S. racial wealth divide*. New York, NY: The New Press.

Mandela, N. (1994). *Long walk to freedom: The autobiography of Nelson Mandela*. New York, NY: Little, Brown.

Morris, M. (2012). *Race, gender, and the school-to-prison pipeline: Expanding our discussion to black girls*. Retrieved from http://www.aapf.org/2013/2013/01/race-gender-and-the-school-to-prison-pipeline-expanding-our-discussion-to-black-girls

Parker, P. (1990). For the white person who wants to know how to be my friend. In G. Anzaldúa (Ed.), *Making face, making soul* (pp. 297–298). San Francisco, CA: Aunt Lute Foundation Books.

Romney, P. (2000). Can you love them enough? Organizational consulting as a spiritual quest. *Journal of Feminist Family Therapy, 11*(4), 65–81.

Warren, M. (2010). *Fire in the heart: How white activists embrace racial justice*. New York, NY: Oxford University Press.

9

WHITE WATER

Gary R. Howard

In much of my previous writing on race I have employed the metaphor of rivers. With their twists and turns, undercurrents and eddies, wild rapids and risk-prone possibilities, rivers are an apt image for describing the journey of a white person into racial awareness and social justice activism. With my son, Benjie, who's been a boatman for over 20 years on the Colorado River in the Grand Canyon, I've invited many educators to step into this metaphorical picture and actually join us on an eight-day river trip, where they feel the shock of the cold Colorado on their bodies, deal with the fear of torrential white water, and learn to survive in a setting where the immensity of the context and the immediacy of the moment can dwarf one's sense of self.

No one who has joined us on this adventure into the wilderness has ever come out unchanged. In the face of the awesome truth of that landscape, the initial human response is often a shuddering experience of one's own smallness, a very personal confrontation with inadequacy in the context of such power. Like the journey of a white person coming to terms with race, the actual experience is not theoretical, metaphorical, or comfortable. There is no risk-free way to run a river like the Colorado and no clearly defined channel for us white people to reconcile the truth of our painful history of racist oppression. In the stories and reflections that follow, I have attempted to map some of the key markers and lessons from the early stages of my own journey, while simultaneously acknowledging that my actual lived experiences at the time were more complex than I can yet fully understand.

The Drought: Fundamentalist White Identity

Before a river forms, there is only dryness. I lived the first 18 years of my life in a drought of dis-consciousness, in utter ignorance of issues of race. During college in the 1960s, my limited reality was gradually flooded with new perceptions in the firestorms of the Civil Rights Movement. That deluge later fed streams of experience that eventually washed away most of my previous sense of self and society and eroded any inculcated beliefs in America as the limitless land of freedom and justice for all. These streams over time have transformed my identity and coalesced into a broad river of work and learning, a river whose rapids I have now been running for more than 50 years.

I was born in 1945 at the close of World War II, in the first cohort of the boomer generation. My childhood was idyllic in an isolated white sense, as scrubbed and dried of racial diversity as the new media we were just beginning to watch: *Ozzie and Harriet, Father Knows Best,* and *Leave It to Beaver.* The new American suburbs of the 1950s were a haven of white isolation, opened up by the GI Bill to upwardly mobile white folks and closed to the soldiers of color who fought in the same war.

In high school my family moved from the white suburbs of Spokane to the white suburbs of Seattle. When my parents asked real estate agents to show them homes in "good neighborhoods with good schools for Gary," they were speaking the carefully coded language of racial segregation, euphemistically sparing the good white folks of Seattle the embarrassment of appearing explicitly racist. I don't know whether, or to what extent, my parents were aware of the racial implications of the redlining real estate practices of the 1960s, but the system of segregation at that time, like all structures of white dominance, could function efficiently with or without consciousness. As I was to learn later in my journey, the perpetuation of racial injustice feeds on white ignorance. If you are benefiting from a system of oppression, it is better for your self-righteous sensibilities not to know about it. *Lesson: There is no innocence to be found in my white ignorance. The fact that I didn't know what was happening does not release me from complicity in a system that awarded privileges to my race.*

As a product of this system of informal, yet powerfully enforced, racial segregation, my educational experience was also structured for isolation and ignorance, colored only in shades of white, with the predetermined foundations of racism remaining outside my conditioned awareness. What this meant in practical terms was that I had almost no opportunity to interact with Black, Latino, Asian, or Native American adults or peers during my formative educational years. I can, however, recall two rivulets of experience that served as harbingers of hope that the drought might someday end.

Fernando Cortinez came to our high school as an exchange student from Uruguay in my senior year. We played sports together and became friends, yet I cannot recall ever learning much about his cultural experience or his feelings about being the only student of color in our whitewashed school. Within the first week of his arrival, we had renamed him Freddie, thus transforming him in our own image and protecting ourselves from the reality of his difference, his authentic otherness. It was a function of our privileged ignorance that we could interact with an exchange student in our midst without ever having to learn much from him. I did not have an intellectual understanding of it then, but this was one of my first experiences with the "luxury of ignorance," a concept that has been central in much of my subsequent writing and teaching about race and whiteness. *Lesson: Our way of relating to Fernando taught me that white folks can be brought into the direct experience of racial realities different from ours and never learn a thing.*

I also recall an assembly in high school where the guest speaker was Wing Luke, the first person of color elected to the Seattle City Council and the first Chinese American ever elected to a major political office in the continental United States. I don't remember the specific content of his speech, but I remember the tone. He was a progressive thinker. He was different from me. He articulated a vision that things could be different, society could be better. His speech was like a time-release capsule, his message percolating beneath my consciousness, surfacing only later when the waves of the Civil Rights Movement first hit my reality and began to wash away the outer layers of entrenched ignorance. The fact that some adult in our school had invited Wing Luke to address our sea of whiteness inspired me later when I was teaching in a predominantly white school. A cornerstone of my teaching became the practice of exposing my students to people and places that might increase the likelihood that they would experience racial realities other than their own. In this way, the Wing Luke story provides a hopeful counterbalance to the Fernando Cortinez experience; sometimes the cross-border connections do pay off. *Lesson: As educators, it is important to acknowledge that providing our white students with even seemingly minor experiences of racial differences can plant the seeds for later awareness and growth.*

I now refer to this period of drought as the Fundamentalist White Identity Orientation (WIO). As an anthropologist of white folks, using myself as the primary subject of study over the past seven decades, I have come to understand there are different ways of being white, and I have termed these the *Fundamentalist, Integrationist,* and *Transformationist WIOs* (Howard,

2006, Chapter 6). The Fundamentalist WIO, in which I lived the first 18 years of my life, is characterized by ignorance, isolation, and the assumption that white social reality is normative. I had no sense of race as a salient aspect of my identity, even though my entire social context from birth through high school was constructed around a white space of racial segregation in 1960s America. *Lesson: From within this Fundamentalist WIO, I could view reports of the civil rights struggle on TV but not personalize those images in any way that had an impact on my own reality or caused me to think about my racial identity.*

Although I was reared primarily in an environment of ignorance regarding the structural dynamics of race, there is a more consciously supremacist and explicitly racist version of the Fundamentalist WIO, characterized by white folks who think often about race and construct their reality in opposition to people of color. Some signs of this surfaced in my childhood, as I heard relatives speaking in racist terms and telling racist jokes. Not knowing any people of color at the time, these experiences seemed disconnected from my daily existence, yet they also became time-release capsules that I would have to revisit farther down the river. *Lesson: Although I would like to think of my white ignorance as morally superior to the more explicit racism of white supremacists, I need to remind myself that both forms of white identity grow from and reinforce the same oppressive structures.*

The Flood: Integrationist White Identity

Social reality shifted significantly for me in 1964 when I moved from Seattle, Washington to New Haven, Connecticut to attend Yale University. Early in my freshman year, I stopped by an informational meeting of the Yale Volunteer Services organization, which was recruiting Yalies to work with social service programs in the city's poorer neighborhoods. I signed up for a YMCA program, agreeing to meet once a week with a group of eight 10- to 12-year-old boys living in the Hill, one of New Haven's most marginalized communities. This experience with Black, Puerto Rican, and low-income white inner-city kids gradually unhinged much of my previous ignorance and challenged most of my assumptions about the country I thought I lived in.

Initially, the decision to volunteer as a small-group leader clearly grew out of my desire to "help the less fortunate." This motivation was rooted in my religious upbringing, reflected in a lifetime of Sunday school lessons repeating that tune white Christians love to sing but too rarely follow:

red and yellow, black and white,
they are precious in his sight,
Jesus loves the little children of the world.

Unconscious of the analytical issues at the time, I was entering the Integrationist WIO, which is characterized by a beginning-level recognition of racial differences and a desire to help and to serve the *other*. In this formulation there is an inherent sense of one's own goodness and superiority, an asymmetry of power, and a unidirectional flow from one's generosity toward the need of the other. From within this assumed goodness, the other remains other. In spite of my naïveté at the time, however, this experience was a new baptism of sorts, immersing me in a river inevitably flowing toward an alternative social narrative. *Lesson: Even though I now distance myself from this white missionary mentality, I need to honestly acknowledge that it is always present just below the surface of my consciousness, particularly when I am tempted to put myself above other white do-gooders, whom I deem to be less evolved in their racial awareness.*

I had grown up in a working-class family, my dad working two jobs for much of my childhood and my mom always having a job outside the house in addition to all the tasks of child rearing and homemaking. We didn't have much, but I had never experienced the abject poverty that defined the lives of the kids in my YMCA group. I had also never experienced the vast generational wealth of many of my Yale peers. Both economic extremes were mind bending for me, and they existed just a 10-minute bike ride apart, the route I took every week between the Yale campus and the Hill. The racial demographic changed radically on this ride as well, Yale students being almost exclusively white at that time and the Hill mostly Black and Brown.

These polar images of racial and economic division washed over my psyche throughout my freshman year. On the conscious level, I was just giving back by spending time with a group of "disadvantaged" kids, taking them to the gym, on field trips, and on an occasional visit to the campus. At a deeper level, however, my personal and political reality was being systematically deconstructed. I had entered Yale in the fall of 1964 campaigning for Barry Goldwater against Lyndon Johnson. Having been reared in Spokane and the northern suburbs of Seattle, I was steeped in the red-meat political rhetoric of self-reliance, the wacko mythologies of the John Birch Society, and the Calvinistic theological dogma of salvation by works. In other words, you worked hard and you got what you deserved. This context was not a supportive environment for Johnson's Great Society "giveaway" programs for people who weren't white and wanted, as the adults around me said, to "live off the government." *Lesson: On our journey to white awareness of racial realities, it is important to name and confront the more caustic aspects of our early socialization.*

In stark contrast, the flood of racial and economic perceptions hitting me in 1960s New Haven, on both ends of that 10-minute bike ride, seriously eroded and finally washed away my imagined world of Goldwater simplicity and my lovingly inculcated notions of Christian goodness. By my sophomore year, I came to realize I was learning more from the kids in the Hill than I was giving back to them. My first lesson in white privilege, in fact, came from one of my 12-year-old group members. On one of our visits to the Yale campus, he said, "You know, Gary, when you finish college, you'll be moving away from New Haven, but we'll still be here." That was a sharp truth and felt like a slap in the face coming from a kid to whom I felt I had given so much. He saw the differences between our social positions, and he got it about my privilege. This came 20 years ahead of Peggy McIntosh's (1989) powerful article "White Privilege: Unpacking the Invisible Knapsack," which made the same point for many white people in the late 1980s. *Lesson: There is a tendency to be defensive and resist the truths about our privilege that come to us from people of color, but the proper stance for white folks ought to be one of humility and gratitude rather than humiliation.*

By junior year, I had been with my group of guys for three years and become connected to a network of civil rights activists on campus and in the community. By then, I had begun to see the structural issues that had predetermined the racial and economic landscape on either end of my bike trip. I realized that only the accident of birth separated my group members in the Hill from my wealthy peers at Yale. Neither generational wealth nor generational poverty was a function of worth or degrees of effort. The kids in the Hill didn't deserve to be stuck in poverty, and my rich classmates hadn't earned their elevated status. Privilege was differentially bestowed by the structures of power, and race was the most powerful determining force in these arrangements of dominance. It was this growing awareness that launched me into the Transformationist part of the journey.

Deeper Water: Transformationist White Identity

People often asked me how and why I became involved in a lifetime of work for racial justice. I have never been able to find a simple or clear way of responding to that question. In part, the preceding narrative offers a beginning answer to the *how* part of the question: I volunteered to work with inner-city kids of color, and that opened my eyes to racial and economic injustice and broke apart my previous paradigm of worth and goodness. Then I connected with a social movement for racial justice, and that set the direction for the rest of my life.

But the *why* aspect of the inquiry has always been more illusive. In part, I think my spiritual upbringing played a key role. As a teenager I was a serious follower of Jesus. I bought the whole program from Reverend Carr, an evangelical Presbyterian minister who regularly exhorted his flock of young people to accept Jesus into their hearts. At the age of 13 I was born again in a Christian sense, an experience that significantly affected my life throughout high school and into my first two years at Yale. While my peers were opening up to drugs, sex, and the wildness of the mid-1960s, I was studying, praying, and reading my Bible. As a staunch Calvinist, I was more into effort than grace, so being a good person was a powerful driving force.

While volunteering in the YMCA program, I was also studying comparative religions as part of Yale's distributive curriculum requirements for undergraduates. This intellectual exploration of the roots of Christianity, Judaism, and Islam began tweaking my religious sensibilities in the same way that the work in the Hill was challenging my political paradigms. I learned that the dogmas of my faith were not fixed truths but merely decisions made by male leaders of the church, often centuries after Jesus's life and teaching. The "truth" of the virgin birth is one such example. As my studies expanded into indigenous and non-Western spiritual traditions, it occurred to me that all spiritual truth is culturally embedded, and my previously held belief structures were not universally true but only one of many options. I know now that I could not have moved away from my Fundamentalist WIO without simultaneously releasing my fundamentalist Christian assumptions of rightness. And ironically, the farther I moved away from my narrow Christian certainty, the closer I came to understanding Jesus's message of radical and inclusive love. *Lesson: Embracing the validity of multiple perspectives and releasing one's grip on single-dimensional truths is an essential step in the evolution of any white person toward authentic engagement with race, even if that means giving up one's most cherished former beliefs.*

The deluge of new awareness and experience that washed over me during these formative years opened the floodgates of perception, spiritually and politically. The social and political landscape was rapidly changing, and so was I. Though I did my requisite share of experimentation, I truly did not need drugs to rearrange my psychic space at this time in my life; bouncing between Yale and the Hill was about all the psychedelic distortion I could take. In the confluence of personal and social history, the forces were aligned for me to join the civil rights activism of the 1960s. My intellectual immersion in liberal arts education and my experiential engagement in the Hill neighborhood connected with the deeper currents of change that were shifting the national terrain at that time. My drug of choice became the movement itself.

It Takes a Community to Run a River

It is important to acknowledge that these flood-stage life changes were not a smooth ride. At several points in the journey, I experienced significant dislocations in my sense of self, frightening times of panic and anxiety where I was underwater in muddy rapids without air or clear reference points. As the currents grew swifter, I was leaving behind a social-cultural-racial-religious landscape that had shaped my reality for 18 years and entering a new land of altered perspectives and stark contrasts. Fortunately, my journey into Transformationist white identity has been guided and supported by many people along the way. *Lesson: Because of the dangers involved, it is never a good idea to run a river alone.*

My first teachers were, of course, the young men in my YMCA group. They opened their lives and experiences to me in a way that was profoundly humbling. They invited me into their homes, where I met their families and saw firsthand the human struggle and suffering that fuels the negative stereotypes of the "ghetto" or the "hood." More important, however, I witnessed the resilience, the courage, and the dignity of people who were holding life together for their families in the face of tremendous odds and intense oppression. During the summer before my junior year, I married my high school sweetheart, and for two years we lived in the Hill and became part of the neighborhood. As white college students we could have been rightly and deservedly viewed with suspicion and held at a distance, which did occasionally happen. Remarkably, however, Lotus and I were, for the most part, warmly welcomed into conversations on the sidewalks, on front porches, at markets, and at community gathering places. My regular presence over the years with the guys in the group probably helped open these doors of relationship, but the primary catalyst was the generosity of spirit and openheartedness of the people themselves. *Lesson: In my many decades of work, nothing has impressed or inspired me more than the persistent willingness of people of color to reach out to white folks who express an authentic desire to learn and to contribute to racial healing. Even centuries of oppression have not closed all hearts or crushed all spirits.*

During the long, hot summers of the late 1960s, New Haven became one of more than 100 cities that burned in the fires of an urban revolution that was sweeping the country. Our neighborhood was often rocked by this unrest, which we saw as a legitimate rebellion against the forces of racism and economic oppression that had created these segregated places of urban blight. Lotus and I became active in community organizations working with youth empowerment and employment opportunities. These programs were funded by President Johnson's Great Society legislation, and I saw clearly the wrongheadedness of my earlier political criticism of these efforts. The new resources flowing into the Hill and similar neighborhoods across the country stimulated a sense of vibrancy, renewed possibility, and hope. Community leaders were empowered by this funding to create their own organizations and direct programs aimed at solving the problems they had identified. Even though our streets were regularly occupied by National Guard troops with heavy weaponry, there was a palpable vitality emerging among the people. Through our work in these organizations headed by Black and Latino community leaders, Lotus and I were educated in an entirely deeper and different way than we were experiencing in our college classes. For me, Yale was a great place to learn, but the kids and community activists in the Hill taught the most relevant and profound lessons. One of these came from a friend and community organizer, who was an early spokesperson for the new politics of Black Power. He pulled me aside one day and said, "Gary, you've done a lot here in the Hill, but it's time to go back home and work with the white folks. That's where the real change needs to happen." At first I was hurt by that admonition. I wanted to be where the real action was, in the Black community. And working with white folks seemed far removed from my desire to help. Only later did I understand the power and truth of his message, and it has guided my professional life for the past 45 years. *Lesson: The primary focus and responsibility of white racial justice activists is to engage and educate our families and other white folks.*

The community of student activists that grew up around the Civil Rights and antiwar movements was another source of guidance and support in my transformative journey. The 1960s are often mistakenly characterized, or satirized, as a time when an entire generation of students was in rebellion against the status quo. In fact, the activist community at Yale in the late 1960s was relatively small; the status for most students was quo: study, play, and party. But a small group of us created an intense camaraderie built around Dwight Hall, a center of student organizing and activism for many generations of Yalies. Very important, and also ironically for me, Dwight Hall was also closely connected to the Yale Religious Ministries. The political consciousness and activism that had caused me to distance myself from my earlier Christian conservatism now led me right back to the heart of the church.

The leader of the Yale religious community at the time was William "Bill" Sloane Coffin, a powerful preacher and courageously outspoken champion of social justice. He was in constant legal trouble over his activities in the Civil Rights and antiwar movements and spent a good bit of time in jail with other charismatic leaders of the time. Lotus and I met in his living room every Wednesday night with a collection of other student activists, talking about the work and reflecting on ideas Coffin was spinning for his next sermon. Since most of the people in the room were dealing with identity dislocations similar to what I was experiencing at the time, these evenings became a touchstone for grounding and guiding my journey. And Coffin's large presence in that room and on campus offered an inspirational and robust alternative to the more anemic Christianity of my childhood. *Lesson: Bill Coffin's life and work exemplified the truth that anyone who authentically follows the teachings of Jesus is called into a heavy commitment to inclusivity and social justice.*

This message was further reinforced for me in the words and activism of Martin Luther King Jr. I had been in the drought period of dis-consciousness and Fundamentalist WIO when King delivered his "I Have a Dream" speech during the 1963 March on Washington. I knew about the event from watching the news but had missed the power and meaning of the message. It wasn't until my politics had been tempered in the fires of New Haven that I could begin to understand the significance of his role and the courage of his convictions. The most powerful MLK moment in my life was his April 1967 speech delivered at Riverside Church in New York City: "Beyond Vietnam: A Time to Break Silence." Many leaders in the peace movement had been urging King to come out against the war. Not wanting to distract energy and attention from the Civil Rights Movement, King resisted this invitation for some time. By 1967, four years after the dream speech, his critique of American social reality had deepened. He had gone public with his critique of the war two years earlier, but the Riverside speech unveiled his full, powerful, and prophetic analysis linking the triple evils of racism, militarism, and capitalism to the oppression of poor people both at home and in Southeast Asia. He called for an immediate end to the war in Vietnam, saying, "The world now demands a maturity of America that we may not be able to achieve" ("Beyond Vietnam," n.d.).

King was killed exactly one year later in April 1968. Many of us in the movement at the time looked back at the Riverside speech as the decisive moment that King would no longer be allowed to live. There was widespread civil rebellion in Black communities throughout the United States after King's assassination. It was spring of my senior year at Yale, and the whole block behind our apartment in the Hill burned the night of his death. Those flames and the fire of his words are as fresh to me today, five decades later, as they were then. His comprehensive grasp of the interlocking forces of oppression has guided my work and inspired my vision. Without his teachings and the community of people of color and white allies who informed my journey in these early years, I would never have ventured out of the narrow enclave of my own whiteness. *Lesson: Speaking clear-eyed truth to power is a dangerous occupation in this country that claims to uphold human rights and social justice.*

A River That Never Ends

All these experiences took place in the first 23 years of my life. They are the source water of my river and have fed my journey for the past 45 years of work. There is much more to the story, and that will be written in its own time. In closing, I can share one lesson that has always held true for me: No matter how aware I may be of racial dynamics, no matter how articulate I may become in mouthing the rhetoric of critical race theory, no matter how many articles I may write or speeches I give on antiracist white activism, I am still on the river. The journey never ends. Racial consciousness honed over a lifetime can still never trump my white privilege. It is always there. Racial justice is still a distant dream. The United States and the rest of the world have not yet achieved the maturity that King hoped and died for.

References

Beyond Vietnam: Excerpts from the address by Rev. Martin Luther King Jr. at Riverside Church, New York City, April 4, 1967. (n.d.). Retrieved from Land and Freedom website: http://www.landandfreedom.org/news/22205.htm

Howard, G. R. (2006). *We can't teach what we don't know: White teachers, multiracial schools* (2nd ed.). New York, NY: Teachers College Press.

McIntosh, P. (1989, July/August). White privilege: Unpacking the invisible knapsack. *Peace and Freedom*, 10–12.

10

LOOKING BACK AND MOVING FORWARD

Frances E. Kendall

I have had a remarkable life. Like most lives, it has been filled with rich, happy experiences and devastatingly painful ones. Some of the most emotionally difficult ones have been my greatest teachers.

I am choosing the concept of crucibles as a way to organize what seems important for you, as current and future racial justice activists, to know about me. The word *crucible* refers to a container that can withstand so much heat that it is possible to separate different kinds of metals as they are being melted. In "The Crucibles of Leadership," Bennis and Thomas (2002) define a *crucible* as a "transformative experience through which an individual comes to a new or an altered sense of identity" (p. 40). I have chosen to write about five such experiences, most of which occurred before I was 30 and shaped the trajectory of my life.

The first and most pivotal crucible was growing up in a Southern upper-middle-class Christian environment. I was born in 1947 and grew up in Waco, Texas, in a family that is in the cotton business and has been for generations. At one point, my mother told me they had owned a plantation in Meridian, Mississippi, as well as the slaves who carried out the labor there. (Other members of my family have denied there were slaves, but it is true that the family was wealthy, in the cotton business, and lived in Meridian. The *pickers* of the cotton aren't spoken about.)

The lessons taught me by my mother and the Southern institutions and local culture where we lived were clear and straightforward: Black people were not as good as white people, they were not as smart, nor were they as moral. They bore children out of wedlock; they were not honest or reliable; they ate different food; their houses were different; in fact, nothing about them was the same as us. They were clearly less worthy, less human, less valuable. And yet, my care as a youngster and the care of our household were entrusted to the Black women who worked for us—when we were lucky enough to find "a good one."

One of those women, Marie Jones, became the only person in my life who has ever shown me unconditional love. She was my disciplinarian, my playmate, my mother substitute, and the person to whom I dedicated my first book, *Diversity in the Classroom* (1983). As with so many white girls in the United States, but particularly in the South, my caretaker, Marie, was the first person I bonded with rather than connecting to my mother. My father died when I was four, and my mother fell into a deep grief that lasted until she died 18 years later. She was simply not emotionally available to me. I saw Marie as my most important parent figure until the day she died in 1996. Yet she was always the maid to the adults in my family; she wasn't considered our equal and didn't have any of the race and class privileges we had. Her children never received the time and attention I got from her, so their resentment of me was enormous and understandable.

We attended St. Paul's, the old Episcopal church in downtown Waco, where everyone in the congregation was white. The stained-glass window over the altar showed a white Jesus with blondish hair surrounded by white children and white lambs. Periodically we sang,

> Jesus loves the little children,
> all the children of the world,
> red and yellow, black and white,
> they are precious in his sight,
> Jesus loves the little children of the world.

My mother mentioned one day that the private elementary school my cousins had built for the church in memory of their daughter had a clause in its contract with the church that prohibited Black children from being admitted. (That clause has now been removed.) And Mom had no qualms about the segregation we were living in and in fact moved us to the suburbs so that I would not go to junior high with Mexicans.

Such confusing contradictions were impossible to hold at the same time. So, I did what many white Southern children did—I put the conflicting ideas into a filing cabinet in my mind and locked the drawer.

I moved into greater cognitive dissonance about what was right and what was true when I went to boarding school at the age of 14 at the National Cathedral School for Girls in Washington, DC. My daily life at Cathedral in the early 1960s became my second crucible. For example, there were two Black girls in my class of 63 students, both of whom were upper-middle class and smarter than I was. One was the daughter of the mayor of Washington.

In 10th grade I went to a class party at the house of one of these girls. It was the first time I had ever been in a Black family's home. In a journal I kept at that time, I found this entry: "The bathrooms were clean, the beds were made, and the small children in the family were neatly and cleanly dressed. I was honestly surprised to find things much as they are in my own home." Walking into the kitchen, I was stunned to see a Mixmaster on the counter-top; it was the exact same model as the one we had at our house. Still more of what I had been told was true was turning out not to be. I clearly remember seeing the pieces of my foundational belief system falling into pieces around my head. I thought to myself, "If Mom lied to me about this, what else has she lied about?" I don't think I ever fully trusted what she told me again.

Another experience at Cathedral was equally shaking. I regularly received entirely different instruction about what it meant to be Christian from the messages I had absorbed at St. Paul's. The Washington National Cathedral shares grounds with my high school. A grand and beautiful gothic Episcopal cathedral, it was still being built when I was a student, and I was in it virtually every day. The cathedral was a gathering place for leaders of the Civil Rights Movement who came to speak about the upheaval that was going on in the South. Regularly I heard that what most white Southerners were doing and had done to Black people was evil, sinful, and un-Christian. In 1963, one of the ministers who preached was a man who became my father figure: the Very Reverend H. C. N. Williams, a white South African who had bat-tled apartheid before becoming the provost of Coventry Cathedral in Cov-entry, England. I wrote down something he said in his sermon: "Prejudice is the sign of a delinquent mind." As I listened to him, I understood that he was talking about my family and their belief system. And I began to realize that I would have to choose between my family and living what I was coming to define as a *moral and Christian life*.

After this shift in my consciousness about race, my relationship with my mother and the rest of my family became ever more fractious. My cousins and my brothers-in-law, husbands of my sisters who were 10 and 12 years older than I, ramped up their racist jokes and comments. Mom and I had terrible fights on the phone when I was in Washington and at the dinner table when I was in Waco. Over time I became bolder. In the best way I could manage at the time, I protected my emerging identity from Mom and my siblings by denying Mom the benefits she expected from her youngest daughter. For example, I wore an equality button (a dime-size button with an equality symbol on it from the march on Selma, to which she had forbidden me to go). I wore it to church, to bed, to the country club, out to dinner with her friends. "Please take that off," she pleaded, and I said no. Becoming separated from one's family—whether by defiance or rejection—is not simple. It was extremely painful for everyone.

There is another story from my time at Cathedral. When I was a senior, my mom called to tell me about an idea she'd had. For my graduation present, she and I could each choose a friend to travel with to Europe. I was excited. "Wonderful," I said. "I'll ask Lloyd." (Lloyd Leva was one of my best friends at school. Her parents, both doctors, had been so welcoming to me throughout my four years there, including having Mom to dinner when she visited Washington to see me. The Levas were Jewish.) Without skipping a beat, my mother said, "Francie, I'm not traveling through Europe with a Jew!" And I responded, "Then I'm not traveling with you!" And I slammed down the phone.

Mom was delighted when I was invited to make my debut with the daughters of other prominent families in Waco.

"Can I ask my Jewish and Black friends from Cathedral and have a Black band play?"

"Francie, you know you can't."

"Well then I'm not doing it!"

My mother finished the conversation: "All I ask is that you are gracious to the person who comes to issue your invitation." I complied.

So, on one hand, I was supposed to be gracious to everyone, evidently because if I wasn't it would reflect poorly on our family. On the other hand, there were some people she didn't want to travel with.

If you are thinking to yourself, "How could you have been so mean to your mother?" please try to see it through my eyes. I honestly felt like I was going mad and my heart was breaking. I was being told to "be gracious to everyone" and "be a lady" and "act in ways that are becoming to you and to us" and "represent your family well by following in the ways we see as appropriate." And I was making choices that would force me to leave my family.

On my second day as a freshman at the University of Denver, I went to the Young Women's Christian Association (YWCA) on campus. There I began to learn in earnest about racism. I was groomed and raised and supported by the Black and white women in the National Student YWCA and the National YWCA. They looked at me, this white girl from Waco, Texas—painted fingernails, frosted hair—and they saw something that said, "This young woman is worth our energy." Through my work at the national level I was involved in ongoing training sessions and daily conversations about white privilege. I was taught many things: how systemic racism works, how it is rooted in beliefs that some people have value and others don't, and how racism has been systematically and intentionally embedded in the formal laws and informal norms in the United States and in its actions around the world. As part of looking at how institutional racism shaped the colleges and universities women in the National Student YWCA attended, I created a guide to move campuses to divest themselves of their financial involvement in South Africa and therefore in apartheid. As a way of understanding how the United States exported class and race supremacy, other students were learning about the United States' role in determining the political rulers in Latin America. For example, at the U.S. Army School of the Americas at Fort Benning, Georgia, Latin American soldiers were trained in combat skills so they would be able to destabilize and overturn their country's governments that were unfriendly to U.S. capitalism. While the school's name has been changed to the Western Hemisphere Institute for Security Cooperation, its mission remains the same. Calling that knowledge mind-blowing is an understatement, and still I kept the horror of U.S. atrocities at the intellectual level and at arm's length from real consciousness.

After graduating from college in 1969, I moved to New York to be closer to those who had become my community: the women in the National Student YWCA at its headquarters in midtown Manhattan. My immersion in learning about organizational systems and white privilege deepened, and my willingness and ability to hold painful realities grew. Each new revelation took me farther away from being able to turn back—to *un*know the injustice in this country's present and its history. As one of my teachers had predicted, I had bought a one-way ticket.

One of my most powerful and disturbing revelations occurred in 1972 at the Whitney Museum at an exhibit titled "Executive Order 9066." Nothing I had learned about U.S. history prepared me for the shock to my head and heart of discovering that *we*, the leaders of the country, had interned 122,000 Japanese people, many of whom were American citizens and World War II heroes. How was it possible that I had never even heard of this?

My first job in New York was at the Grail Bookstore, part of a movement run by women pioneers in Roman Catholic feminist theology. There I began to learn about Christians who were leading radical change in the church and speaking out for peace and justice, regardless of the risks: Dorothy Day, Sister Mary Corita Kent, Thomas Merton, Daniel Berrigan, and others.

Their resolve was similar to that of the leaders I was working with in the YWCA—Dorothy Height, Lilace Barnes, Valerie Russell—who were courageous in pushing the 1970 adoption of the National YWCA's One Imperative: "To thrust our collective power toward the elimination of racism, wherever it exists and by any means necessary" (YWCA, 2014). My lifelong journey was beginning to become clear.

I began my professional career at Bank Street College of Education in New York City, a graduate school that specializes in early childhood education. In hindsight, I think I went there to try to figure out how the early death of a parent affects children psychologically. My learning experience there was the best institutional educational experience I've ever had. The school is clearly based on a developmental psychodynamic framework, and all the curriculum supports that. My master's thesis was on racism in children's literature, and I was able to apply and enhance some of my knowledge about white privilege and systemic white supremacy.

I also had my first experience with how white liberals resist acknowledging our personal participation in institutionalized racism, a behavior I call *personal racism*. I challenged the Bank Street Bookstore for carrying Roald Dahl's (1964) *Charlie and the Chocolate Factory*. For those of you who don't know the book, one of the storylines is that the Oompa-Loompas, small African pygmies, were so grateful to white Willy Wonka for saving them from a survival diet of grub worms that they happily left their home and went to work in his chocolate factory. There they continued to do relatively menial tasks. It seemed to me that since Bank Street was putting their seal of approval on the book by carrying it, they ought to rethink their decision. I lost, of course. My hope is that some teachers rethought how they framed the book for young readers, but I'll never know. Criticizing one of (white) children's favorite authors seemed to me to be a fool's errand, but it gave me practice in pushing the limits of white people's thinking. (An interesting historical note: Evidently I was not alone in criticizing the depiction. In later editions of *Charlie and the Chocolate Factory*, the Oompa-Loompas are white-skinned and blond-haired! That fact attests to the value of speaking your mind, no matter how futile it appears to be.)

At the urging of my beloved mentor at Bank Street, Barbara Biber, I decided to get my doctorate. Privilege had everything to do with where I applied and was accepted. With no grades—Bank Street had a pass/fail policy—and very low GRE scores (because of my dyslexia and difficulty in taking tests, my combined GRE scores were around 1,000) I was offered a choice of Harvard, University of Massachusetts Amherst, and the University of North Carolina at Chapel Hill. I expected Amherst would be my choice.

As I was pondering where to go, my fourth crucible occurred. I was at the opening of an art exhibit of Sister Mary Corita's, whose work I had come to love on my sojourns to New York for YWCA meetings. As I walked into the reception, I saw out of the corner of my eye a large black-and-white serigraph of the outline of a tree and its reflection below. Across the middle was a space with the following quote by Carl Jung: "No noble, well-grown tree ever disowned its dark roots, for it grows not only upwards but downwards as well" (Jung, 1982). For the second time, I saw pieces of my life falling around my head, and I thought, "Damn! I have to go back to the South."

Having fled Texas, my family, and, by extension, my Southern roots, I had no desire to get anywhere near the South. Even at the mention of Texas and my cotton-business family, shame and anger rose in my throat. I had carefully locked all that away and intentionally gotten rid of as much of my Southern accent as I could. All the while I envisioned settling in New England, as though racism and white supremacy did not occur anywhere else but in the South. Jung's quotation was a reminder that my literal well-being was reliant on my returning to the part of the world that, for me, brought up enormous guilt, pain, and shame.

I was unable to take myself back to Texas; the closest I could get was North Carolina. In addition to getting a PhD, I went to North Carolina to figure out what it meant to be a white Southern woman working on race. There I took my initial dive into the disabling terror of discovering that my work on race had been a charade and that I was everything I abhorred. In fact, rather than finding that I was a fraud, I began to plant seeds of understanding in myself and in others, which opened the door even further to my purpose in life.

Working on my doctorate was relatively easy, given my white upper-middle-class and academic privilege as well as my instruction at National Cathedral and at Bank Street. As I say in my book *Understanding White Privilege: Creating Pathways to Authentic Relationships Across Race*, my real challenge was the personal excavation I did on two fronts (Kendall, 2013, p. 13). The first and most powerful was accepting myself as a white Southerner. The second challenge, and my fifth crucible, was coming out as a lesbian. While the order might seem odd, that was how it felt to me. Coming to grips with being a lesbian was traumatic, given the 1970s' national culture of revulsion at and fear of things not heterosexual. But I knew that I would not have to give up my chosen families—my friends and loved ones or my YWCA connections—over this issue. It would be painful and it would be a struggle to fully integrate that part of my identity, and I knew I would be fine in the end, despite all the internalized heterosexism I carried. My central identity was race, and while my sex, my gender presentation, my class, and my sexual orientation are vital to me, race has remained the center of my life's work.

My next move was to teach at Tufts University. I learned fairly quickly that I was not cut out for work inside an institution; I was too bound by the "suggestion" that I not say anything about the institutional problems I was seeing until I was granted tenure. I realized my place was on the outside helping institutions and organizations become what they said they wanted to be regarding race and inclusion. Over the past 40 years, I have worked with many dozens of predominantly white colleges and universities, corporations, and nonprofits, facilitating their work on becoming genuinely hospitable to people of color and helping them create systems that would hold that inclusion in place.

So, what have I learned in these 45 years that seems important to pass on? Here are some of my lessons:

- I know that my internal work will never be done; that I resolve, as Rainer Maria Rilke suggests, "to be always beginning, to be a beginner" (Muller, 2000, p. 128).
- I know that I will always wrestle with guilt and shame. (Guilt, remember, is feeling bad about something you've done; shame is feeling bad about who you are.) And I believe that the depth and quality of the personal excavation we step into is directly correlated with our ability to be partners in eradicating racism. Too often, in my experience, white people, and particularly white women, hide behind guilt. Rather than listening to people of color talk about their experience, we recenter ourselves: "Oh, I feel so guilty. It is so painful for *me* that I can't bear to hear you talk about your pain. I feel so guilty." That won't endear ourselves to any people of color and, in fact, will only confirm that we are not worthy of trust. It is our work to help ourselves and others move through the process of dealing with guilt and shame.
- I know that for those of us alive today, the historical creation of white supremacy is not our fault. We didn't create it. We do, however, reap the benefits of those systems. And each of us regularly colludes, through internalized supremacy, with keeping it in place. Rather than feeding guilt, it is far more useful to choose actions that move justice forward.
- I know that shame is related to guilt, yet for me shame is a core part of my being. Shame is deeply embedded in most of us who live our lives with unearned access to power, resources, and the ability to influence—that's all of us with privilege connected to any of our identities. Being able to hold on to the notion that our worth is based on others' lack of worth, that the presumption of white competency sits hand in

glove with the presumption that people of color, particularly darker-skinned people, are incompetent, requires breaking away from our hearts, our minds, and our souls. As the remarkable and daring Lillian Smith (1949/1994) said in her powerful book *Killers of the Dream*,

> The warped, distorted frame we have put around every Negro child from birth is around every White child also. Each is on a different side of the frame but each is pinioned there. . . . What cruelly shapes and cripples the personality of one is as cruelly shaping and crippling the personality of the other. (p. 39)

- I know that the shame of privileged people requires us to cut away parts of ourselves that would otherwise clearly recognize the dehumanization of our actions.

I *believe* and I hope with all my heart that we can end our abhorrent systems of oppression, although I don't believe it will happen in my lifetime. To do that, it is essential for those of us who have privilege to develop the will and the skills to embrace followership from those who bear the wounds of our oppression. If we are serious, we must often quiet ourselves to hear another's perspective and to follow the lead of those whom we oppress, intentionally or not.

We can never know what it is to be *other* if we aren't very clear about our experience as white people. This journey is not simple, nor is it quick. It is continuing work. And while it can be painful, it is essential. Lifelong antiracist activist Anne Braden (1999) talked about it this way:

> We who grew up white Southerners two and three generations ago learned something else the whole society needs to ponder. We found that when we turned ourselves inside out to face the truth, it was a painful process, but it was not destructive. Rather, it became a moment of rebirth—and opened up new creative vistas in our lives. (p. 339)

References

Bennis, W., & Thomas, R. (2002). The crucibles of leadership. *Harvard Business Review, 80*(9), 39–45, 124.

Braden, A. (1999). *The wall between* (2nd ed.). Knoxville: University of Tennessee Press.

Dahl, R. (1964). *Charlie and the chocolate factory.* New York, NY: Puffin Books.

Jung, C. G. (1982). *Dreams.* London: Routledge.

Kendall, F. E. (1996). *Diversity in the classroom* (2nd ed.). New York, NY: Teachers College Press.

Kendall, F. E. (2013). *Understanding white privilege: Creating pathways to authentic relationships across race* (2nd ed.). New York, NY: Routledge.

Muller, W. (2000). *Sabbath: Finding rest, renewal, and delight in our busy lives* (1st ed.). New York, NY: Bantam.

Smith, L. (1994). *Killers of the dream.* New York, NY: Norton. (Original work published 1949.)

Young Women's Christian Association (YWCA) USA. (2014). *Who we are: History.* Retrieved from http://www.ywca.org/site/c.cuIRJ7NTKrLaG/b.7515891/k.C524/History.htm

11

WORKING WITHIN THE SYSTEM TO CHANGE THE SYSTEM

Julie O'Mara

In the early stages of my career, the word *activist* described me better than it does today. Given my gender, race and ethnicity, other diversity dimensions, skills, and personality, I've determined that my role in a movement to address social injustice is better served by working for change from within organizational systems as opposed to taking an adversarial position to them from outside those systems. This is a personal choice, not an opinion on which method is better. Work needs to be done inside and outside the system. I'm just better at working for change inside a system and helping educate others to work inside the system. Working as a diversity and inclusion consultant, I have the objectivity of being an outsider to specific organizational systems, along with the perspective and insight to help educate and coach those inside the system to change it. The opportunity to participate in this book allowed me to explore and put into words why I chose to work from the inside, a view not always present in this field of social justice.

What Led Me to Focus on Working Within Organizational Systems

I was born in 1946 into a middle-class family in St. Louis, raised in the 1950s, and graduated from high school and college in Missouri in the 1960s. We were regarded as a normal White middle-class family—a dad, a mom, three children. I was the oldest and found myself affected by the civil rights events of the times as well as being born in the first year of the baby boomer generation. My parents were liberal Democrats, and while they were not active in the Civil Rights Movement, they believed changes were needed to overcome the injustices of the time. My mom was a college graduate with a degree in journalism, and my father was a salesperson and truck driver without a college education. My father did not allow my mother to work, and there was a lot of tension about that dictate. I always knew I would have a career outside the home, although I always assumed it would be a girl-type career. I then read Betty Friedan's (1963) *The Feminine Mystique,* and my worldview changed. I ended my engagement to my high school sweetheart and went to college. I felt proud that I eventually became a women's libber, although it took me a while to realize that what I was actually involved in was a White women's movement. The White privilege issue sneaked up on me, and I did not recognize it for years.

Right after my college graduation in 1969, I took a job at a Fortune 500 company headquartered in a small town in Michigan. I was the first woman the company had ever hired as a marketing management trainee who was fresh off the college campus. I was on my own in a totally new environment and not bothered by that at all; I should have been, but I wasn't, because I was career focused and naive. With my first-woman-hired status, I became somewhat of a local celebrity who was way too socially inexperienced for something that would cause me to significantly stand out from the crowd. I had no idea about the downside of being the first. Fortunately, it was a positive time for business, and I managed to do well. I gradually became more and more involved in women's issues and realized I wanted to make the equality of women in the workplace, and specifically the advancement of women into management, a significant part of my work. Years later I connected with many others working in the diversity field, learned from and aligned with them, and started doing antiracism work along with work on women's issues. This later expanded into broader diversity and inclusion work. What became clear to me was that many of the organizational interventions and solutions for one dimension of diversity also worked for other dimensions of diversity. It started to make sense that there was a growing need to include other dimensions of diversity in my work.

While doing diversity work, I was firmly convinced that any equation for success needed to go beyond individual growth and development. Even if all individuals were brilliant performers, they still might not be able to excel in a closed system where unearned privilege reigned. Many organizational systems are oppressive and lack inclusivity, and in my experience they need to change; that was true a while ago and is still true today. What I saw most was antisexism and antiracism work focused on individual change. Granted, this approach included individuals who were both the oppressed and the oppressors, but I felt that the work that would effect systemic, institutional, and organizational change was being neglected. I discovered it was systems change that interested me most deeply.

I eventually realized the corporation I worked for seemed to control my life more than I wanted. The time commitment and travel required for my career was significant, and I decided I needed the independence and freedom that being a consultant would bring. I also quickly realized I was not alone. At that time many women were leaving corporate life to become entrepreneurs because the rules, structures, and assumptions of corporate life were not friendly to women or anyone else who did not fit in a world controlled and owned largely by White, heterosexual, wealthy men. I wanted to start a family and needed flexibility. In my view of life and work, if I was going to be this dedicated and work this hard, I wanted to have my own organization, even if it wasn't as potentially lucrative as being part of a Fortune 500 company. I didn't want to be poor or economically dependent, and I felt good about my personal goals and values being aligned with my career and economic goals. I knew that as a White educated professional from a middle-class background, I had an advantage over many others. I wanted to use that advantage to achieve success on my own terms, as a woman, a mother, and a consultant, and to help others have an opportunity to achieve as well through working with them on mentoring and partnership.

As time went on I began consulting with more clients and was doing well. I was active in the American Society for Training and Development (ASTD; now Association for Talent Development) and served on the board of directors as chair of the Women's Caucus, then as a regional vice president, and eventually as national president in 1983. While on the board of directors, I initiated and led an unsuccessful attempt to get ASTD to boycott holding conferences in states that had not passed the Equal Rights Amendment. At the age of 35 and with a 7-year-old son I became ASTD president-elect. This election was monumental as most of the previous ASTD presidents were male and in their 50s.

As things were moving forward in my consulting work, a pivotal event took place. It was 1984, the era of apartheid in South Africa and the U.S. economic boycott, known as the disinvestment campaign, against South

Africa. That year, at a conference for human resource professionals in South Africa, I delivered a keynote speech on the work on racial equity I had been doing in the United States. My experience in South Africa was probably the most important event that opened my eyes to how I personally could best contribute to helping mend social injustice. Although I already thought focusing on systems change was where I wanted to dedicate my time and skills, learning about the powerful strategy being proposed by these human resource professionals in South Africa convinced me I could have a positive impact on change for social justice through the workplace. The inside track became clearer to me as I explored how to best use my skills. Although I briefly considered working in the arena of public policy and running for office, I decided those areas didn't match my skill sets and energy. I am glad to say that in this case hindsight is good, and I believe I made the right decision.

Approaching Social Justice Work as a Diversity and Inclusion Organizational Change Agent

One of the greatest impacts on my work was the opportunity to start O'Mara and Associates, a small, independent consulting firm serving large- and medium-size corporate and government clients in the United States and Canada. The firm's clients are from a variety of industries, although usually my client is a member of the human resources, organizational development, or diversity and inclusion department. Some of the contracts are large, and to best serve the clients I may hire other consulting partners to work with me or others to assist. I am also fortunate enough to sometimes be included in a colleague's contract. Working on the inside means I sometimes do only a onetime event, but I am often asked to consult for an extended period. As with many other diversity and inclusion consultants, the design, development, delivery, and training of trainers is a substantial part of my work. But I also often guide strategic diversity and inclusion consulting and change initiatives. In addition to this consulting work in diversity and inclusion, I perform general organizational development, change management, team building, and facilitation. Change is needed in every aspect of our society, and social justice activists have to follow their strengths and work where they can have the most impact. For me, it is from within, where I can delve into the structure of the system and work for change.

As a way of passing on suggestions, the following are some of the best practices I've developed over more than two decades. These are examples of what worked for me as I journeyed through the corporate world, the feminist world, and finally through the world of White privilege. We each have to find our own path.

Model the desired outcomes while doing the work. The desired outcome of this work is for people of all races and all dimensions of diversity to work together as social equals. As a White woman, therefore, it is extremely important that I model this behavior in all aspects of my work within the organization. I had to learn that many times I needed to be second instead of first. This was not just for the sake of appearances; it had to be, and always was, genuine. Sometimes this meant that although I received a request for proposal, I would invite one or more colleagues of color to respond as the primary consultant, and that's how we operated throughout the contract. Other times the contract was in my name, and I would invite several other people of color as senior consultants, and we worked with the clients as equals. It may be a little tougher with a White woman being the owner, as there is no denying that the structure makes it appear that I am in charge, but if we are modeling equity in the ideas, approaches, and every single detailed aspect we can think of, the equality message does come across. Also, I am not always the one who receives or carries the contract. Many times I subcontract with a team. Those I work with are almost always people of color or have primary diversity dimensions different from mine. We talk about this among ourselves and propose the differing dimensions to the client as an asset. In the day-to-day basis of doing the work, I learned not to be the first one with the answer, and that it is essential I always check my dominance and wait for others to offer ideas. Fortunately, most everyone I work with is assertive, so practically speaking, checking my dominance isn't a problem. I strive, however, to be extra sensitive to conversational dynamics and the metamessages of social equity that are being sent.

Meet clients where they are. One of the main mistakes consultants and leaders make is to get frustrated when their clients or coworkers don't understand the points they are striving to make.

I recall the moment when a White male executive ally said to me: "Julie, I'm on your side. Just tell us what to do." My first reaction was to rebut his statement. Why did I have to tell him what to do? Couldn't he see what needed to be done? But I decided instead to ask him what he meant. He said he thought I needed to get the participants' attention on what they as leaders needed to model and do (I worked mostly with leaders and managers inside large organizations including corporations, government agencies, and nonprofits). Then he said that once I had their attention, and what was expected of them was clear, they would likely be more ready to delve into the rationale—go deeper, as we often say in diversity and inclusion work—behind why those behaviors and organizational system changes are necessary. In other words, he was suggesting I spark them *to ask* me for the depth of the rationale and to learn more about race, gender, and other diversity issues.

This idea struck me as a useful approach I really had not considered. I was skeptical that many would not care to ask, and some didn't, but many did. And I learned that meeting them where they were gave me greater insight into what they needed. Even though I wanted these leaders to grasp the depth of the issues and to feel and understand oppression, I was really focused on actual systems change. I wanted my clients to take action to open doors and fix organizational structural issues. I encouraged them to not just recruit at White schools, not make women employees wait an additional three years to join the pension program, and not direct advertisements to men or women according to gender-based assumptions that weren't necessarily valid. I had to learn to appreciate their viewpoints and give them an opportunity to work through their issues before I worked with them to change.

See the scope of diversity and inclusion as broad and deep. Many organizations think of diversity and inclusion work as belonging primarily to the human resources function. It doesn't. It belongs to the entire organization—marketing, services and product development, social responsibility, philanthropy, training, compensation, accounting, information technology, every possible function and department. It is essential that I coach those inside an organization to see diversity and inclusion work as involving all departments, functions and units, and stakeholders, including all levels of employees. Social justice work is too often seen as work that only affects others. To bring about systemic change, all components of an organization must agree to it. To that end, a major open-source document, *Global Diversity and Inclusion Benchmarks: Standards for Organizations Around the World* (O'Mara & Richter, 2014), contains five conceptual frameworks for diversity and inclusion, 13 categories, 280 benchmarks, and a model that shows the systemic relationships. The benchmarks are outcomes and results of quality diversity and inclusion work. I'm proud to say that this document is being widely used, it's free of charge, and can easily be accessed through the Internet.

Become partners with a diverse team and model inclusion. I believe a solid approach to working inside an organization is to model the inclusion behaviors that are the desired end result. For an excellent discussion of inclusion behaviors, see Ferdman (2014, pp. 37–40).

This inclusive behavior usually includes cross-level and cross-functional teams working with a mind-set filled with a variety of differences to achieve a better outcome. It's important to work in consultant teams whose members are diverse in as many ways as possible and who model working together and demonstrating respect for their colleagues. There will be times when an older White male is the owner of the consulting firm and will need to be in the role of leader and owner during parts of the work. However, to be effective, that owner must appreciate modeling inclusion behaviors and know how to step back, listen, and not take the lead on everything. Presentations, as well as the groundwork, need to be shared based on talent and skill. Too many times I have seen an older person dominating a younger person in a meeting when the younger person is just as, or even more, skilled. These types of meetings are too often based on issues of privilege in the corporate world, such as race, gender, or other oppressive ideologies.

Listen to others as if they are wise. Years ago a colleague, Toni Wilson, said something that had a huge impact on me: "Listen to others as if they are wise." I continue to see this as a way to check my assumptions and become more patient. I have learned that when I made the choice to regard others as being wise, I then took the time to listen deeply to them. I'm not especially proud that I needed to have this shift in attitude and behavior pointed out, but it has worked well for me. If I was offering advice to those entering the field, I would echo the words of Toni Wilson.

Go slow to go fast. Michael Doyle, author and founder of Interaction Associates, an outstanding systems thinker and expert on collaboration, always said, "Go slow to go fast." What he meant by this statement was to take the time to assess a situation and get people ready for the work ahead. Plan and strategize. Don't jump in without thoughtful analysis. In diversity and inclusion work we need to be careful not to just jump in and do the first thing we think about or pull the same things out of a bag of tricks. In diversity and inclusion work, problems and opportunities present themselves in different ways. An issue may present itself as gender or race based, but it may not be. And, of course, there may be gender- and race-based issues that present themselves as performance issues. Real or perceived accusations of racism can be devastating to individuals and organizations. Proceed cautiously. Gather the facts. I recall a workplace issue investigation I did in which I believed the accuser, who, as it turned out, was lying. Be careful and gather your facts.

Thoughts for Those Considering a Career in Social Justice

Consider working for business or government. I hear many young people today say they will never work for a corporation; businesses are corrupt, they just want your money; they produce dangerous, polluting products; they harm others and will fire you on a whim; and they would rather work for a nonprofit, which feels more important. I have great concerns about these statements. Business needs the talent of young people. Society needs business and government to work. The goods and services provided by business and government are vital to how we live our lives. And businesses, like many other organizations, need thoughtful, talented employees to improve and create a better world for all. The ability to be working from inside the system has given me a skill set those on the outside don't have, which enhances my ability to create change.

Gain depth of knowledge about organization development and being a change agent. The knowledge and science of the theory and practice of change including organizational development, conflict resolution, managing resistance, communication techniques, organization systems, appreciative inquiry, styles and assessments, behavioral management, organizational anthropology, and many more topics are critically important. In my view they are as important to the work of systems change as are diversity and inclusion and social justice concepts such as oppression, privilege, unconscious bias, and others. Consider getting an advanced degree in change management, organizational development, or a similar field. The depth of knowledge will help you design and navigate challenging change strategies.

Earning a good or great income is not selling out. Some people believe a person making more money than 95% of the rest of the U.S. population is corrupt, evil, or being paid too much. Probably some are but not all. I learned pricing strategy by thinking about the value of the work to the organization. When I first entered the diversity and inclusion consulting business I saw no reason that I should be paid less because I am a woman or because I was doing work that was a cause. Many assumed that I would take less. I recall a situation where I was asked to help an organization write a business case for diversity and inclusion, but upper management decided to bring in a top-notch large consulting firm to do this, as it would have credibility. I had written diversity business cases before and had some models to follow to customize their case. The Big Eight firm was charging a lot more than I bid. This angered me. I wondered, "If I had charged more, would they have valued me more?" Ironically, because the project was taking too long and became too complex, I was brought in to finish the work. From that moment on, I understood the politics of pricing and usually didn't hesitate to charge rates comparable to what men and large firms would charge. I began to price jobs similar to other management consulting firms. I no longer felt compelled to charge a lower rate because my work was "for a cause." As you think about entering this field, remember your importance to success, and don't let others undermine you. This work is essential.

Conclusion

There are many ways to do social justice work, and all of them are valuable. My hope is that by contributing my experiences and best practices to this collection of chapters by White social justice activists, I've offered another option for how social justice work can be done. As I stated at the beginning of the chapter, I believe the word *activist* describes how I got into this work. There are many paths and many roles in social justice work. I believe we all need to use our strengths where they can best serve, whether it is inside the system, outside the system, on the outskirts, or deep in the heart of it. The key is that we value different approaches and support others in this important social justice work.

References

Ferdman, B. M. (2014). The practice of inclusion in diverse organizations. In B. M. Ferdman & B. R. Deane (Eds.), *Diversity at work: The practice of inclusion* (pp. 37–40). San Francisco, CA: Wiley.

Friedan, B. (1963). *The feminine mystique.* New York, NY: Norton.

O'Mara, J., & Richter, A. (with 80 Expert Panelists). (2014). *Global diversity and inclusion benchmarks: Standards for organizations around the world.* Retrieved from http://diversitycollegium.org/globalbenchmarks.php

12

INSIDE AND OUTSIDE

How Being an Ashkenazi Jew Illuminates and Complicates the Binary of Racial Privilege

Warren J. Blumenfeld

Sometimes I don't know which side of the wall I'm on. (Szpilman, in Harwood & Polanski, 2002)

As I sit here visiting my ancestral town of Krosno, Poland, thinking about issues of race and privilege, I am again reminded of two key issues that came to light for me a number of years ago. First, this socially constructed notion we call "race" (with its privileges and restrictions based on individuals' assigned race) must be seen in the contexts of place and time. Second, components of race need to be charted along a wide continuum and not as polar opposites within a binary frame (e.g., people of color and white people).

In this regard, I can never truly know the racialized experiences of those currently constructed in the United States as people of color. Having studied and traveled to Poland five times and to the Ukraine twice, I can now at least begin to understand what it is like to be on the receiving end of prejudice and racialized violence: from the offensive and stereotypical iconography to the comments to the hesitation of some to shake my hand believing I and all Jews were fathered by the Devil to the feeling that I am seen as an odd curiosity at best. To be quite frank, while I see real changes occurring in Poland in terms of Polish people's relationships with Jewish people, and I have hope for an even better future, at times I don't feel safe here, emotionally or physically. In Eastern Europe, Jews are racialized as nonwhite.[1] This racialization is very

---

clearly about race and not merely about being subject to the prejudices of others based on our othered religious beliefs.

I must, nevertheless, be very clear: My intent is *not* to erase the reality and enormity of dominant group privilege that white-skinned Jews receive in the United States. Nor do I want to ignore its effects on those with this privilege and those denied it. I hope, however, that we will not only continue, but also, more important, expand our examination of the issues in the day-to-day lived experiences of people and communities. I hope that as we move forward, we will undertake a somewhat more nuanced approach. As I have done this in my inner personal work and in my teaching, I have discovered a deeper, more complex understanding of unearned privilege, and I have experienced less resistance within myself and within my students when addressing it. By taking into account context and intersectionalities, I believe we will come to a fuller and deeper awareness of issues of power and privilege, marginalization, and oppression as we work toward a more socially just society and world.

Coming to Consciousness

On numerous occasions, I have attended the annual National Gay and Lesbian Task Force's Creating Change Conference, bringing together grassroots activists from throughout North America as well as from other countries around the world. At one of the conferences in the early 1990s, I was a participant in a well-attended workshop titled Activists of Color/White Activists Dialogue facilitated by two highly respected activists: a woman of color and a white Christian man.

When the workshop began, the woman outlined the agenda for the next one and a half hours. The workshop would concentrate on the concepts of race and dialogue across racial divides and include two separate panels of participant volunteers: one composed of four people of color, the other of four white people. Panel members were to each answer four questions from the facilitators; first, the people of color panelists, followed by the white panelists.

As she explained the intended focus and agenda, great confusion came over me: Should I volunteer? Well, maybe, but I really can't because I'm not sure if either of the categories for panelists include me. I know for certain that I am not eligible to volunteer for the people of color panel. But also I feel somehow that I don't belong on the white panel either. Maybe I should just listen to the panelists, which I did.

But what caused my bewilderment? What got in my way of self-defining myself as white? Where was this feeling of not belonging on either panel, or my feeling of in-betweenness coming from? Thinking back, I came to realize that it stems, I believe, from my personal and collective experience.

On the personal level, one day when I was a very young child, I sat upon my maternal grandfather Simon (*Szymon* in Polish) Mahler's knee. Looking down urgently but with deep affection, he said to me through his distinctive Polish accent, "Varn, you are named after my father, your great-grandfather, Wolf Mahler. I lived in Krosno, Poland, with my father, Wolf, and my mother, Bascha Trencher Mahler, and 13 brothers and sisters, aunts, uncles, and cousins."

Simon talked about our *mishpocheh* (family) with pride, but as he told me this, I saw an obvious sadness on his face. I asked him if our family still lived in Poland, and he responded that his father and most of the remainder of his family were no longer alive. When I asked him how they had died, he told me that they had all been killed by people called Nazis, except his mother, Bascha, who died of a heart attack in 1934. I asked him why the Nazis killed them, and he responded, "Because they were Jews." Those words have reverberated in my mind, haunting me ever since.

Jews Constructed as Racialized Other

Looking back to the historical emergence of the concept of race, critical race theorists remind us that this concept arose concurrently with the advent of European exploration as a justification and rationale for conquest and domination of the globe beginning in the fifteenth century of the Common Era (CE) and reaching its apex in the early twentieth century (see, e.g., Cameron & Wycoff, 1998). Geneticists tell us that there is often more variability *within* a given so-called race than among races and that there are no essential *genetic* markers linked specifically to race. They assert, therefore, that race is discursively constructed—a historical, scientific, biological myth, an idea— and that any socially conceived physical racial markers are fictive and are not concordant with what is beyond or below the surface of the body (see, e.g., Zuckerman, 1990).

Although biologists and social scientists have proven unequivocally that the *concept* of race is socially constructed (produced, manufactured), "the knowledge that race is an ideological, social/material construct does not take away the consequences when one is faced with actual racist incidents or practices" (Sefa Dei, 2000, p. 35).

In European society, according to social theorist and author Sander Gilman (1991), Jews were thought of as the "white Negroes" (Gilman, p. 30). And to Thandeka (1999a): "In the eyes of the non-Jew who defined them in Western [European] society the Jews became the blacks" (p. 37). Thandeka adds that "the male Jew and the male African were conceived of as equivalent threats to the white race" (p. 37).

This supposed racialization of the Jews was codified in American writer Madison Grant's (1916) influential book *The Passing of the Great Race,* in which he argued that Europeans were composed of four distinct races, which he ranked in a racial hierarchy. On the bottom he placed the most inferior of all the European so-called races: the Jews. Referring specifically to the Polish Jew, Grant asserted that "the Polish Jews, whose dwarf stature, peculiar mentality and ruthless concentration on self-interest" (p. 16), present themselves in "swarms" (p. 63).

Analogous to the notion in the United States that one drop of black African blood makes a person black, according to Grant (1916),

> The result of the mixture of two races, in the long run, gives us a race reverting to the more ancient generalization and lower type. The cross between a white man and an Indian is an Indian, the cross between a white man and a Negro is a Negro, the cross between a white man and a Hindu is a Hindu, and the cross between any of the three European races and a Jew is a Jew. (p. 18)

The Nazis accepted and advanced the "scientific" view that Jews of European heritage, in fact all Jews of every so-called race, constitute a separate and lower race as justification for extermination as if we were vermin.

Following Hitler's invasion of Poland on September 1, 1939, Nazi troops isolated all 2,071 Jewish residents of my ancestral town of Krosno into a strictly demarcated area and frequently took large numbers of them into the surrounding woods, where they forced them to dig their own mass grave before Nazis shot them. Eventually, troops ordered those who remained to board packed and virtually airless train cars for shipment to the Auschwitz-Birkenau and Bełżec concentration camps, where virtually all perished. None of my Krosno relatives survived. I have since returned to Krosno many times to recover the missing pieces of the jigsaw history of my ancestral past.

So for me, anyway, it seemed to have taken somewhat longer than, for example, many Christians of European heritage to come to accept that by dint of my skin color, hair texture, facial features, and, most important, my European genealogy, U.S. society grants me a host of privileges denied those constructed as people of color. My initial and continuing questions for years were the following:

- In European society, my *mishpocheh*—in fact, all Jews then and in many areas today—were and are still not considered white. If this is so, if the Nazis ruthlessly murdered my Polish and also Hungarian family because they were *not* white, then how can I have white privilege?

- In discussions about race, how can I find my voice and be heard when carrying this feeling of not belonging completely to either group on the current racial binary?

Coming to Consciousness

I grew up in a mixed Christian and Ashkenazi Jewish community during the 1950s and 1960s, and, before I experienced any informal or formal discussions or readings specifically related to the topic of dominant group privilege, I began to question these things known as race and privilege through personal encounters.

I witnessed other students in my third-grade classroom whispering and talking behind the back of the only black student in our class. I heard students saying, "I'm having a party at my house, but I'm sure my father won't let me invite him," and "I'm glad the teacher didn't seat me next to him because I hear *they* smell." And they asked him, "How do you comb that kind of hair?" and, "If there were a pill that would make you white, would you take it?" And through it all, I saw how students consciously marginalized him. I'm sure I had lots of excuses, but although I did not engage in the gossip or add to the offensive comments, I also did not reach out to befriend this student or in any way intervene to counter the marginalization.

Later in school, teachers talked about slavery, Jim Crow, and the Civil Rights Movement. Teachers showed us pictures of white people cheerfully posing for the cameras after hanging black people in the South. I saw the red glow in the night sky over the hills where I lived and the National Guard vehicles driving through my neighborhood en route to the Watts district of Los Angeles. I too experienced the trauma and utter shock (though not surprise) over the murders of Bobby Kennedy and Rev. Martin Luther King Jr. in the span of a mere three months. And I noticed that no black person took any advanced-track courses (today known as advanced placement) in my high school, but in reality, when I attended school in Los Angeles County from 1955 through 1965, racial segregation was the rule and not the exception. Very few people of color attended our high school.

I had begun to see during these incidents the types of benefits or privileges I had that people of color in my youth did not have. This became crystallized in my mind when one day standing in line at the grocery store, I witnessed the cashier asking for three forms of picture identification from the black woman in front of us as she pulled out her checkbook; the same cashier required only one from my mother. In addition, I watched as two security guards tailed a black man as he entered a department store, but as I looked behind us, no guards followed me and my father in the same store.

So fairly early in my childhood, I at least became aware of how my life was relatively easier for me because of my skin color, although I remained confused about how I fit in this thing called race. For example, my father often talked about his childhood and the ways he suffered the effects of anti-Jewish prejudice. One of only a handful of Jews in his schools in Los Angeles in the 1920s and 1930s, he returned home injured from a fight on many afternoons. During recess period in elementary school, to avoid attack by the other boys who targeted him as "the Jew" or "the dirty Jew" or "the killer of Christ," he found an opening under one of the buildings where he hid each day. To get a decent job, his father, my grandfather, Abraham, anglicized the family name, changing it from Blumenfeld to Fields, so he could find a job in this highly discriminatory society.

My mother related how in high school another female student approached her and accused her of lying by claiming that she was Jewish. "You can't be a Jew," the student asserted. "My mother told me that Jews were fathered by the Devil, and they have horns and tails. Since you don't have horns and a tail, you can't be a Jew!"

I eventually learned about "the talk" that black and brown parents have with their children, especially with their sons. Police officers and also white residents of the United States routinely profile and target black and brown boys and men for harassment, arrest, and accusations of violence and murder simply for walking down the street or driving in cars while being black or brown. Parents warn their young people that if ever approached by police, walk toward them and never run away, keep hands out of your pockets in plain view, don't raise your voice, be polite, and never show anger or use derogatory language.

My parents never gave me *that* talk, but my mother did sit me down for a talk. When I was born in 1947, my maternal uncle's friend gave my parents a small gold chain for me with the fifth letter of the Hebrew alphabet, *Hei*, representing "G*d" in Hebrew, or *HaShem*.[2] Upon my Bar Mitzvah at the age of 13, my mother presented me with the *Hei*, saying: "Warren, you are old enough now to wear this. Remember, though, to always wear it *under* your shirt out of view. There are still many people who hate Jews, and I don't want you to get hurt if these people see the *Hei* around your neck."

While today a number of so-called blond jokes circulate around the United States that depict people with blond hair as essentially superficial, bland, and ignorant, I believe this covers an underlying blond standard of physical beauty and privilege (as well as a reified value system) of white people—a standard that many Jews, including members of my own immediate family, attempted to emulate. According to Norman Podhoretz, if one is not a WASP, one had better become a "facsimile WASP" (quoted in Thandeka,

1999b). If one wants to make it in American society, and if one is female, one must aspire to what Brodkin (1998) terms "blond-people standards of female beauty" (p. 17)—that is, to embrace mainstream white standards.

My sister, Susan, who had naturally sandy brown and very curly hair in junior and senior high school in the 1950s and 1960s, bleached her hair to a golden blond. In addition, once or twice a week for a number of years, she asked me to smooth out the curls with a hot iron by placing her long hair upon an ironing board. She pleaded with my parents to allow her to have nose reduction surgery (a so-called nose job), and she reacted in tantrums of despair when they refused. To be quite frank, as a college sophomore at age 19, I also straightened my hair with a drugstore remedy. While it did, indeed, relax my curls, it also seriously burned my scalp. I picked at the scabs on my scalp for the next month, all in an attempt to look like them—the blond people.

The black Civil Rights Movement during the 1960s reconnected and strengthened my ties to *my* past and *my* culture. People like Rosa Parks, Martin Luther King Jr., Stokely Carmichael, Bobby Seale, Angela Davis, Huey Newton, and Eldridge Cleaver presented a visible alternative to blond-people mainstream standards. Events during this time seriously challenged and even somewhat reversed white standards of beauty and culture, such as the Black Power and Black Is Beautiful movements.

In terms of standards of beauty, straight hair was out, curly hair was in. The African 'fro (Afro) hairstyle brought the natural look and curly hair into fashion. I could now wear my hair in a 'fro. I used a pick and let it grow out in all its dark curliness. For the first time in my life, people envied *my* hair, and I actually liked it myself.

From White Negroes to Off-White Whites

Throughout my graduate studies at the University of Massachusetts Amherst, I had the opportunity of first enrolling in, then co-facilitating with a black colleague, weekend undergraduate courses focusing on the long history of persecution against the Jewish people. One semester, following a lecture I presented to the class on the history of anti-Jewish prejudice, a student responded, "I understand about the brutal persecution of Jews in Europe. So why have Jews had an easier time in the United States?" I immediately thought of Allport's (1954) words:

> In Europe, where there is no Negro minority, it is the *Jew* who is blamed for the lechery, filth, and violence. Americans, having the Negro to personify these traits, do not *need* the Jew for this purpose. The Americans, therefore,

can build up a more specialized stereotype of the Jew embracing only the "superego" qualities of ambition, pride, adroitness. (p. 194)

Without hesitation, I pointed to my co-facilitator, an African American man, and I said, "Americans don't *need* me to oppress. They have Torin." (Yes, Torin and Warren co-facilitated the workshops, and as we told the students, "It isn't going to be borin'.")

Because Torin and I had worked multiple times in Jewish oppression workshops, and in workshops covering larger issues of racism, we were able to realize that while the experiences of Ashkenazi Jews and people currently constructed as people of color in the United States are *very* different, we understood that in some ways, considering context, while different, some of our communities' experiences run parallel and at points intersect. By my understanding and acknowledging the white privilege accorded me today in the United States—relative, at least, to white mainline Protestants—I have found that at those points of intersection, I see the greatest potential for developing empathy and forming coalitions.

Seeing Race in Context Along a Continuum

Because of historical and social conditions, Jews have a sort of "double vision" (Brodkin, 1998, p. 102) or "insider/outsider" status (Biale, Galchinsky, & Heschel, 1998) in contemporary U.S. society. According to Brodkin, "In the last century, Jews in the United States have spent about equal amounts of time on both sides—the not white and the white—of the American eth-noracial binary" (p. 102). And Melanie Kaye/Kantrowitz (1995) concludes, "The truth is, Jews complicate things. *Jewish* is both a distinct category and an overlapping one. . . . The problem is a polarization of white and color that excludes us" (p. 125).

Michael Lerner (1992) resents this racial polarization as well: "The linguistic move of substituting 'people of color' for oppressed minorities, coupled with the decision to refer to Jews as 'whites,' becomes an anti-Semitic denial of Jewish history" (p. 123).

The irony is that as Jewish ethnoracial assignment has increasingly moved to the white side of the racial divide, according to Peter Langman (1995), "Putting Jews and neo-Nazis in the same racial category is probably offensive to both" (p. 236).

Once constructed as the other in European society, Jews of European heritage and Jewishness in the United States—while certainly not fully embraced by the ruling elite as one of their own—acquired a sort of middle status, "standing somewhere between the dominant position of the White majority and the marginal position of people of color" (Biale et al., 1998, p. 5). And this change in Jewish ethnoracial assignment has occurred only within the past 60 or so years.

While I and other Jews of European heritage clearly understand that we have been accorded white privilege vis-à-vis minoritized racial communities, we also understand the history and legacy of anti-Jewish persecution and, yes, how dominant groups have *racialized* us as well. I see anti-Jewish prejudice and discrimination *as* a form of racism.

Well into my college years, foundational, gnawing, and, for me, unanswered questions still often remained unanswered: Do Jews of European heritage in fact have the privileges accorded to, say, mainline white Protestants and other white people in the United States? And even more fundamental: How can we Jews of European heritage have white privilege when dominant groups justified the murder of our *mishpocheh* for not being white? In other words, What *is* my race?

The last question became a central focus for my doctoral dissertation in which I interviewed a cross section of Ashkenazim of different generations and regional locations in the United States. I recorded responses to my question, What is your race? along a continuum from "not white" to "Jewish" to "white, but . . . ?" to "white enough to have white privilege" to "white."

Although I have much left to learn, certain ideas I have found that inform my current perspective may be helpful for those entering this work. With my Ashkenazi experience, I have come to see how racial categorization has not merely been social, assigned by physiognomy (outward body characteristics), as much as it has been perception and assumptions. For example, an orthodox Hasidic Ashkenazi Jewish man and I may have similar or even identical physical features, but I may appear to others as *whiter* and accorded a greater degree of white privilege since I have assimilated closer to the mythical norm of whiteness in my presentation.

In terms of context, I have learned to carry my physiognomy wherever I go. In larger U.S. cities, for example, my whiteness and white privilege would probably not be denied. While living and working in a small midwestern city for nine years, however, my physiognomy and religious background placed my whiteness and privilege under scrutiny in an area where "Don't Jew me down" and "That's *so* Jewish" surfaced regularly on the school yard and in the home. When traveling in Poland, I certainly do not feel my white privilege.

With these lingering questions, with the occasional acts of anti-Jewish violence, with the continued categorization of Jews as racially inferior and as so-called "mud people" (along with people of color) by extremist white racist groups, and possibly because I continue to carry a collective memory of the long history of persecution toward the Jewish people, I come close to Brodkin's (1998) placement of Ashkenazi Jewish American ethnoracial assignment as white, but not completely. I now choose, therefore, to plot my own current placement as off-white or whiteish on the American ethnoracial scale as it is currently constructed. Along with two of my dissertation participants, I agree that I am white enough to have white privilege, although there remains within me the lingering hesitation of white . . . but?

I have picked up a large array of jewels along the road of understanding issues of race, racism, dominant group privilege, and how I have begun to see my placement along the wide continuum. I have used these jewels to create a strand I wear, sometimes under my garments, sometimes over them in clear view. For me, my racial understanding is not only fluid and contextual but also ever evolving. I continually investigate and analyze my racial identification, the ways that race constantly emerges, changes, constructs, and deconstructs within a social context.

While I compare and contrast my racial standing as constructed with others around me, I have learned how important it is to raise questions about my Ashkenazi racial positionality, at least initially, only with other Ashkenazim who might have asked themselves similar questions and have come to their own conclusions. For me anyway, I believe these sorts of questions need to be raised as an internal discussion within our larger Ashkenazi community.

I have also come to firmly believe we need to know our history, not only of our persecution but also of how we have overcome many of the impediments placed in our way and the benefits we have accrued. To do this, I truly believe we need to look at the larger timeline of Jewish history in its entirety. If we investigate merely the timeline of U.S. American Jewish history while neglecting the larger historical international timeline, I have found that we come away with a somewhat distorted and incomplete understanding of ourselves and our communities.

Notes

1. When I speak of Jews of European heritage, I refer in particular to Ashkenazi Jews. I try throughout the chapter to make it clear that I am referring only to this group. I am aware that there are many Jews of color from around the world, including many Sephardim, Mizrachim, and African Jews, who remain in many nations categorized as people of color.
2. In Judaism, we do not spell out the name of G*d.

References

Allport, G. W. (1954). *The nature of prejudice.* Cambridge, MA: Addison-Wesley.
Biale, D., Galchinsky, M., & Heschel, S. (1998). *Insider/outsider: American Jews and multiculturalism.* Berkeley: University of California Press.

Brodkin, K. (1998). *How Jews became white folks & what that says about race in America.* New Brunswick, NJ: Rutgers University Press.

Cameron, S. C., & Wycoff, S. M. (1998). The destructive nature of the term *race:* Growing beyond a false paradigm. *Journal of Counseling & Development, 76*(3), 277–285.

Gilman, S. L. (1991). *The Jew's body.* New York, NY: Routledge.

Grant, M. (1916). *The passing of the great race: Or the racial basis of European history.* New York, NY: Charles Scribner.

Harwood, R., (Writer), & Polanski, R. (Director). (2002). *The pianist* [Motion picture]. United States: Universal Studios.

Kaye/Kantrowitz, M. (1995). *The issue is power: Essays on women, Jews, violence, and resistance.* San Francisco, CA: Aunt Lute Books.

Langman, P. F. (1995). Including Jews in multiculturalism. *Journal of Multicultural Counseling and Development, 23*(4), 222–236.

Lerner, M. (1992). *The socialism of fools: Anti-Semitism on the left.* Oakland, CA: Tikkun Books.

Sefa Dei, G. J. (2000). Towards an anti-racism discursive framework. In G. J. Sefa Dei & A. Calliste (Eds.), *Power, knowledge, and anti-racism education: A critical reader* (pp. 34–40). Halifax, Nova Scotia, Canada: Fernwood.

Thandeka. (1999a). The cost of whiteness. *Tikkun, 14*(3), 33–38.

Thandeka. (1999b). Middle-class poverty: Race- and class-passing within white America. *World: The Journal of the Unitarian Universalist Association.* Retrieved from http://www.uuworld.org/1999/0999feat1.html

Zuckerman, M. (1990). Some dubious premises in research and theory on racial differences: Scientific, social, and ethical issues. *American Psychologist, 45*(12), 1297–1303.

13

OF WHITE AND HEARING PRIVILEGE

Jane K. Fernandes

We are living in a pathology of socially interwoven oppression and privilege systems. If we leave the interweaving (or intersections) of these systems unexamined, the result is like trying to pull our fingers out from the ends of a woven bamboo Chinese finger puzzle. The weaving tightens and entraps. Without awareness of the interconnecting parts of oppression systems, we remain trapped too, and struggling only tightens their grip, preventing us from pulling out and then unraveling the systems to better understand and transform them. Among these multiple systems, I examine in more depth the two interwoven systems of White privilege and hearing privilege.

My Entry Into the Systems of White Privilege and Hearing Privilege

My mother was born deaf into an all-White family. She learned how to speak and speechread and had her own speech teacher at home. When she and my father, a White hearing man, married, they spoke English at home with my mother relying completely on speechreading with some writing to communicate. The origins of my privilege were in my having been born into an extended middle-class White family, with a deaf mother and a hearing father.

Unlike the class and skin color privilege that I received at birth, I developed, after inordinate work, speaking privilege, through which I can make myself understood without dependence on a sign language interpreter. Hearing parents of deaf children, please note: I am not suggesting this hybrid path would work for everyone, although it clearly worked for me as it developed organically out of my particular set of circumstances. What I can do now is reflect on the hearing privilege none of us consciously understood or addressed while I was growing up.

Since my mother never learned American Sign Language (ASL), when I was born deaf and one of my brothers was later born hard of hearing, she taught us the same way she had learned to communicate because it was the only way she knew. I learned, after struggle and a lot of work, to speak, speechread, read, and write English. I lived at home and went to local public schools and received at-home instruction prior to the passage of state and federal laws requiring reasonable accommodations. Growing up, understanding and being understood were a constant uncertainty. This barrier resulted, as I later learned, from hearing privilege. As a result of this lack of access, I unconsciously saw my difference as a deficit.

In contrast, I saw how my brothers easily converted what they heard and spoke into what they read and wrote. Through an accident of birth, they easily acquired a language built for their ears and expressed in speech and writing, which in turn gave them ready access to all kinds of information essential to life.

Anyone dismantling privilege understands, just as with other accidents of birth, it is not their fault that my brothers had hearing and thus enjoyed the privilege it offers. But I have come to understand that, once aware, we all bear the responsibility of choosing whether we perpetuate a system that benefits hearing people solely because they can hear. As I was growing up, we were not aware of and did not address this privilege in everyday life. But I did understand another system enough to work to change it: racism and White privilege.

The Anthropology of Friendship

At my local public school, friendships were hard to cultivate because I could not easily communicate with hearing peers. As I look back on my life, I realize difference and discrimination based on difference helped me make one of my best friends, an African American girl. LaToya (not her real name) was one of the few African American students, and I was the only deaf one. In junior high school, we were like fish out of water or birds without air. The school was not made for us. We forged a bond based on a shared desire to succeed in school, both struggling against the odds.

Our bond of friendship tested other bonds, however. I upset our White neighbors who asked my mother why I was "bringing the Blacks in." LaToya risked losing her African American friends by including me in her circle. Our relationship challenged me to understand more about myself as a White person and a deaf person.

One incident stands out. While LaToya and I often sat together in the cafeteria despite otherwise racially segregated tables, one day I ate alone. Finishing, I threw on my bulky winter coat, cleaned up my tray, and went outside. A few minutes later, a White assistant principal summoned me back inside, where I saw our African American principal talking with several Black students I had seen sitting behind me at lunch. My heart pounded because I could not understand what they were saying but sensed I was in trouble.

I figured out that my bulky coat must have knocked the Black students' milk cartons onto the floor. Since I heard neither the cartons falling nor the girls calling me to pick them up, and they did not know I was deaf, they must have thought I had deliberately dismissed them.

Somewhere in the discussion, I saw clearly on the principal's lips, "Now, girls, this appears to have been an accident." But they were having none of it. My whiteness, I saw much later, clearly figured in their disbelief. But at the time, their reaction astounded me, and I felt bad that the principal, believing it an accident, still asked me to clean up the cartons. By this time, everyone outside was looking in the window to see what was happening.

I remember this incident as a clear example of White and hearing privilege, not intersecting with but crashing into each other. At that time none of us had enough courage or understanding to discern all that was happening. Instead we lived out the roles that the White and hearing systems had created for us.

In high school I became clearer about racial privilege, although I had not grasped the nuances of hearing privilege beyond a gut level. I can recall another incident that demonstrated a complex but important intersection of White and hearing privilege involving the use of pity.

LaToya and I planned that each of us would write a required paper but swap them and put our name on the other one's paper. When we got our traded papers back, the one with my name on it but authored by LaToya had an A, whereas she normally would have received a B or B minus. And hers, which I wrote, bore a B minus. We felt we had proof of racism in our school and told everyone we could about it. With the benefit that comes from a long view of years, I know now that we also had proof of hearing privilege. That is the privilege of knowing that the grade you are given is a reflection of your demonstrated skill, rather than of the pity that your deafness engenders. I knew even then that teachers often would give me an A because they could not imagine how anyone could deal with being deaf. In their mind, deafness caused such a deficiency that I deserved an A, regardless of the merits of my work. Much later I came to understand how this pity sits at a unique intersection of White and hearing privilege that has helped create a hierarchy among deaf people.

Hearing people allow themselves the authority to extend pity to children born deaf. These children receive rewards given out of pity, and deep down inside, or sometimes by very public and embarrassing incidents, the children know that hearing people are lying to them about their achievements. At the same time, the deaf children grow up wanting the rewards they are given. Having internalized their denigration through pity, they perhaps half believe or may fear they cannot get these rewards authentically. Intensifying their sense of inadequacy are barriers to learning English as well as ASL.

Despite the denigration of pity, White deaf people and White hearing people unconsciously align with each other, thus sharing in the power of White privilege. Most White deaf people focus on their deaf oppression, to the exclusion of any awareness of the privilege granted them by being White in a system conducive to White people, wherein being White is considered the norm.

White hearing people, out of pity but also because of White privilege, bestow positions and other benefits on White deaf people. This systematic practice enables White deaf people to share in unearned benefits of whiteness and in the belief that they, as White people, are better than deaf people of other races. It is in this way that their whiteness somewhat mitigates the devastating effect of pity. Examining the pity factor and race explains how White deaf people and deaf people of color experience different effects of that pity. Accustomed to the elevated position that a system advantageous to White people has put them in, White deaf people begin to believe they are owed that privilege, even at the expense of deaf people of other races.

Some White deaf people have become aware of how pity ultimately serves to undermine them and reinforce hearing privilege, but this awareness emphasizes only their difference from White hearing people, not their similarity with other deaf people of color. Intersections of privilege systems, when they are not unfolded and opened to full view, become a bastion for maintaining White power and privilege. In many cases, they take place out of the view of the majority of people and thus many, even those committed to social justice, do not see or understand the role of intersections in the maintenance of White supremacy.

Framework of Intersectional Discrimination

In 1980 as a graduate student at the University of Iowa, I walked into the Cedar Rapids Deaf Club—that's *Deaf* with a capital D^1—and my whole world changed. For the first time, I met Deaf people who signed. My journey into the Deaf world began at the age of 23. At that time, however, I had not yet grasped that it was White Deaf people's ASL and Deaf culture that I was learning.

Deaf people in Iowa helped me learn that as a deaf person, ASL is my language and that I belong to the deaf community. Why did it take me 23 years to know that I am proud to be deaf? That's the result of an *ism* for which a new word has been coined: *audism*. Audism, or discrimination based on the ability to hear, has a systemic version called institutional audism.[2]

Renowned philosophers like Aristotle believed that without speech there could be no thought and that speech made us human. This belief has come down to us through the centuries, fostering an almost universal conviction that it is better to be hearing than deaf and that if you have the misfortune to be deaf, it is better to speak and speechread than to sign.

I began my career with this new awareness of hearing privilege and audism, and immediately saw it manifested institutionally during my tenure at the Hawaii School for the Deaf and the Blind. Despite a critical mass of deaf students at a school designed for them, deaf people continue to experience diminished access to information. For example, at meetings with mostly deaf people, a hearing person would gain the floor by using voice to interject a comment, not waiting first to gain visual attention as well or in place of voice. At the same time, White privilege also existed at this institution with a predominance of children from many ancestries and cultures, including Hawaiian, Japanese, Chinese, Filipino, and Samoan. Each group has its own unique sign language, yet all had to use English and ASL at the school.

The interplay of White and hearing privilege within the deaf community became intensely clear once I worked at another institution with a large population of deaf people: Gallaudet University in Washington, DC. Within this critical mass of deaf people, I understood clearly the hierarchy arising from the intersection of hearing privilege, with its concomitant pity factor, and White privilege.

Advantaged White Deaf Core

Children from multigenerational Deaf families, known as Deaf children of Deaf parents (DOD), have unearned advantages of early access to full communication in ASL and transmission of cultural norms within family life.

While it may seem to hearing people that being a Deaf child of Deaf adults might be a disadvantage, there is a way that such children get positioned as the most legitimate members of the Deaf community, with all other experiences of deafness being inferior. Those Deaf families that are also White gain a synergistic blend of advantages. While aware of their advantages as DODs, these DODs are not as aware of their White privilege. At the time I was growing up in the 1950s and 1960s, most deaf schools, like hearing schools at the time, were segregated. White deaf students attended a school designed for them, while Black deaf students attended a segregated school. Linguistic and sociolinguistic work on Black ASL and Black Deaf schools finally began only in the past few years, with the first empirical study published in 2013 (McCaskill, Lucas, Bayley, & Hill, 2013). Yet the preponderance of research-backed descriptions of DODs rests on the study of White Deaf people.

The early scholarly focus on these White Deaf people gave respectability to *their* norms and ASL, thus solidifying their prestige and influence among all Deaf people (for more discussion of the narrowing of Deaf life based on the study of White Deaf people, see Fernandes & Myers, 2010, pp. 18–19). It is this group that prescribes markers of authentic deafness as devaluing speaking while valuing loud sounds and vibrations as helpful for communication purposes, using the form of ASL that White Deaf people use, considering reading and writing in English important, and marrying other Deaf people. Even valuing reading and writing in English enforces DOD power because educational research has found that DODs who sign achieve higher results on all measures of achievement and acquire a better command of both written and spoken English than children without early signing. Many other deaf people who have not had full and early access to ASL have not benefitted from an education resulting in English fluency. This accident of birth into an all-Deaf White family is a certain insider track prescribed as the core of Deaf life.

Indicative of this insider-track status is the confidence these core Deaf culture members exhibit. While some might think that deaf children of hearing parents gain privilege from their parents' capacity to navigate the hearing world, it is the DODs who benefit from parents who serve as a buffer between the children and the audist hearing world, provide strategies for dealing with it, and instill a positive identity for their difference.

In addition, advantage-inspired confidence underlies DODs' enormous influence at any school for the Deaf. Even at a very young age, DODs teach their peers ASL and enculturate them with the norms, behaviors, customs, and values that go along with being Deaf. The White Deaf native signers sit at the top of a hierarchy, a privileged position they acquired through an accident of their birth, a position that gives them power and privilege maintained for life within any organization or institution with a Deaf majority.

In the recent past, while DODs stood at the top of the Deaf hierarchy that informally organized life outside the classroom, the predominantly hearing authorities, who valued speech, hearing, and English above all else, slapped deaf children on the hands with a ruler or forced them to kneel on a broomstick as a consequence for signing. They rewarded those able to demonstrate good speech and speechreading skills over those with an excellent mastery of academic content through ASL but without facility in English. White Deaf people continue throughout their lives to fight for and assert their position at the top of the hierarchy of deaf people, which results from audism and racism, especially because of the tremendous counterpressure the hearing world puts on them.

Intersections of Institutional Audism and Racism

Working at Gallaudet University, I again witnessed manifestations of institutional audism that I had seen in Hawaii, such as the hearing norm of using voice to gain the floor at a meeting. But now, from my position as vice president overseeing improvements in primary and secondary deaf education on campus and throughout the nation, I confronted a complicated manifestation of audism and its nuanced intersection with racism.

At Kendall Demonstration Elementary School, I discovered a segregated program. All White deaf children, the vast majority of whom had Deaf parents and siblings, were taught in a regular curriculum. Black deaf children were grouped into a separate program called the Special Opportunities Program. Under my guidance, and at the direction of the assistant secretary of the U.S. Department of Education, we dismantled this discriminatory program and gradually integrated all children into one school. Startling results emerged: White parents fled with their children from Kendall to Maryland School for the Deaf in Frederick. One of these parents said her daughter pointed uncomfortably, even disparagingly, at all the new people (Black children) in her classes as "not her peers." But they also said their children were going to the Maryland School for the Deaf in Frederick to get a "better" education. How prepared are they, I wonder, to enter the twenty-first century global village?

Promoted to the position of provost in 2000, I continued to work on inclusive academic excellence. Among other academic initiatives, I created a group of diversity leadership fellows, and, guided by Frances E. Kendall, we developed a comprehensive diversity strategic plan designed to unravel the threads holding together racism and audism on the Gallaudet campus. We pushed people hard, and like the White parents at the dismantling of tracking (grouping children according to their academic ability) at Kendall School, the privileged core became uncomfortable. Rather than fleeing, however, those belonging to this core fought to retain dominion over Gallaudet University, considered to be their nation or home. They wanted to create a piece of the world that belonged to them, that was perfect for them. A world created by them, for them, is a privilege and a power that only White people, including White Deaf people, have.

White Deaf privilege was rampant at the university, and challenges to it enraged the most privileged. One infamous example occurred after the Homecoming Ball at a hotel in downtown Washington, DC, in the fall of 2005. Students booked rooms, and ran up and down the halls into the night yelling, pounding on doors, and pulling fire alarms, causing the entire hotel to evacuate a few times. The police and firefighters came repeatedly to the scene. I received many letters from guests questioning how Gallaudet could support such behavior. One woman said she opened the door to her room, holding her infant to show Deaf students that the noise was keeping her baby awake and crying. The students, according to her letter, laughed and derided her. The hotel demanded payment of damages in the thousands of dollars. When I wrote to the students criticizing the privilege they had granted themselves to destroy property and prevent other guests, including infants, from sleeping, the response from Deaf students and adults was outrage. They claimed to be the victims of my authoritarian ways. I did not treat them respectfully as equals. Having been born into a White family (half deaf and half hearing), and having attended hearing schools, learned to speak English, married a hearing man, and given birth to two hearing children, I was not at the top of the deaf hierarchy. I was viewed through the lens of White Deaf culture as a colonizer with hearing behaviors.

Another incident occurred that fall of 2005. The football team, disappointed at the lack of a celebration of their no-loss record, enlisted others to help pull dormitory fire alarms and direct the evacuated students to drag down the goalposts. The ensuing chaos included copious amounts of alcohol and drugs, flying beer bottles that hit some people in the head, and an overturned car. Citing reluctance—born of pity—to traumatize Deaf students with arrest but fearing the falling goalposts could seriously injure them, campus police only asked students to disperse. Egged on by several adult leaders, the spared students raged at the request to disperse and diverted attention from their own actions by assuming the role of victim and faulting the signing skills of the campus police. When I attempted to talk with them about their actions and failure to disperse, I was once again the "schoolmarm,"

oppressing Deaf life with my humorless hearing ways. Not one of them realized their attack against the campus police was made easier because the majority of the officers were African American. Their youthful White privilege saw
and took advantage of vulnerable targets they could disregard and blame.

The following spring, I applied to become the university's ninth president, advocating that Gallaudet dismantle its system of privileging the White
Deaf core and become an inclusive deaf university of academic excellence: an
academic culture where all kinds of deaf people and diverse ideas and opin-
ions are welcome. I was honored and humbled when the board of trustees
appointed me as the second deaf president and the first deaf woman president in the university's history.

Rather than avowing their opposition to Gallaudet University's becoming a university inclusive of all kinds of deaf people, those who wanted a
university molded to White Deaf norms sought publicly acceptable reasons
for protesting my appointment. At first they attempted to marginalize and
exclude me, saying I was "not deaf enough." When asked about the reasons
for the protest, one demonstrator was quoted in the *New York Times* as saying, "She married a hearing man" (Schemo, 2006). Flyers distributed during
the protest listed the following reasons for it: "Her mother is deaf but oral;
her father is hearing; she went to hearing schools; her children are hearing;
she did not play with us at the youth leadership camp."

When the not-deaf-enough standard failed to play well in the media, the
protesters tried to disavow it and instead turned to my management style—
itself code for challenging White Deaf norms. Many (to be sure, not all)
White Deaf people were so threatened by my vision of inclusive academic
excellence and by my challenge to the current power structure, they resorted
to a powerfully organized resistance to my shining a bright light on what was
happening at the intersection of hearing and White privilege.

As a result, a seven-month maelstrom of hate, anger, death threats, and
ridicule ensued against me, my two children, my husband, and the many
deaf/Deaf and hearing people who stood beside me. The protesters responded
to the cumulative effects of my actions over 12 years; chief among them
was naming White privilege and racism at Gallaudet University as crucial
issues and addressing them. The protest was like suddenly lifting the lid off
a long-simmering pressure cooker. Changes at the elementary and secondary
schools, the football field and hotel fiascos, and my substandard status as a
deaf person with speaking privilege within the Capital D Deaf Culture and
community, for example, boiled over and erupted like hot lava spewing from
a volcano. Although publicly the protest tried to appear peaceful and based
on principles of civil rights, it masked the private expression of unchecked
rage and the height of White privilege in action.

One searing memory was a YouTube video that the protesters posted in which an African American hearing campus security officer entered Hall Memorial Building, home to many campus classrooms. As he entered, he signed to protesters that he was coming in and directed them to stand aside and let him do so. They posted the film to show proof that he was not signing ASL, but the irony was that the officer signed, if not in White ASL, at least in a manner that clearly stated his intention, and the protesters understood him quite well. As the African American security officer walked through the building, a growing number of young White Deaf men and women surrounded and stalked him, holding a camera in his face and gawking at him the whole time. The film showed the terrified look on the security officer's face as it dawned on him that the protesters were setting him up to do something on film that would embarrass him. I could almost see etched on his face thoughts like, "I have family, and I need this job to support them; please don't get me fired." He looked all around for a way to escape while the young White men and women surrounding him just stared. Finally, he found an opening, turned, and ran to get out of the building before something happened. I will never forget how terrified he appeared; equally memorable was the privileged position of the young White Deaf men and women who were able to arouse that fear in a campus security officer—who knew what they were deliberately doing and why.

Many deaf people of color challenged the invisibility of White Deaf privilege. One of the six semifinalists for Gallaudet president was Glenn B. Anderson, an African American Gallaudet alumnus who had served successfully as chairman of the board of trustees for 12 years but was not one of the final three candidates. Given their assessment of the strengths and weaknesses of the final group, students of color began protesting almost immediately. One scene emblazoned on my memory is their march across campus carrying a mock coffin with these words on it: Diversity Is Dead. Deaf and hearing people of color held meetings, rallies, press conferences; they also appealed to the National Association of the Deaf and other advocacy groups but received no significant or visible support.

The main groups, predominantly White, had already accepted the three named finalists and counted on one of the two White DOD male candidates to be selected. When I was announced as the board's choice to serve as the ninth president of Gallaudet University, the protest representing White Deaf interests erupted immediately. Those protesting my appointment knew that my platform involved creating a more diverse and inclusive university, precisely what they did not want Gallaudet to become.

Despite competing viewpoints, the two groups of White protesters and protesting people of color attempted to join forces at the beginning.

Messages appeared from the protesters in strong support of diversity, such as a banner in front of campus saying, "Honk if you support social justice." These messages originated with the group who could not see the presidential candidate finalists as legitimate without the highly accomplished Anderson among them. While some White protesters offered a semblance of agreement with this social justice message, they in fact appropriated the message, using it to mean having the board do what they wanted so they could reap the most benefit from Gallaudet for their own. This perversion of social justice for self-interest dovetailed with other messages from the protest that were more focused on me personally, such as, "JKF is killing our future." But when I became the target of personal attacks, many deaf people of color broke from the ranks and started speaking out on their own.

After the Gallaudet University Board of Trustees rescinded my contract, a news story broke on television about a group of White Deaf students at the Model Secondary School for the Deaf on the Gallaudet campus who forced a Black deaf boy to the floor and held him there against his will, writing KKK and drawing Nazi swastikas all over his body. Cathy Lanier, chief of the Metropolitan Police Department, issued a statement that the incident was being investigated as a possible hate crime because of the different races of the White perpetrators and Black victim. In that moment, I felt the protesters were sending me a powerful message about who is in charge at Gallaudet.

At Gallaudet University, the framework of intersecting oppression systems I observed was virtually flipped from what it looked like when I was growing up. Rather than living in a world of predominantly hearing people where racism was apparent and audism virtually invisible, now I worked in a university of predominantly deaf people. The critical mass of deaf people made personal and institutional audism crystal clear. And racism, even within the Deaf culture, was virtually invisible. The Gallaudet community ultimately had no ability to understand racism; White Deaf people in support of the protest go went far as to say that all deaf people are united in their experience of deafness and are thus immune to racial differences among them.

My growing understanding of audism, particularly how we deaf people internalize it, was enhanced. Likewise, I saw an oppressed people, in this instance Deaf people, become fixated on their deaf oppression. And this institutional audism made it impossible to recognize any privilege they are granted, particularly that which comes from having White skin. For the same reason, the ability and willingness to work on racism, personally or institutionally, becomes impossible. This is exactly the outcome that the White people who put this system into place wanted. Yet, when we understand what happens at the intersections of privilege, we are morally obligated to do everything possible to expose, understand, and change that.

Manifestations of the Intersection of Audism and Racism Today

Today, social conditions are intensifying the contradictions crashing into each other at these intersections. Despite ASL becoming more widely known by hearing people and accepted as a language worth learning, hearing parents continue to want their deaf children to speak rather than sign. Receiving cochlear implants during the brain's critical language learning years, more and more deaf infants and toddlers hear and learn to speak in a way very similar to a hearing child. Furthermore, more of these children are likely to be White because in general their families can afford cochlear implants; other forms of support more readily available to White children include hearing aids, speech teachers, and audiologists. Disparities in access to health care also contribute to a decrease in the birth of White deaf babies but an increase for children of color. Protesters supportive of the White Deaf core transferred onto me their fear of sharing power with other kinds of diverse deaf people, seeing me as somehow allowing genocidal forces against Deaf people that cochlear implants and all things non-Deaf represented to them.

Beyond Gallaudet, my voice box sits at the intersection of hearing and White privilege, a pawn in the struggles for control. Each time I set out to speak in public, I review the litany of advice I receive over how I should communicate:

- I should use my own voice and sign at the same time.
- I must not use my own voice but ask an interpreter to voice for me while I sign because I am representing all deaf people, and the audience will assume that all deaf people can and should use their own voice if I do.
- Even if I sign only, without speaking, and ask interpreters to voice for me, I have to have ASL interpreters on the stage at the same time because my ASL is not pure.

I go to bed most nights with a pain in my side over my voice.

In essence, I would prefer not to talk at all—and there is the rub exactly. This complex intersection of hearing and White privilege is designed to shut me up. I cannot imagine any hearing person under the kind of pressure I feel every time I open my mouth. James Baldwin (2010) once made the scathing remark that "it is astonishing that in a country so devoted to the rights of the individual, so many people should be afraid to speak" (p. 14). I am not going to be afraid to speak, to tell my truth.

Joining Hands

Rather than pulling away from each other, I ask you to join me in examining the Chinese finger puzzle of interwoven oppression systems. In that examination and the subsequent efforts of dismantling and transforming, I ask that you consider the role of hearing privilege in the maintenance of the trap of White supremacy and that you include deaf, hard of hearing, and deaf-blind people in your work. I am grateful to many African American, Latino, Asian, Native American, and White hearing women and men who have become the strongest allies I have in the examination and transformation of audism.

I dream of a day when all public schools require ASL and Deaf Culture classes in grades 3, 5, 8, and 11, for example. Doing so would go a long way toward an individual and societal examination and transformation of audism. I look forward to the day when White Deaf/deaf people become clear about their own White privilege and the adverse impacts of hearing privilege on the complexity of their lives and their relationships with deaf and hearing people of color.

Together we will expand the small body of work on intersections and help ourselves and others learn to respect and cherish differences within our families, workplaces, schools, and communities. Poet and author Muriel Strode (1903) wrote early in the nineteenth century, "I will not go where the path may lead, but I will go where there is no path, and I will leave a trail" (p. 506). Together, let us blaze that trail.

Notes

1. The term *Deaf* when capitalized refers to the cultural group of deaf people who use ASL and take pride in their Deaf identity. The word *deaf* with a lowercase *d* denotes people who have a significant audiological degree of hearing loss regardless of cultural identity. Identifying as a Deaf person is independent of the amount of usable hearing the person possesses. For example, a child with very mild hearing loss born to Deaf parents and growing up using ASL would self-identify and be recognized by others in the culture as Deaf despite having enough hearing ability to understand spoken language and talk on the telephone.
2. *Audism* is "the notion that one is superior based on one's ability to hear or behave in the manner of one who hears" (Humphries, 1977, p. 12). *Institutional audism* is "a system of advantage based on hearing ability. This definition allows us to detect the privilege allotted to hearing people. Such privilege, many would argue, makes sense. After all, Deaf individuals make up a miniscule fraction of the world's population. . . . But what about those

environments that are designed to work for the betterment of the Deaf individuals?" (Bauman, 2004, p. 241). The clearest examples of institutional audism happen in medical and educational institutions serving deaf populations (Bauman, 2004).

References

Baldwin, J. (2010). *The cross of redemption: Uncollected writings.* New York, NY: Pantheon.

Bauman, H.-D. L. (2004). Audism: Exploring the metaphysics of oppression. *Journal of Deaf Studies and Education, 9*(2), 239–246.

Fernandes, J. K., & Myers, S. S. (2010). Inclusive deaf studies: Barriers and pathways. *Journal of Deaf Studies and Deaf Education, 15*(1), 17–29.

Humphries, T. (1977). *Communication across cultures (deaf/hearing) and language learning* (Unpublished doctoral dissertation). Union Institute and University, Cincinnati, OH.

McCaskill, C., Lucas, C., Bayley, R., & Hill, J. (2013). *The hidden treasure of Black ASL: Its history and structure.* Washington, DC: Gallaudet University Press.

Schemo, D. J. (2006, May 13). Protests continue at university for deaf. *New York Times.* Retrieved from http://www.nytimes.com/2006/05/13/us/13gallaudet.html?_r=0

Strode, M. (1903). Wind wafted wildflowers. *The Open Court, 17*(567), 506–507.

14

HANDS-ON ACTIVISM

Paul Kivel

My work grows out of 45 years of living in community; raising children; working with various social service and social justice organizations; and doing education, activism, and writing, all focused on one primary question: *How can we live and work together to sustain community, nurture each individual, and create a multicultural society based on love, caring, justice, and interdependence with all life?* I still don't know the answer to that question. But I feel more strongly than ever that it poses the most important challenge we face in the world today.[1]

I grew up in a white, upper-middle-class, assimilated Jewish family in the suburbs of Los Angeles in the 1950s and early 1960s. My family carried the scars and trauma from the violent anti-Jewish riots (pogroms) in Russia that my foreparents escaped by immigrating to the United States and away from the Nazi Holocaust that killed almost all those who stayed in Eastern Europe. Keeping quiet, claiming whiteness, adapting to a dominant Christian culture, and adopting racist attitudes were all part of my family's survival.

I came of age during a period of major world liberation struggles (Vietnam, South Africa, Cuba, Zimbabwe) and the Civil Rights, women's, and gay liberation movements. These struggles confronted us with the moral choice of whether we supported colonialism, segregation, and inequality, or liberation, equity, and justice. I had to ask myself the question, What do I stand for? Of course, I knew I stood for all things good including liberty, equality, and democracy. Who ever proudly claims to stand for tyranny or exploitation? I soon learned that my platitudes were not enough.

I was attending a small, almost all-white liberal arts college in the Northwest in 1968 when 25 African American students, awarded scholarships by the Rockefeller Foundation, arrived for classes. Within weeks they were outraged at the racism they were experiencing on campus and in the wider community. They approached some of us who were white. My first response was to say, "I'm not racist. I treat everyone equally; I'm color blind." I was claiming to be a good (and innocent) person and certainly not part of the problem.

They said, in brief, that they appreciated that I was against racism, but they were experiencing racism in the educational system, the housing system, the job market, and the media. Did I stand with them in the struggle to end racism?

They were asking me how I was showing up in the struggle—what was I doing? Was I acting as an ally? In response, a few of us white students and staff put together a group to support the mobilized black students when they took over the administration building demanding an independent black studies program. When we asked these fellow students what they needed from us, they responded that they needed logistical support—food; messages to family, friends, and the campus community (this was before the days of computers and the Internet); and supplies. So we set up a system to provide these items. They also said they needed us to talk with the white students and faculty who didn't seem to have a clue about what the issues were and why their struggle was important. The white students, faculty, and administration were overwhelmingly against addressing the needs of the black students and angry that they were being inconvenienced by the protest. I immediately realized that I was unprepared to address white people about racism given how little I knew about it myself. It took me 25 years of self-education and activism to feel qualified to address this topic in my book *Uprooting Racism: How White People Can Work for Racial Justice* (Kivel, 2011b). But not having all the answers didn't stop me from stepping up as an ally in the ways that were needed.

My work on campus that year taught me a couple of important lessons about being an ally. An ally listens to the leadership of those on the front lines of struggle, those who are best situated to know what is needed and who will take the harshest backlash from the efforts of others. In addition, intervening in my own community, in this case the white community, was an essential contribution for allies to make.

But such learning is slow to come and difficult to absorb. Nearly 10 years later, when women approached some of us men with their anger and outrage over the levels of inequality and male violence they were facing, my response was little changed. I again threw up my hands in innocence and protested that I didn't hit my partner, I did my share of the housework and child care in our family, and I stood for equal rights. These women responded by affirming my personal behavior but pointed out that every year one million to two million men in the United States battered their partners. Did I stand with them in the struggle to end male violence? Again I had to step back and ask myself, beyond my personal practice, what was I actually doing to promote gender justice?

Prompted by these women and inspired by their work, a group of us formed the Oakland Men's Project in 1979. We went to women involved in the movement and asked them what they needed men to do. They outlined specific needs such as donations, child care, advocacy, and our presence at rallies and events. In addition, and perhaps most important, they said that they needed men to intervene with, educate, and mobilize men. Some men set up batterer's programs to work individually or in groups with men who were violent. Others, including myself, established the Oakland Men's Project to educate and mobilize men to end sexism and male violence.

In the early years of the Oakland Men's Project, we were asked to take our prevention work into the schools to address violence against women and to give young people alternatives to violence. We went into schools with a simple message for the young men: You are hitting your girlfriends; that's wrong, so stop it! This was the message we were receiving from women in the male violence prevention movement, so as allies we passed it along. Not surprisingly, the young men were not too receptive to our message. But they were, in fact, very concerned about the violence they experienced and were very honest in their responses to us. They admitted that they sometimes abused their partners, but they added that if we were serious about addressing the violence in their lives we had to talk about family violence, fights on the playground, gangs, hate crimes, and gay bashing. In addition, they said, what about racial profiling, the dismal state of their schools, lack of jobs, and toxic dumping in their neighborhoods? They were aware of having to deal with institutional levels of violence that caused or exacerbated the interpersonal ones. Since we were serious about listening and responding to their feedback, we had to rethink everything we were doing. Listening, responding, rethinking, doing, listening—my life has been a recurring set of this cycle, trying to figure out the next useful step as I engage with family, friends, colleagues, and young people.

During the 1980s and early 1990s I was developing a more complex and nuanced understanding of what it meant to be an ally, to be in solidarity with others. I was not Vietnamese, but I understood the tremendous cost of U.S. imperialism in Southeast Asia (and elsewhere). I could also feel the impact of the glamorization and glorification of war and violence in our culture as well as cutbacks in social services in our communities and increased repression of our civil rights and privacy in the name of national security. I was not female but could see the devastation of male violence; male socialization; and the economic, emotional, and sexual exploitation of women in my family and community. I experienced directly the constant competitiveness, violence, and emotional dysfunction of many men in personal relationships and organizational settings. In those years of doing solidarity work on issues of gender, race, war, and economic inequality, I began to understand that solidarity was something I was doing not for other people but because we are all mutually affected by the systems of exploitation and violence that we live within. Solidarity was about more than understanding the costs of oppression on those most immediately affected and more than understanding the privileges I attained from these very systems of oppression. Solidarity stemmed from my understanding, to use a metaphor that my friends Hugh Vasquez and Victor Lewis have developed, that we are all in the same boat. We may be on different decks. We may even have different access to benefits on the same deck. But the boat has a massive hole in it, and it is sinking (H. Vasquez & V. Lewis, personal communication, 1996). My understanding of interdependence and mutuality increased in the 1980s when I became more acutely aware of the devastation to the environment caused by Western industrial societies. I learned that the impact of global capitalism and the policies of the overdeveloped countries were leading toward the catastrophic destruction of the natural environment and the potential inability of humans to live viably on Earth. These understandings led me to reconsider the very human-centered, materialistic basis of Western civilization itself and its dominant Christian foundations (see my book *Living in the Shadow of the Cross*, Kivel, 2013). Not only does the human ship have a gaping hole in it, but also the oil, smoke, garbage, and other toxic pollution leaking from it is poisoning the natural environment.

As I began to shift my understanding of what it means to be human in a complex, multilayered world at the center of a declining empire, new questions came up. Is what I am doing commensurate with the magnitude of the challenges we face? Who benefits from my work? To whom and what am I accountable? How can I sustain myself, live sustainably, and nurture family, friends, and the broader human and natural environments? These questions guide the everyday decisions I make about what to do and how to live. They keep me honest about the gap between how I live my life and my aspirations.

I see my work as a platform for leveraging my class, race, gender, and other forms of privilege to work for social and environmental justice. Even the names of some of the groups I've been a part of reflect these efforts— Americans Against the [U.S.] War [in Vietnam], the Oakland Men's Project, Angry White Guys for Affirmative Action, Jewish Voice for Peace, Progressive Jewish Alliance, Hand in Hand: The Domestic Employers Network, and Showing Up for Racial Justice. (Even the names can educate and inspire to help break through the silence and collusion of the privileged.) I leverage my privilege not out of charity or compassion but because this is my life, my community, my world. I am responsible for being present, for leading a life of integrity, and for doing what is within my capacity to do to bring healing and justice into the world. Besides a responsibility, it is also my joy, my pleasure, my inspiration, my connection to others, my creative expression, my healing.

None of this means that it is easy to know what to do. In the real world, I believe there are multiple truths; I try to remain humble and embrace complexity. If those of us at the Oakland Men's Project had not been able to learn from the young people we met, we would have remained completely irrelevant to their lives. If Jewish Voice for Peace was not flexible and responsive to the shifting needs of the Palestinian liberation movement, it would no longer be useful or effective. Listening and learning are the foundation of any effective social justice work.

Many of us listen, learn, and may even experience a profound transformation in our understanding of the economic, racial, gender-based, and other pillars of our society. However, ultimately it comes down to our practice—how we show up, every day, in the world. This is where the concept of being an ally is useful but inadequate. *It is not an identity; it is a practice.* It is the act of being present, showing up and working with others that defines the activity of an ally. I call it *getting together for social justice* because it is so much more effective—and human—when we come together to build community, end exploitation and violence, and stand for justice.

When we get together I think we need to have long term vision and goals, middle-term strategies, and short-term tactics. Our long term vision might include a healthy, just, inclusive, and sustainable society. Our goals might cover transforming capitalism into a people-centered economic system, ending patriarchy, eliminating racism, and so on. But what strategies do we need? What tactics?

If one of our goals is to build an inclusive society and eliminate all forms of racism, we have to use strategies that create inclusive structures; change consciousness; educate, train, and mobilize people into specific projects, campaigns, and movements; challenge power; and attack specific forms of exploitation and segregation. When we have long-term, sustainable movement building as a goal, then any issue or project might contribute—or not, depending on whether we are accomplishing some of these strategies. Tactics are simply planned and organized actions to move our strategies forward.

My support for the National Domestic Workers Alliance (NDWA; see www.domesticworkers.org) and my work with Hand in Hand: The Domestic Employers Network (domesticemployers.org) is based on the importance of clear vision, strategy, and tactics. NDWA's vision is of a society in which all those who need care receive quality care, and all those who provide care have living wages and good working conditions. Its strategy is to build a long-term, cross-generational, cross-class, and interracial movement to build the political power and cultural change necessary to achieve its vision. More specific strategies include national and local coalitions of workers, elders, people with disabilities, and other progressive organizations (Caring Across Generations); statewide bill of rights campaigns (already victorious in New York, California, Hawaii, and Massachusetts); federal legislation reform; organizing domestic workers at a grassroots level; organizing employers; working-for-living-wage legislation; and immigration reform. Tactics follow from each strategy. There are multiple ways that allies can get involved locally and nationally.

Not all political work is so visionary or so complex. Much of it is not grassroots nor led by people from disenfranchised communities. I have learned that when I am not working from a long-term vision ambitious enough to create serious change and led by people most affected by the issues, no matter how good I feel about my work, I am not responding to the magnitude of the challenges we confront. I may be standing for the right things, but I am not standing *with* the right people as an effective ally in the appropriate struggles. In other words, an ally for social justice is someone who gets together with others to mobilize people and resources to accomplish strategies that build movements for social, economic, and environmental justice and move us closer to the vision of the society we want to live in. This is lifelong work.

It took 350 years for enslaved and freed Africans and their white abolitionist allies to eliminate slavery in the United States and nearly 75 years for women and male allies to win (white) women's right to vote. We need to understand ourselves as a generation that continues the legacy of social justice struggles on the shoulders of those who have gone before us. We also do this work for our children, our children's children, and future generations. An inspiration to me in this work is Generation Five, an organization that was started with the goal of eliminating child sexual assault within the next five generations—a 100-year goal. Its members defined their work as consciousness raising, leadership development, and practice in transformational justice in this current generation that would provide a foundation for the next generation to build on.

I have identified a few essential elements for a lifetime as a participant in building community and working for justice. We need to take care of each other, our natural environment, and ourselves physically, emotionally, and spiritually. And it should go without saying that we need to eat healthily, exercise, relax, have fun, play, enjoy, and smile—there is much to be grateful for. We have to not only sustain ourselves, but also decolonize our minds and bodies and begin to create alternative forms of community and cultures of healing, connection, creativity, and love to provide sustenance and hope for our communities. Living our values and vision allows us to prefigure the kind of society we want to create and inspires others to continue the work. At the same time, living our values cannot become a substitute for effective political action.

We can't create social justice by ourselves. Cultural activities and broad-based community support and action networks are essential to sustain us in this work. They help us maintain perspective on who we are and what we can do. Taking care of ourselves through healthy lifestyles and support networks sustains a community of people dedicated to social justice.

Parenting and mentoring are essential components for such community building. I have written extensively about both, because an ally, in fact any effective leader, supports the emergence of the leadership of others, especially that of young people. Younger people's courage, caring, creativity, and passion for justice can inspire and challenge those of us who are older. Only in cross-generational alliances can we build successful long-term movements for social justice.

Finally, we need to celebrate our successes, no matter how small, our victories, no matter how tenuous. We have made progress, things have changed. They have changed because multitudes of courageous people have resisted and refused to be overwhelmed by challenges. They have changed because the human spirit is indomitable, and we each share that spirit. We can sustain our efforts only by building on and celebrating the achievements of those who have contributed to moving us as far as we are today, adding our own efforts to creating a multicultural society based on love, caring, justice, and interdependence with all living things.

To conclude I want to return to the questions I raised at the beginning of this chapter:

What do you stand for?
Whom do you stand with?
If you stand for economic, social, and environmental justice, and if you stand with people who are under attack, how are you showing up each day

in your community? How are you getting together with others for our collective liberation?[2]

Notes

1. This chapter may be quoted, adapted, or reprinted only for noncommercial purposes and with an attribution to Paul Kivel, www.paulkivel.com. Creative Commons Attribution–Noncommercial 3.0 United States License. To view a copy of this license, visit http://creative commons.org/licenses/by-nc/3.0/us/. My thanks and appreciation to Micki Luckey and Ali Michael for editorial suggestions that improved this chapter and to the entire editorial and production group that has made this book possible.
2. *Collective liberation* is a phrase I adopted from the Catalyst Project (http://collectiveliberation .org).

References

Kivel, P. (1998). *Men's work: How to stop the violence that tears our lives apart* (2nd ed.). Center City, MN: Hazelden.

Kivel, P. (1999). *Boys will be men: Raising our sons for courage, caring and community.* Gabriola Island, BC: New Society.

Kivel, P. (2011a). *Helping teens stop violence, build community and stand for justice* (2nd ed.). Alameda, CA: Hunter House.

Kivel, P. (2011b). *Uprooting racism: How white people can work for racial justice* (3rd ed.). Gabriola Island, BC: New Society.

Kivel, P. (2013). *Living in the shadow of the cross: Understanding and resisting the power and privilege of Christian hegemony.* Gabriola Island, BC: New Society.

Piercy, M. (1980). *The low road.* Retrieved from http://www.pacifict.com/ron/ Piercy.html

AFTERWORD

Resisting Whiteness/Bearing Witness

Michelle Fine

In the winter of 2014, my friend and colleague Tamara Buckley and I attended a People's Institute for Survival and Beyond workshop in New York City titled *Undoing Racism* at Saint John the Divine. The room filled with the classic diversity the institute cultivates, a sampling of participants varied by age, ethnicity, biography, gender, sexuality, (dis)ability. I listened as well-educated, otherwise articulate young White women stumbled awkwardly when asked the question, "What do you like about being White?" I laughed as one of the facilitators, my age, offered, "As an older White woman, I would make a perfect drug mule." And then I teared up when a young woman of color attending a private upstate university, well known for its diversity and inclusion, explained, "I used to be comfortable speaking with anyone . . . but at college I hear what White people really think about us when they are drunk so I find myself not really trusting White people. No offense."

White people don't have a language for thinking about their skin, privilege, sense of entitlement, shame, guilt, and rage that dance just under the surface. We rarely have to explain who we are, based on color, because we float through the world as if it didn't matter. But it does. Our embodiment, experience, and enactment of whiteness differs obviously in intersection

162

with class, geography, gender, sexuality, and (dis)ability, but whiteness is the unmarked signifier of deservedness. And we never talk about it in school, at work, on the streets, with friends or family. When the question, What do you like about being White? is raised, we have no words.

So why do we need this book?

We need this book because it is now 60 years past *Brown v. Board of Education* (1954), and our schools are more segregated than in the past; the Supreme Court has hobbled Affirmative Action and sustained all the policies that make whiteness an easy pass privilege into higher education; prisons fill up with bodies of color; inequality gaps are stretching; and White men are standing their ground as Black bodies are gunned down. We need this book because youths of color are attending schools with metal detectors, aggressive policing, and equally aggressive high-stakes testing, and they are witnessing the closing of their schools. White people of affluence think they are simply witnesses to injustice but are really profiting in the short term and are increasingly vulnerable in the long term. Together we are losing our humanity, security, trust, and radically new opportunities for breathing antiracist, that is, clean air.

Young White people, and the rest of us, need to understand how to wear our skin critically. We need to understand how to develop what Du Bois (1903) called "double consciousness" (p. 351), a sense of living in our skin, and at the same time thinking critically about why the world treats whiteness like a badge of honor. We need to think about how to metabolize privilege into activism and not fumble (too badly). We need to learn why racial injustice is our problem too. We need to work through all the White muscle memory that has attached to our personal biographies, our work, and our political engagements, the moments when we are proud and the moments when we feel shame. We need to be humble and listen.

And so these chapters are a gift to White people like me who are repeat offenders of privilege, eager to break the habit, and hungry to engage in antiracist justice movements.

But looking forward requires looking back on how we came to embody White.

Whiteness and Families

Becoming White

In 1921 my mother, Rose, the youngest of 18 children, and my dad, Jack, an orphan, arrived separately at Ellis Island, each at the age of seven, escaping the pogroms of Poland. They entered the country at a moment "when the

Jews became White," as Karen Brodkin Saks (1998) has written. My father, then called Yankel Yankelovich, saw his name circumcised by an immigration officer. As he exited the doors of Ellis Island holding hands with his grandmother, Jack Fine moved into Harlem, where his childhood was nourished by the American dream. A decade older, in the same neighborhood, Langston Hughes was writing poetry about the crushing of his dreams. Deferred in Harlem, that dream must have hopped the No. 1 train downtown to the lady in green and nestled in the bodies of little White boys and girls coming across the Atlantic. Having eaten their first bananas on boats of nausea, loss, and adventure, they were welcomed by our country, and a few landed in the manicured suburbs of White New Jersey.

Thirty years later, in the 1950s, the Fine family moved into a suburban ranch home in New Jersey with

four

steps

down

to the sunken living room, ironically a signifier of upward mobility. The house at 510 Summit Street in Englewood Cliffs filled with the existential weight of injustice, despair, and depression embodied in the migraines of my mother who took to bed more often than I wished, and the rusty, metallic scent of plumbing supplies circulating in and out of the front door attached to the flannel shirts my father wore. We were first-(and a half)generation American Jews: hard work, assimilation, love, laughter, and accumulating privilege without noticing.

Taunting White

In the 1990s we would laugh at the idea of White, as our family consisted of David (the dad; my loving partner, whom I did not formally marry; and White Jew from Missouri), Demetrius (our oldest, African American, brought to us through the foster care group home adjacent to our house in Philadelphia, now in his late 30s), Sam (our C-section boy, White, now in his late 20s), and Caleb (yet another C-section, also White, now in his late teens). We would count in airports as we entered planes how many people would recognize us as a family and let us pass as a group and how many would stop our group when they got to Demetrius. We would tally White stops and stares versus Black stops and stares (sorry, I think there weren't many Latino flight checkers those days). Whites won. Black flight attendants were able to make sense of the laughter of family in many shades. Whites seemed to encounter a cognitive processing problem, not quite able to figure out that we were together.

Whiteness and Shame

I bumped into White when I was writing *Framing Dropouts* (Fine, 1991) and interviewing young African American students who had been pushed out of their high schools. Andrea, age 16 and out of school, suggested we conduct the interview in the park.

"Which park?" I asked.

"Morningside," she replied.

I attended Columbia University, and the first day of graduate school we all received a flyer in our mailboxes alerting us to stay out of Morningside Park because of rapes, muggings, and violence.

"Okay, sure," I said hesitantly.

I arrived, surrounded by children, families, balls, laughter, swings, and my own shame. It was after all a park.

In the middle of the interview, Andrea asked me directly, "How do you feel here? Everyone thinks you are a nurse or a social worker, but when I go to your neighborhood, I feel like people don't want me there, they want me to move fast and get out" (A., personal communication, 1991).

Later in the interview, still not fully aware of how drenched in White my biography and consciousness have been, I asked, "So, when you were in school were you the kind of student who participated a lot in class?"

"No, not me. I was a good kid."

Fifteen years later I ran into another version of White. I was hired as an expert witness in a lawsuit when the White male principal of a school in Wedowie, Alabama, canceled the prom because of what he called cross-race dating and told a young biracial student that she was, in his words, a mistake (see Fine et al., 2004), and he couldn't tolerate more mistakes like her. As the expert for the U.S. Department of Justice documenting racial dynamics in and around the school, I visited the local Black church on a hot Sunday evening to meet the families that had been boycotting the school and attending freedom schools instead. Expecting to confer with a small set of elders, I drove up the gravelly road at dusk to a small church and surprisingly spotted three buses and scores of cars. I entered the church through what I hoped was the back entrance and noticed quickly all seats were occupied, and rows of young Black men lined the walls; it was standing room only. Trying not to draw attention to myself, I hid in the back. I heard the seemingly 150-year-old preacher say, "Praise Jesus, Dr. Fine is here," and I was welcomed, hugged, fed, and cheered on by community members. The next morning when I arrived at the school to interview students and educators, I encountered the same churchgoers from the night before, the school aides and food service employees. But this time, in daylight and around other Whites, there was no eye contact, no sign of recognition. I learned much about southern racial politics and the danger of eyes meeting eyes, lips part-ing in a smile. I stifled my characteristic hugs of familiarity. We won the case. The principal was removed. Within a few years, the same man who was found guilty of racism was elected by the general population to be the district's superintendent of schools.

Learning the Limits of White Privilege

I learned the limits of White privilege with another family. Together we tried to combat the bulimia of structural racism consuming Black families in fam-ily court and throwing them up in new homes, on the streets, in disarray, all in the name of protection. Somehow, White privilege fed my fantasy that I could slay this dragon.

In 2009 a first-year brilliant doctoral student, let's call him Akom, asked me to accompany his mother and siblings to family court. The woman's hus-band had just been released from prison, and the state decided in the name of protection to remove the couple's three foster sons after eight years, even though the husband assured the court he would not live in the same house but in an apartment upstairs. Unsure of my role, but sensing that my skin and maybe my PhD might matter, I of course agreed, honored and humbled.

Clearing the metal detectors that welcome visitors into Brooklyn Family Court, we wandered upstairs where families of color wait on benches, while White and a few Brown lawyers huddled making deals. Serious Black court officers call the names of the cases. There was no laughter in the hallway; and it could have been 1909 or 2009. One can only imagine that the stone walls know little has changed within the structural racism of family court.

We entered the courtroom. The only other White woman in the room was the judge. In a room full of Black faces, the judge asked the lawyer my name and turned to me, saying, "Dr. Fine, do you have a report?"

Shot through with a sense that I was to explain and exploit racism to defeat racism, I called up a "report" from my belly, explaining the strength of this family and the integrity of this mother's commitment to her boys, and the intellect and character exhibited by Akom and his mother. In my "expert" opinion (an expertise granted me largely in the absence of melanin), I concluded that the children would be developmentally disrupted if they were moved again, that the strength of attachment was significant, that this is family.

The judge let me speak my piece, but my whiteness did not trump the cumulative weight of racism that has built the brick and mortar of Brooklyn Family Court. My whiteness caught her eye but not enough to bend the hard-wired racist tentacles of three systems strangling us in that room: the prison industrial complex, the foster care system, and family court. Ashamed that I tried to summon up privilege, and embarrassed that I lost, I turned to Akom and we all cried. I understood then that my whiteness had been Akom's last hope. Perhaps graduate school and a doctorate in social psychology fueled a sense that movements matter, that change is possible, and it all might have been otherwise.

Soon thereafter, Akom dropped out of a program that very few ever leave. According to his Facebook page, he joined the Marines. The boys were eaten by the system.

My outrage, disbelief, and shock were drenched in the flaccid privilege of whiteness, unable to disrupt a well-oiled machine.

Education Reform, or Dangling the Tragedy of the Black Child as Foreplay to Privatization

Most recently, I despair at White privilege when I witness elite White privilege, embodied in the education reform movement, parading the "tragedy of the illiterate Black child" who needs to be saved from his or her mother and community, removed from a local school and unionized teacher to attend a charter school, earn a voucher, or be swept away to a private boarding school. In the interim, these philanthropists who largely send their children to private schools are advocating charters, vouchers, testing, and technology while dismantling public education. I despair more when I hear these words now being spoken by very smart, very well-educated young adults of color, graduates of the Ivies, whose student debt has been paid by Teach for America or Charter Network or Broad Academy, whose pain of miseducation, or luxury of having been plucked as a member of the "Talented Tenth," has been exploited into opportunity for a privatizing disruption of public education, unions, pensions, and community schools.

Where Are the White Prisoners?

I learned White in a sea of green in 1994 when I worked closely for four years with women in green in Bedford Hill Women's Correctional Facility in New York, where we collaborated on resurrecting college in prison after Bill Clinton withdrew Pell Grants from prisons. We were involved with a participatory evaluation of the college program, and we learned that White people are allowed to make mistakes and learn from them; Black people are required to pay (with long sentences) for their mistakes.

Sweet Intimate Privileges

I was told about my whiteness when Donnie, Linda, and I (all psychologists, two involved with a Black church, one a White atheist) used to go on vacations, and I would walk into sections of restaurants that had signs that said closed, or I would grab a chair on a pool deck from a roped-off section of the cement, and they laughed at my privilege.

Across my 60 years, I have come to know White privilege, shame, entitlement, disappointment, and the unearned advantages we receive when we walk into court, into school, on the street, and even in forbidden places. And now I know that a single White antiracist woman just turns into white noise in court. But for 30 years I have engaged in feminist, antiwar, racial justice, and education justice movements, and in struggles against the prison industrial complex, high-stakes testing, gentrification, and exclusion from higher education, and in these delicious, sweaty settings I have learned there is strength when antiracist White allies link arms in coalitions for justice. I take wisdom from Gloria Anzaldúa, reinterpreted by Maria Elena Torre and Jen Ayala (2009), when they call for us coming together as *nos-otras*, us/others.

White people need to think about how they have come to embody and breathe in White privilege so they may exhale White responsibility. Our lives are filled with messy contradictions. Our debt to justice is to interrogate our privilege and our li(v)es of whiteness.

So we need this book because it is a self-help manual for recidivist Whites, those of us who exercise our privilege as repeat offenders but are willing to try to change our ways as individuals, in our families, at work, and in social movements. Read these chapters and think through your own biographies of embodying, enacting, and resisting whiteness and bearing witness. You may periodically relapse into White privilege, but you will develop the muscle of reflexivity, of double consciousness that Du Bois (1903) so eloquently described for African Americans. We end with the wisdom of Tim Wise (www.goodreads.com/quotes/851927):

> After all, acknowledging unfairness then calls decent people forth to correct those injustices. And since most persons are at their core, decent folks, the need to ignore evidence of injustice is powerful: To do otherwise would force Whites to either push for change (which they would perceive as against their interests) or live consciously as hypocrites who speak of freedom and opportunity but perpetuate a system of inequality.
>
> The irony of American history is the tendency of good White Americans to presume racial innocence. Ignorance of how we are shaped racially is the first sign of privilege.
>
> In other words. It is a privilege to ignore the consequences of race in America.

There is a master's thesis, I have been told, at Bank Street College titled *Did You Know Michelle Fine Isn't Black?* I'm not sure it's true, but I laughed so hard when I heard that, honored of course, and much more so than when people tell me, "You don't look Jewish," which is supposed to be a compliment but just feels kind of anti-Semitic.

In the language of my dear friend Maxine Greene, who passed away as I was writing this, we are all not finished yet.

References

Brown v. Board of Education, 347 U.S. 483 (1954).

Du Bois, W. E. B. (1994). *The souls of Black folks.* New York: Dover Publications.

Fine, M. (1991) *Framing dropouts: Notes on the politics of an urban high school.* Albany, NY: SUNY.

Fine, M. (2004) Witnessing whiteness/gathering intelligence. In M. Fine, L. Weis, L. Powell Pruitt & A. Burns (Eds), *Off-White: readings on power, privilege and resistance* (2nd ed., pp 245–256) New York: Routledge.

Brodkin, K. (1998) *How Jews became white folks and what that says about race in America.* New Brunswick, NJ: Rutgers University Press.

Torre, M. & Ayala, J. (2009) Where PAR and borderlands scholarship meet. *Urban Review, 41*(1): 66–84.

Appendix

The following are examples of work from authors of color recommended by the authors and editors of *Everyday White People Confront Racial and Social Injustice: 15 Stories*. Only one work by each author is listed, although all the authors on this list have multiple works readers are urged to consult. This is also only a beginning, and readers should continue to search for opportunities to learn about multiple perspectives.

Akbar, N. (1996). *Breaking the chains of psychological slavery*. Tallahassee, FL: Mind Productions & Associates.

Alexander, M. (2013). *The new Jim Crow: Mass incarceration in the age of colorblindness*. New York, NY: The New Press.

Anzaldúa, G., & Keating, A. (Eds.). (1984). *This bridge we call home: Radical visions for transformation*. New York, NY: Routledge.

Asante, M. K. (2009). *Erasing racism: The survival of the American nation*. Amherst, NY: Prometheus Books.

Brewer, R. (2002). *A special issue on gender, color, class, and caste*. London, UK: Routledge.

Collins, P. H. (1998). *Fighting words: Black women and the search for justice*. Minneapolis: University of Minnesota Press.

Crenshaw, K., Gotanda, N., Peller, G., & Thomas, K. (1995). *Critical race theory: The key writings that formed the movement*. New York, NY: The New Press.

Davis, A. (1984). *Women, culture & politics.* New York, NY: Random House.

DeGruy, J. (2005). *Post traumatic slave syndrome: America's legacy of enduring injury and healing.* Portland, OR: Uptone Press.

Du Bois, W. E. B. (1994). *The souls of Black folk.* New York, NY: Dover. (Original work published 1903.)

Freire, P. (1970). *Pedagogy of the oppressed.* New York, NY: Continuum Press.

Higginbotham, E. (2001). *Too much to ask: Black women in the era of integration.* Chapel Hill: University of North Carolina Press.

hooks, b. (1999). *All about love: New visions.* New York, NY: HarperCollins.

Hull, G. T., Scott, P. B., & Smith, B. (Eds.). (1993). *All the women are White, all the Blacks are men, but some of us are brave: Black women's studies.* New York, NY: The Feminist Press at City University of New York.

Kunjufu, J. (2012). *There is nothing wrong with Black students.* Chicago, IL: African American Images.

Lorde, A. (1984). *Sister outsider: Essays and speeches.* Trumansburg, NY: Crossing Press.

Mandela, N. (1995). *Long walk to freedom.* New York, NY: Little, Brown.

Roy, A. (2014). *Capitalism: A ghost story.* Chicago, IL: Haymarket Books.

Singleton, G. (2005). *Courageous conversations about race: A field guide for achieving equity in schools.* Thousand Oaks, CA: Corwin Press.

Steele, C. (2011). *Whistling Vivaldi: And other clues to how stereotypes affect us and what we can do.* New York, NY: Norton.

Walker, A. (2013). *We are the ones we have been waiting for: The promise of civic renewal in America.* Oxford, UK: Oxford University Press.

West, C. (1993). *Race matters.* Boston, MA: Beacon Press.

Additional Resources

Albrecht, L., & Brewer, R. M. (1990). *Bridges of power: Women's multicultural alliances*. Santa Cruz, CA: New Society Publishers.

Anzaldúa, G., Cantu, N., & Hurtado, A. (2012). *Borderlands/La frontera: The new mestiza*. San Francisco, CA: Aunt Lute Books.

Collins, P. H. (2005). *Black sexual politics: African Americans, gender, and the new racism*. New York, NY: Routledge.

Collins, P. H. (2008). *Black feminist thought: Knowledge, consciousness, and the politics of empowerment*. New York, NY: Routledge.

Davis, A. (1983). *Women, race, & class*. New York, NY: Vintage.

Du Bois, W. E. B. (1994). *The souls of Black folk*. New York, NY: Dover. (Original work published 1903)

Ferber, A. L. (1999, May 7). White/Jewish/other: What White supremacists taught a Jewish scholar about identity. *The Chronicle of Higher Education*, B6–B7.

Ferber, A. L. (2003, October 1). Increasing synergy between the conservative movement and the far right [Web log post]. Retrieved from http://mobilizingideas.wordpress.com/2013/10/01/increasing-synergy-between-the-conservative-movement-and-the-far-right/

Ferber, A. L. (2012). The culture of privilege: Color-blindness, post-feminism and Christonormativity. *Journal of Social Issues, 68*(1), 63–77.

Higginbotham, E. (2001). *Too much to ask: Black women in the era of integration*. Chapel Hill: University of North Carolina Press.

hooks, b. (1999). *Ain't I a woman: Black women and feminism.* Boston, MA: South End Press.

Hull, G. T., Scott, P. B., & Smith, B. (Eds.). (1993). *All the women are White, all the Blacks are men, but some of us are brave: Black women's studies.* New York, NY: The Feminist Press at the City University of New York.

Ignatiev, N. (2008). *How the Irish became White.* New York, NY: Routledge.

Ignatiev, N., & Garvey, J. (1996). *Race traitor.* New York, NY: Routledge.

Kimmel, M., & Ferber, A. (Eds.). (2014). *Privilege: A reader* (3rd ed.). Boulder, CO: Westview Press.

Lorde, A. (2007). *Sister outsider: Essays and speeches.* Berkeley, CA: Crossing Press.

McIntosh, P. (1988). *White privilege and male privilege: A personal account of coming to see correspondences through work in women's studies* (working paper no. 189). Wellesley, MA: Wellesley College Center for Research on Women.

Moradi, B., & Huang, Y. (2008). Objectification theory and psychology of women: A decade of advances and future directions. *Psychology of Women Quarterly, 32*(4), 377–398.

Morraga, C., & Anzaldúa, G. (1984). *This bridge called my back: Writings by radical women of color.* New York, NY: Kitchen Table/Women of Color Press.

Naison, M. (2009, March 17). Is "Schwartze" a racial slur? Reflections on Jackie Mason's comedy and Yiddish vernacular speech [Web log post]. Retrieved from http://withabrooklynaccent.blogspot.com/2009/03/is-schwartze-racial-slur-reflections-on.html

Roediger, D. R. (2007). *The wages of whiteness: Race and the making of the American working class.* London, UK: Verso.

Romero, M. (2002). *Maid in the USA* (10th anniversary ed.). New York, NY: Routledge.

Saxton, A. (2003). *The rise and fall of the White republic: Class politics and mass culture in nineteenth century America.* London, UK: Verso.

Schur, E. (2007). Sexual coercion in American life. In L. O'Toole, J. Schiffman, & M. Edwards (Eds.), *Gender violence: Interdisciplinary perspectives* (2nd ed., pp. 86–98). New York: New York University Press.

Stelle, C. M. (2010). *Whistling Vivaldi: And other clues to how stereotypes affect us.* New York, NY: Norton.

Sue, D. W. (2010). *Microaggressions in everyday life: Race, gender, and sexual orientation.* Hoboken, NJ: Wiley.

Warren, M. R. (2010). *Fire in the heart: How White activists embrace racial justice.* Oxford, UK: Oxford University Press.

Zinn, M. B., Cannon, L. W., Higginbotham, E., & Dill, B. T. (1986). The costs of exclusionary practices in women's studies. *Signs, 11*(2), 290–303.

Glossary

Ableism: "Ableism is a term meaning prejudice and discrimination—against people who have disabilities. It's the belief that disability itself makes one in some way lesser, less deserving of respect, equal treatment, equality before the law. [Thomas Hehir (2002)] defines ableism as 'the devaluation of disability' [p. 3] that results in 'societal attitudes that uncritically assert that it is better... to walk than to roll, speak than [use] sign [language], read print than read Braille' [p. 3]" (Johnson, 2006, p.9).

Antiracism: "Being an antiracist begins with understanding the institutional nature of racial matters and accepting that all actors in a racialized society are affected *materially* (receive benefits or disadvantages) and *ideologically* by the racial structure. This stand implies taking responsibility for your unwilling participation in these practices and beginning a new life committed to the goal of achieving real racial equality" (Bonilla-Silva, 2009, p. 15).

Ethnicity: A social construct that divides people into groups based on characteristics such as shared sense of group identity, values, culture, language, history, ancestry, and geography.

All definitions not directly referenced are from the glossary created by Dr. Abby L. Ferber for the White Privilege Conference.

Gender: Socially constructed categories of masculinity and manhood, femininity and womanhood.

Gender identity: A person's internal sense of a specific gender.

Heteronormative: "The expectation that all individuals are heterosexual. Often expressed subtly through assumptions that everyone is or will grow up to be straight" (Human Rights Campaign Foundation, Welcoming Schools, 2012).

Heterosexism: The system of oppression that assumes heterosexuality as the norm, favors heterosexuals, and denigrates and stigmatizes anyone whose gender or sexual behavior is considered nonheterosexual.

Homosexual: A person who experiences attraction to and/or sexual relations with a person of the same sex/gender. Some may be offended by this term and prefer one or more of the following: lesbian, gay, bisexual, transgender, intersexed, queer, or questioning (LBGTIQQ).

Inclusiveness: A commitment to foster a climate that represents and values members of diverse social identity groups. Inclusive practices occur at the individual, cultural, and institutional levels, creating a culture where all members feel they are welcome and belong.

Intersectionality: An approach largely advanced by women of color, arguing that classifications such as gender, race, class, and others cannot be examined in isolation from one another; they interact and intersect in individuals' lives, in society, and in social systems, and are mutually constitutive.

Oppression: A systemic devaluing, undermining, marginalizing, and disadvantaging of certain social identities in contrast to the privileged norm; when some people are denied something of value, while others have ready access.

Privilege: "The dominant group takes or easily receives benefits because of their group's power—such as good jobs, high income, access to money, physical safety, good education, quality health services, good housing, respectful treatment, being held in high regard, favorable historic interpretations, and so on. Privilege can show up in 'simple' ways such as being able to catch a cab when you need one; or not to be treated with suspicion while shopping. It also shows up in 'not-so-simple' ways such as being reasonably sure you'll find a place to live where your neighbors are welcoming or at least neutral;

or, that you will be treated fairly when stopped for a traffic issue" (Mattheus & Marino, 2003).

Race: A social construct that divides people into groups based on factors such as physical appearance, ancestry, culture, history, and so on; a social, historical, and political classification system.

Race as a social construct: "(Race is) a recent idea created by western Europeans following exploration across the world to account for differences among people and justify colonization, conquest, enslavement, and social hierarchy among humans. . . Ideas about race are culturally and socially transmitted and form the basis of racism, racial classification and often complex racial identities" (American Anthropological Association, 2011). There is no biological basis for race; in fact, there is more similarity among people across racial groups than within racial groups. Race carries tremendous social meaning that significantly impacts the lives of all people as a result of the myths, ideas, and systems that reinforce the concept.

Racism: A system of oppression involving the systematic subordination of members of targeted racial groups by those who have relatively more social power. This subordination occurs at the individual, cultural, and institutional levels.

Sexism: A system of oppression that privileges men, subordinates women, and denigrates women-identified values. This subordination occurs at the individual, cultural, and institutional levels.

Sexual orientation: A concept referring to sexual desire and preference for emotional and sexual relationships with others based on their sex/gender; often implies that sexual object choice is an essential, inborn characteristic, so may be problematic to some.

Social class: (as in upper class, middle class, lower class, working class). A concept that refers to people's socioeconomic status based on factors such as wealth, occupation, education, income, and so on.

White privilege: An institutional set of benefits, including greater access to resources and power, bestowed upon people classified as white.

White supremacy: The assumption or theory that whites are superior to all other races and should be in power and control.

References

American Anthropological Association. (2011). *RACE—Are we so different?* Retrieved from http://www.understandingrace.org/resources/glossary.html#r

Bonilla-Silva, E. (2009). *Racism without racists: Color-blind racism and the persistence of racial inequality in America.* Washington, DC: Rowman & Littlefield.

Hehir, T. (2002). Eliminating ableism in education. *The Harvard Educational Review, 72*(1), 1–32. Retrieved from http://rtcudl.edublogs.org/files/2010/01/Eliminating-Ableism-in-Education.pdf

Human Rights Campaign Foundation, Welcoming Schools. (2012). *A few definitions for educators and parents/guardians.* Retrieved from http://www.welcoming-schools.org/pages/a-few-definitions-for-educators-and-parents-guardians

Johnson, M. (Ed.). (2006). *Disability awareness: Do it right.* Louisville, KY: Advocado Press.

Mattheus, A. & Marino, L. (2003). *Whites confronting racism: A Manual for a Three-Part Workshop.* Philadelphia, PA: Training for Change. https://www.trainingforchange.org

Index

(Continued from the following page)

The Nigger in You

Challenging Dysfunctional Language, Engaging Leadership Moments

Dr. J. W. Wiley

"This book is inspiring, challenging, informative, and a timeless resource for educators, parents, and community leaders. It's the real deal. You'll learn something every time you read it."—***Eddie Moore Jr.***, *Founder/Director, The White Privilege Conference*

"Whether in a classroom, campus, or community setting, Dr. J. W. Wiley always enlarges the conversations we need to be having about diversity, social justice, and leadership. He does so compellingly with *The Nigger in You*. As an educator and community activist, I know I will turn to his book as a trusted friend and guide, and recommend you read it. It is right on time."—***Martha Swan***, *Executive Director, John Brown Lives!*

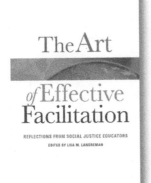

The Art of Effective Facilitation

Reflections from Social Justice Educators

Edited by Lisa M. Landreman

How can I apply learning and social justice theory to become a better facilitator?

Should I prepare differently for workshops around specific identities?

How do I effectively respond when things aren't going as planned?

This book is intended for the increasing number of faculty and student affairs administrators—at whatever their level of experience—who are being are asked to become social justice educators to prepare students to live successfully within, and contribute to, an equitable multicultural society.

It will enable facilitators to create programs that go beyond superficial discussion of the issues to fundamentally address the structural and cultural causes of inequity, and provide students with the knowledge and skills to work for a more just society. Beyond theory, design, techniques, and advice on practice, the book concludes with a section on supporting student social action.

22883 Quicksilver Drive
Sterling, VA 20166-2102

Subscribe to our e-mail alerts: www.Styluspub.com

Also available from Stylus

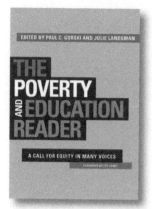

The Poverty and Education Reader
A Call for Equity in Many Voices
Edited by Paul C. Gorski and Julie Landsman

"*The Poverty and Education Reader* is a top pick for teachers and educators as well as social issues readers, and packs in essays, memoirs, and poetry with the idea of analyzing the schooling experience of poor and working-class students. Low-income family experiences are targeted with the idea of profiling proven strategies teachers and schools have used for closing educational gaps, and contributions come from a range of writers, from teachers and students to parents and scholars, discussing views of poor students and their families and approaches that have made a difference. Don't consider this a 'fix' for poor students: look at it as a series of articles on ways youth is alienated by education practices—and how to overcome this with new school and classroom routines."—*Midwest Book Review*

Cultivating Social Justice Teachers
How Teacher Educators Have Helped Students Overcome Cognitive Bottlenecks and Learn Critical Social Justice Concepts
Edited by Paul C. Gorski, Nana Osei-Kofi, Jeff Sapp, and Kristien Zenkov
Foreword by David O. Stovall

"Packed with honest stories that document the missteps, mistakes, and rethinking of courses that focus on issues of social justice, *Cultivating Social Justice Teachers* offers all of us—professors, teachers, researchers, and students—strategies for teaching and learning how to face the inevitable bumps and obstacles that get in the way of full inclusion and understanding of multiple perspectives. Engaging in brave and frank discussions, the editors and contributors of this text are a model of what is needed if we are to change how teachers are prepared to teach in our diverse classrooms."—*Sonia Nieto, Professor Emerita, School of Education, University of Massachusetts, Amherst*

(Continued on preceding page)